Foucault's Archaeology of Political Economy

Foucault's Archaeology of Political Economy

Iara Vigo de Lima

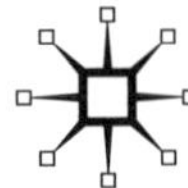

First published 2010 by
PALGRAVE MACMILLAN

Palgrave Macmillan in the UK is an imprint of Macmillan Publishers Limited, registered in England, company number 785998, of Houndmills, Basingstoke, Hampshire RG21 6XS.

Palgrave Macmillan in the US is a division of St Martin's Press LLC, 175 Fifth Avenue, New York, NY 10010.

Palgrave Macmillan is the global academic imprint of the above companies and has companies and representatives throughout the world.

Palgrave® and Macmillan® are registered trademarks in the United States, the United Kingdom, Europe and other countries.

ISBN 978–0–230–24261–6   hardback

This book is printed on paper suitable for recycling and made from fully managed and sustained forest sources. Logging, pulping and manufacturing processes are expected to conform to the environmental regulations of the country of origin.

A catalogue record for this book is available from the British Library.

Library of Congress Cataloging-in-Publication Data

Vigo de Lima, Iara.
  Foucault's archaeology of political economy / Iara Vigo de Lima.
     p. cm.
  ISBN 978–0–230–24261–6 (hardback)
  1. Foucault, Michel, 1926–1984.—Views on economics.   2. Economics—
  History.   I. Title.
  B2430.F724V54 2010
  330.1—dc22

                                                            2010023943

10   9   8   7   6   5   4   3   2   1
19 18 17 16 15 14 13 12 11 10

Printed and bound in Great Britain by
CPI Antony Rowe, Chippenham and Eastbourne

To the memory of my mother and father

Dorilde Vigo de Lima (1929–1991)
Ari Ibairro de Lima (1923–2004)

Contents

List of Diagrams and Tables

Note on Abbreviations

References to the following texts are abbreviated in citations as follows:

AK: Foucault, Michel (2002) [1969] *The Archaeology of Knowledge*. London: Routledge.

BC: Foucault, Michel (1973) [1963] *The Birth of the Clinic. An Archaeology of Medical Perception*, A.M. Sheridan Smith (trans.). London: Tavistock Publications.

HA: Smith, Adam (1986c) [1799] 'The principles which lead and direct philosophical enquiries; ilustrated by the history of astronomy', in Robert L. Heilbroner (ed.) *The Essential Adam Smith*. With the assistance of Laurence J. Malone. New York and London: W.W. Norton & Company.

OT: Foucault, Michel (1970a) [1966] *The Order of Things. An Archaeology of the Human Sciences*. London: Tavistock Publications.

TMS: Smith, Adam (1986a) [1759] 'The theory of moral sentiments', in Robert L. Heilbroner (ed.) *The Essential Adam Smith*. With the assistance of Laurence J. Malone. New York and London: W.W. Norton & Company.

WN: Smith, Adam (1986b) [1776]. 'An Inquiry into the nature and causes of the wealth of nations', in Robert L. Heilbroner (ed.) *The Essential Adam Smith*. With the assistance of Laurence J. Malone. New York and London: W.W. Norton & Company.

Acknowledgements

This book owes much to the continuous and kind support of many people over a number of years. I would like to begin by dedicating it to the memory of my mother and father, Dorilde and Ari, for making this all possible.

I would like to offer my deepest thanks to friends and family, especially to Iana and Sirlange, together with Ron and Angela Fox. I would particularly like to thank Charles Richard Fox for his continuous encouragement, support and advice throughout the publishing of this book.

This book owes a great deal of acknowledgement to Professor Sheila Dow, to whom I offer my deepest gratitude – for her kind guidance, dedication, encouragement and friendship, during and after my PhD, I am truly grateful.

I would also like to thank Dr Jeremy Carrette, Professor Ramón García Fernandéz and Professor Dipak Gosh for all their kind support. To all my friends and colleagues in the Department of Economics at the University of Stirling and at the Federal University of Parana, an offer of thanks for the support and encouragement and for providing the propitious environment in which the accomplishment of this work would otherwise have not taken place. I would also like to thank the Coordenação de Aperfeiçoamento de Pessoal de Nível Superior (CAPES), within the Ministry of Education of Brazil, for awarding me the financial assistance during the period of my PhD research.

I would like to offer my deepest thanks to the publisher, Palgrave Macmillan, together with those involved in the analysis of the initial proposal and the people who helped with the editing and production of this book, particularly Taiba Batool, Jon Lloyd and Gemma Papageorgiou, who provided prompt and efficient support throughout this entire project.

I am also indebted to the various anonymous referees for all the attention that they have paid to my work and for all their invaluable comments, feedback, critical reflections and suggestions. I would also like to offer my special thanks to Professor Keith Tribe for his timely consideration of my work during the assessment stages.

Finally, the author and publisher of this book would like to offer their deepest thanks to the following companies for the permissions to reproduce copyright material:

From: *The Order of Things* by Michel Foucault. Copyright © 1970 Random House, Inc., New York. Originally published in French as *Les Mots et les Choses*. Copyright © 1966 by Editions Gallimard. Reproduced by permission of Taylor & Francis Books UK.

From: *The Archaeology of Knowledge* by Michel Foucault. Copyright © 2002 Routledge, London. Originally published in French as *L'Archéologie du Savoir* © 1969 by Editions Gallimard. Reproduced by permission of Taylor & Francis Books UK.

From: *The Order of Things* by Michel Foucault. Copyright © 1970 Random House, Inc., New York. Originally published in French as *Les Mots et les Choses*. Copyright © 1966 by Editions Gallimard. Reprinted by permission of Georges Borchardt, Inc., for Editions Gallimard.

Every effort has been made to trace rights holders, but if any have been inadvertently overlooked the publishers will be pleased to make the necessary arrangements at the first opportunity.

1
Introduction

This book presents three primary objectives. The first objective is to pursue a detailed reading of Michel Foucault's writings on the archaeology of knowledge, focusing on the emergence of political economy. The second is to examine some of Foucault's contributions to three main areas of research in economics: the methodology of economics, the historiography of economic thought, and studies on Adam Smith's context and writings. The third and overall objective is to argue that Foucault's archaeology of political economy provides possibilities for a reassessment of the historiography and methodology of economics. A consideration of his work is not solely pertinent in current debates regarding the methodology of economics: it is also indispensable. It aims to illustrate how Foucault went beyond offering a reinterpretation of the history of political economy. He raised new questions and provided a novel method, a range of inspiring notions and concepts, and a consideration of the history of epistemological and ontological conceptions since the sixteenth century, which should not be ignored by those intending to study the methodology and historiography of economics.

Very few assessments have been made of Foucault's archaeology of economics, both within the field of economics and within philosophy and the history of thought. Although it may be possible to find allusions to his work in economics, in particular, by applying some general ideas, notions and concepts introduced and made prominent by him, they do not follow a critical analysis of his writings and they are probably more often related to his genealogy of power/knowledge relations.

In the Anglo-American literature of economics, in particular, there appears to be little or no engagement with the works of Foucault. It is possible to find some examples exploring the relationship between Marx and Foucault's ideas, and this interaction appears to be the basis upon which most discussions take place (for instance, Poster, 1984 and Marsden, 1999). The same interaction has also inspired some of the economists behind the journal *Rethinking Marxism*, such as David Ruccio, Richard Wolff, Jack Amariglio and Stephen Cullenberg. The one interesting article written in English that explicitly performs an analysis of Foucault's archaeology is the paper by Amariglo, 'The body, economic discourse and power: an economist's introduction to Foucault', published in the *History of Political Economy* in 1988. Amariglio's statement remains valid to this day:

> With the exception of a few economists, such as Antonio Callari, Stephen Resnick, Richard Wolff, Keith Tribe, and Athar Hussain [...], most economists are distinctly unaware of Foucault's writings [...] And yet [...] the opening up of the philosophy of economics and the history of thought to the questions raised by philosophers of language, aestheticians, and literary theorists *makes our reading of Foucault a must.* (Amariglio, 1988, p. 584, emphasis added)

Keith Tribe (1978), who is included in Amariglio's list, is usually depicted as the most evident example of someone having been influenced by Foucault's archaeology of knowledge on the writing of the history of economic thought. Foucault has been a major influence in the whole of Tribe's intellectual work.

The lack of a conscientious study and assessment of Foucault's archaeology of political economy does not only apply to economists. In philosophy, interpreters of and commentators on Foucault's archaeology do not form a critical approach to the case of economics (for instance, Cousins and Hussain, 1984, Kusch, 1991, Hacking, 1981, Gutting, 1989, Shumway, 1989, Major-Poetzl, 1983 and O'Farrell, 1989 and 2005). Ian Hacking, for instance, wrote an article to celebrate 40 years of the publication of *The Order of Things*, referring specifically to Foucault's archaeology of biology, economics and linguistics, in which he declared:

> From time to time I rethink for my own ends something about the evolution of biology, or of linguistics. I always [*sic*] astonished by what a rich source Foucault's story is, of a fairly sharp creation of new sciences. I always find illumination. *I cannot vouch for economics because I do not think about it much.* [...] *I am not sure this works so well for the labour theory of value, but that is just ignorance on my part.* (Hacking, 2005, pp. 23–4, emphasis added)

Although attempts have been made to initiate renewed discussions relating to the importance of Foucault's writings in economics, these attempts have been limited to a mere handful of scholars. Generally speaking, economists are still considered to be missing out on a wide range of opportunities opened up by Foucault's reconsideration of the history of political economy and of the role played by it as a founding discourse of our modernity.

Foucault was one of the greatest thinkers of the twentieth century, having strongly influenced a large number of disciplines, such as history, rhetoric, philosophy, sociology, politics, psychiatry, medicine, psychology, linguistics, semiotics, law and literature. In particular, his work has been one of the most persistent examples of resources used in the humanities and social sciences. He has played a fundamental role in the construction of new ways of thinking, emerging as a consequence of the radical changes in the development of Western thought. Indeed, Foucault's work reflects and promotes a definite transformation in the context of post-linguistic turn and critical theory.

Dissatisfaction with the neoclassical approach to economic phenomena has led to a debate amongst economists regarding method, discourse and the study of history. It has been argued that the current hegemonic formalist conception of method in economics has led to less and less attention being attributed to the study of history. Much of what Foucault had to say to us is about our history and, when approaching history, he introduced and developed both a theory of discourse and a new method of approaching it.

Hodgson (2001, p. xiv), addressing the issue of the importance of studying history in economics, argued that without a knowledge of the past, we are condemned to repeat the same mistakes. We can certainly learn from the past and avoid repeating what has been done previously. Foucault's declaration, when referring to the fact that he was not familiar with the work of the Frankfurt School, is clearly appropriate here: 'I would not have said a number of stupid things and I would have avoided many, if the detours which I made while trying to pursue my own humble path – when, meanwhile, avenues have been opened up by the Frankfurt School' (Foucault, quoted in Best, 1995, p. 195).

The past may be a source of information and inspiration; however, there continues to remain another very important contribution in understanding the history that Foucault's archaeology stresses. The knowledge of our past can enhance the level of consciousness regarding who we are today, which Foucault called 'the history of the present'. Although this may appear rather obvious, it is clear that many economists have overlooked this point. Foucault's archaeology, as part of his genealogical project, aimed to provide us with elements required to understand who we are today. This has enabled us to unravel such questions as why we think some thoughts and not others, how the meaning and the scope of some concepts in their historical context affect us, and which fundamental rules were and are used to underpin the formulation of such concepts. As Baert (2005, p. 198) remarks, Foucault followed Nietzsche's genealogical approach with the intention of not simply gaining access to the unfamiliar past, but also to articulate and illuminate the familiar present, the past then becoming a means to access the present. Therefore, throughout his intellectual life Foucault declared that he was indeed interested in 'the history of the present'. His studies of the past were not simply aimed at an understanding of how we became what we are today, but were also intended to provide elements for an intervention. Foucault followed Nietzsche's belief that history itself would indeed only make sense insofar as it could alter the present. It was Foucault's intellectual project to accomplish and promote a 'historical ontology' of ourselves, meaning 'an attitude, an ethos, a philosophical life in which the critique of what we are is at one and the same time the historical analysis of the limits imposed on us and an experiment with the possibility of going beyond them' (Foucault, 1984c, p. 50). This prompts us to question: 'in what is given to us as universal, necessary, obligatory, what place is occupied by whatever is singular, contingent, and the product of arbitrary constraints' (ibid., p. 45). Looking for answers to this kind of question, he provided elements to improve our understanding of how historically economics adopted some epistemological figures, rhetorical schemes, methods of investigation and linguistic devices.

Beyond some internal contributions of Foucault's archaeology regarding the rethinking of the history of political economy, he provides elements for studying historical contexts through their specific 'discursive practice'. For instance, works on the history of methodology of economics focus on what economics imported from other sciences and, in particular, explore the relationships between economics and physics (for instance, Mirowski, 1984 and 1989, Deane, 1978 and Redman, 1991).

One important contribution to the understanding of the history of economic methodology was provided by Philip Mirowski, whose intellectual project was established to trace the origins of mathematical economics through the influence of physics on the method employed in economics. Mirowski (1984) argues that, in a process that might be called 'abduction', the protagonists of the marginalist revolution promoted a 'methodological revolution' in economics, employing a metaphor imported from physics (more precisely from energetics) as it was being developed in the middle of the nineteenth century. It is particularly interesting to notice here that Mirowski presents the process as discontinuous and investigates what, in Foucault's approach, is a 'region of interpositivities' or an 'interdiscursive domain'. For Mirowski, there was a discontinuity in the history of economic thought in the years 1870–80, which led to the genesis of neoclassical theory, and it was a process that also followed a discontinuity in physics. Instead of what is usually believed to be the case, that neoclassical theory was inspired by Newtonian physics, Mirowski shows that it was indeed built upon an analogy to energetics. All the main protagonists of the marginalist revolution (Jevons, Walras, Edgeworth, Fisher and Pareto) were familiar with the developments in energetics, which provided them with a metaphor (utility = energy), the mathematical techniques and the new attitudes in theoretical construction (Mirowski, 1984, p. 366). Mirowski argues that this allowed them to apply mathematical language to the construction of theories and promote the first great point of inflection of mathematical economics.

From a Foucauldian perspective, we can see that Mirowski's investigation of the marginal revolution was touching on an inquiry into the historical interdiscursive practice that gave rise to it, which may also help us to understand why these thinkers, though working independently, followed the same approach. Mirowski's study is an example of different domains of knowledge being determined by the same epistemic context. Therefore, the conscious possibility of such underlying configurations of thought may also shed light on the historiography of economic thought.

Mirowski was actually investigating the consequences for economic theory of the existence of a certain historical 'discursive practice', as Foucault would define it. In this expression, 'practice' means 'a way of doing things' and 'discursive practice' comprises a set of regularities regarding the form by which certain fields of objects are demarcated and norms about how to elaborate concepts and theories are established (Foucault, 2000b, p. 74). Hence, each historical 'discursive practice' presupposes a play of prescriptions that govern exclusions and selections (Foucault, 2000a, p. 11). It is through the analysis of 'discursive practices' that we can unravel 'a type of systematicity' that characterizes different 'systems of thought'. For Foucault, this 'systematicity' could not only be found out through a logical or linguistic analysis. Furthermore, the transformations of discursive practices could not be reduced to 'a precise individual discovery'. According to him, the 'systematicities' of thought change according to a complex set of historical modifications that may occur either outside it (in the form of production, social relations and political institutions), within it (as in techniques for determining objects, refinement and adjustment of concepts and the accumulation of data) or alongside it (as in other discursive practices). They do not refer to a subject of knowledge (historical or transcendental) and they are derived from a 'will to knowledge' which, argued Foucault, had been studied thus far according to anthropological and psychological notions. He intended to investigate them through a 'set of relations', which he defined in his archaeology of knowledge and which will be explored in further detail following this introduction.

This notion of 'discursive practice' is related to Foucault's work and his perception of 'thought', to perceive it as an action, to say that every human institution or action comprises a form of thought and that even when individuals are seen to be exercising it, they are indeed unaware of it. As O'Farrell (2005, p. 71) remarks, Foucault is actually challenging the 'theory/practice' split, since theory is already a practice, which occurs in a particular time and place. Without doubt, he manages to destroy any usual distinction made between theory and practice. This is why historical investigations, if they are to produce a rewarding outcome, need to compare and treat all the different fields at the same level, even those traditionally considered to be hermetically divided, such as literature and scientific research, together with the cultural and human activities.

One should also emphasise in the distinctive character of Foucault's approach the expression 'historical specificity' and what is meant by this in economic methodology. Hodgson (2001, p. xvi) exemplifies this point, arguing in favour of a restoration of the historical alternative, pointed out by the German Historical School at the end of the nineteenth century. He argues that theories should consider the historical, institutional and socioeconomic context, highlighting that when economics abandoned its historical orientation, it lost its emphasis on the study of real, socioeconomic systems and instead became a deductivist exploration of 'individual choice'. Foucault's approach shows that theories are built according to some historical conditions of possibility, which allow them to emerge, exist, coexist, change and disappear. This is to say that, if economists opted for a formalist approach instead of a historical perspective when formulating theories, then that would be because there were some historical conditions attributed to this, which

Foucault went on to investigate. While Hodgson was in fact emphasising a concern with the method, empiricism versus rationalism and induction versus deduction, Foucault pursued an explanation as to how and why these were privileged in time. The discussion relating to historical specificity that Hodgson promotes engages on a methodological level, while Foucault focuses on answering such questions as why empiricism or rationalism was privileged in a certain spatiotemporal context. We could extend Foucault's questions to our moment and ask why it is that we contemplate a crisis in the science of economics. In a Foucauldian terminology, what is it that we have managed to establish that defines the limitations of our discourse? Is it possible to go back to our past methods in order to surpass the current crisis? Foucault's archaeology of knowledge offers answers to these questions, which can radically change the way methodology has been studied in economics.

Furthermore, Foucault talks about discontinuous and non-teleological history, and these remain as missing categories in the historiography of economic thought. Economists still consider their history as continuous and progressive. For example, Cantillon may be regarded as a precursor to classical and neoclassical economics. However, there is a fundamental line of thought which needs to be determined before such similarities can be professed. The similarity established between Cantillon, physiocrats and Smith's work may well be explained via a project of establishing a taxonomy of elements of wealth (a general science of order), although Cantillon was not actually setting up 'a model of general equilibrium' in his *Essai*, as some may presume. This interpretation of his work is purely down to a desire to see continuity and progress established in thought.

Schumpeter's *History of Economic Analysis* is another classic example. Schumpeter analysed economic thought as continuous, made affirmations such as 'there is an unbroken line of development between Galiani and J. B. Say, Quesnay, Beccaria, Turgot, Verri, Condillac' and maintained that Galiani was a predecessor to marginal utility theory, Ricardo and Marx (Schumpeter, 1954, p. 302).

We could ask ourselves the question of what it would mean to consider economic thought in a non-teleological and non-progressive way. For Foucault, concepts, notions, theoretical frameworks, methods and so on are all bound by time and culture. For example, what 'wealth' meant to mercantilists and physiocrats is not considered to be the same as it meant for Smith or Ricardo. This means that concepts like 'value', 'money', 'exchange' and so on all need to be understood according to the context in which the economic thought was originally construed.

Although this appears obvious on the surface and very little controversy exists regarding this view, there undoubtedly still remains a missing factor in economic theory. Perhaps the problem stems from the question as to how we interpret this context in order to unveil such differences. Taking the two examples mentioned above, Hodgson on the one hand proposes to analyse social institutions and Mirowski on the other hand suggests that we should look at what was occurring in physics. However, instead of concentrating on the surface similarities, Foucault declares, it could be interesting to establish an answer as to why they are connected, since while upon initial examination it would appear that they are quite similar on the surface, they do in fact have fundamental differences. Instead of drawing upon the conclusion that the concepts of 'labour', 'scarcity' and so on were already clearly established by Galiani or Petty, it would be extremely beneficial for economists to examine if they were indeed talking about the same thing and, if not, why not? Even in the case of Schumpeter and his view on 'continuity', the reflections he makes indicate to us that his interpretation may well be hiding some crucial differences. When he claimed (1954, p. 184) that none of Smith's ideas were actually new to his age, it would be interesting to clarify and examine this to see if they were definitely talking about the same thing. Schumpeter also remarked upon Smith's main contribution and enlightenment as the building of a system reflecting a moment of 'co-ordination' of ideas (ibid., p. 185). This raises a deep question: what does this 'moment of co-ordination' actually mean? When Schumpeter states that Smith's *The Wealth of Nations* did not contain a single *analytic* idea, principle or method which could be considered as being entirely new at the time of its publication in 1776, he implies that there was actually some form of continuity (ibid., p. 184). Although Schumpeter sees a continuity of ideas, he also recognised that Smith followed a moment of change that led him to co-ordinate them. This leads us to the question of on what basis could Schumpeter have argued that the ideas were the same and what was meant by 'a moment of co-ordination'? In other words, how would he define continuity and the moment of co-ordination had he elaborated on it? It seems that Schumpeter's statements touched on a number of questions that Foucault raised in his archaeological investigations. This is to say that it was necessary to go beyond the surface and to investigate the existence of continuity or the lack of it, and to suggest that continuity implies that the problems, notions and concepts formulated by Smith's predecessors were the same as Smith's own views. Foucault wanted to know if they really understood 'wealth' in the same way and if it was truly being analysed according to the same set of standards. Furthermore, did they indeed all have the same understanding regarding the concept of money, value, labour and production?

These questions disturbed Foucault and in order for him to consider them, he needed to develop a new set of conceptual frameworks (articulated in *The Archaeology of Knowledge*) together with a very detailed empirical work. This new conceptual framework has revealed a completely new range of options within the rethinking of various fields of investigation, therefore suggesting that we should explore these and provide a critical reading of Foucault's contributions towards economics.

It is the hope of the author that this book will provide some of the basic elements required for a renewed thinking to take place regarding both the historiography and methodology of economics. It is believed that this will shed some light on the question as to why a rhetorical, linguistic or methodological scheme is made in preference to others. Comparisons will be made with case studies in economics using Foucault's approach, with the focus being placed on two specific areas. The first will examine the context of antipositivist reflections on economic methodology and the relations between the Kuhnian concept of 'paradigm' and the Foucauldian notion of 'episteme', and how this may help us to think about economic discourse. The second analyses the transition from pre-classical economic thought to political economy according to Foucault's notion of episteme. It is suggested that Foucault's approach bears a close resemblance to other ways of thinking of economic discourse that are more 'radical', in the strict sense of the word, such as the way to think of economic discourse regarding 'paradigms', 'modes of thought' (as introduced to economics by Sheila Dow, 1985) and different historical matrices (such as the 'modern' and 'postmodern' matrices). It may also be possible to adopt this method of thinking when looking at the different modes of approach towards the economic phenomena and when identifying closed and open conceptions of systems and the consequences for theorising economy, in accordance with one or other of these standards. Although these approaches may appear disparate, they do have something fundamental in common from which they then depart. Beyond an explicit criticism of a rationalist project for science, they all embrace the efforts to enhance our understanding of the current character of economic discourse, through the searching for deep conducive factors, which culminate in a certain state of affairs in economics. Sheila Dow, for example, defines 'mode of thought' as:

> [T]he way in which arguments (or theories) are constructed and presented, how we attempt to convince others of the validity or truth of our arguments. It is concerned as much with the rhetoric used as means of communication as with the logical structure of the argument. It is a *broader* concept than 'methodology', and indeed influences our judgement as to what constitutes an acceptable methodological position. (Dow, 1996, p. 10, emphasis added)

These current perspectives all beg the same question: is there any underlying configuration that determines our way of thinking, theorising, speaking, writing and so on? This question is not only implied by these approaches but has also been raised by current works in economic methodology. For example, it was pointed out by Klamer (1995, p. 332), when he wrote that a crucial question that needed to be investigated by economists was why certain rhetorical devices are privileged over others. Henderson, Dudley-Evans and Backhouse (1993) also called attention to the limitations of McCloskey's analysis of rhetorical devices in the introduction to one of the few works dedicated exclusively to language studies in economics: 'If we ignore linguistic structures, and *if we do not explore the reasons why these have been adopted*, there are important aspects of economists' writing that we cannot understand' (Henderson *et al.*, 1993, p. 9, emphasis added).

Foucault's particular way of thinking about history, which he preferred to call the 'history of systems of thought', offers elements that provide us with the ability and the insight to consider specific questions in the history of economic thought. According to him, every age has its way of producing 'the truth', which can be uncovered as we consider history. Through extensive archival work and analysis of theories and practices of an age, Foucault tried to disclose the conditions that made knowledge possible, and in a specific way. He wondered about the possibility of knowledge having historically followed a kind of well-defined regularity':

> [I]f empirical knowledge, at a given time and in a given culture, *did* possess a well-defined regularity? If the very possibility of recording facts, of allowing oneself to be convinced by them, of distorting them in traditions or of making purely speculative use of them, if even this was not at the mercy of chance? If errors (and truths), the

practice of old beliefs, including not only genuine discoveries but also the most naïve notions, obeyed, at a given moment, the laws of a certain code of knowledge? If, in short, the history of non-formal knowledge had itself a system? That was my initial hypothesis – the first risk I took. (*OT*, pp. ix–x, original emphasis)

Instead of looking for the rules of good science, Foucault focused his study on how these rules were formulated and how they change in certain empirical forms of knowledge. He actually believed that systems of thought and knowledge are governed by rules, although these rules are 'beyond those of grammar and logic' and functioned 'beneath the consciousness of individual subjects', defining 'a system of conceptual possibilities that determines the boundaries of thought in a given domain and period' (Gutting, 2005, p. 4).

Besides the writing of history, Foucault also offers an insight into the economic methodology. It will later be suggested that his perspective was very close to that of rhetoric. Their similarity may well stem from the fact that they are not posing the question about the true value placed upon what is said, but rather are aimed at discovering how, against other possibilities of discourse, one succeeds in imposing itself. Foucault's archaeology has also provided elements for the rethinking of rhetoric. *The Order of Things* can even be seen as a history of rhetoric, so much so that Corbett and Connors (1999, p. 541) even call Foucault a 'rhetorician' and state that when the next chapter in the history of rhetoric is written, books like *The Archaeology of Knowledge* will need to be discussed. These authors then place Foucault beside great contemporary rhetoricians such as I.A. Richards, Richard Weaver, Stephen Toulmin, Chaim Perelman and Kenneth Burke, as a writer who has to be considered by rhetorical scholars.

Indeed, Foucault's archaeology, in particular the concept of episteme, has bolstered the development of a movement in rhetoric called 'epistemic rhetoric'. His notion of 'episteme' in *The Order of Things* and his metatheory of discourse in *The Archaeology of Knowledge* have provided scholars with many elements in this movement in rhetoric.

Much has been said about the density of Foucault's work (for example, Carrette, 2000, White, 1973 and 1979, and Leary, 1976). It is claimed that this is drawn from his interdisciplinarity and the profound character of his writings, and that they are the result of an exigent mind in continuous reflection. Foucault constantly pushed his thinking beyond what he and others knew (Lemert and Gillan, 1982, p. 134). To this is added a great erudition, a singular style, a specific language and, as Shumway (1989, Preface) points out, a work that usually 'challenges our assumptions, beliefs, and expectations'. Foucault did have a very singular style. Caws (1971, p. 34) declared that *The Order of Things* could be blamed for three 'deadly sins in French intellectual prose': verbosity, pomposity and preciosity. White argues that Foucault's thought is still more difficult to define in short, since it 'comes clothed in a rhetoric apparently designed to frustrate summary, paraphrase, economical quotation for illustrative purposes, or translation into traditional critical terminology' (White, 1979, p. 81). Part of this 'idiosyncrasy', White argues, reflects a kind of rebellion of Foucault's generation against the clear Cartesian style.

The difficulty found with his work is still attributed to the sometimes arguable problems of language translation, and although the translations earn no particular praise, it is commonly agreed that the fault lies buried in the original French (Leary, 1976, p. 290). O'Farrell (2005, pp. 7–8) also makes a point about the problems of translation, drawing attention to some French words that are crucial in Foucault's texts which have been inadequately translated, all adding to the problem of the interpretation of his writings. For example, the expression *'le savoir de connaissance'* is a real dilemma, since *savoir* and *connaissance* have only one equivalent translation in English: 'knowledge'. She even concludes that there are actually two different Foucaults, depending on the language used, and makes the distinction between a French and an English-language Foucault.

One reason for Foucault's lack of prominence in economics could be somewhat due to the fact that he was part of a French movement that has been ignored by most Anglo-American literature. McCloskey (1992) raised this issue when commenting on Rossetti's (1992) paper on deconstruction, implying that economists could well be frightened by the difficulty of such readings. She wrote: 'you could frighten someone away from modern criticism by telling them that French leftwing criticism was its essence. I worry that focusing on something so terrifying as deconstruction will give economists a cheap excuse to go on ignoring the other half of their intellectual culture' (McCloskey, 1992, p. 262).

Foucault's work has emerged in the context of intense debate about epistemology and the history of thought. In opposition to Cartesian and Hegelian arceptions of these subjects, Foucault developed his own system based upon Nietzsche. Primarily, he adopted the 'genealogy' from Nietzsche as a tactic of investigation to emphasise the emergence of historical events through relations of forces. His objective was to establish the conditions leading to an emergence (and coexistence, maintenance, modification and disappearance) of discourses, comprising two stages: archaeology and genealogy. In the former, Foucault searched for an underlying historical set of relations that defined such conditions within the system of discourse. In his genealogical project, he was looking for external conditions, particularly derived from the social relations that determined discourses, focusing on the power-knowledge relations.

Unlike 'discourse' used in linguistic, grammar or rhetoric studies, Foucault's interpretation of discourse differs from the conventional term, since it does not regard discourse as a linguistic system or a text built to persuade. Foucault was not searching for the answer to how some concepts were formed; instead, he wanted to know how some conditions of possibility determined them, in such a way that they (the conditions) could define a common group of different domains of knowledge (different discourses). 'Discourse' means 'discipline', which can be understood as the bodies of knowledge (archaeology) or disciplinary institutions (genealogy). This book focuses on his archaeology. Discourse is hereby taken as 'discourse-as-knowledge'. Furthermore, Foucault's approach to discourse was not formalist or empirical, but 'critical' in two senses. Firstly, Foucault, like Kant, was looking for 'the conditions of possibility', although Foucault's 'critique' had some major differences compared to those of Kant, in particular the historical character of such conditions. Secondly, his approach was critical in the sense that he intended to establish the possibilities of change.

In particular, Foucault has been considered a 'structuralist' because: he did see a 'structure' underlying discourse; he did employ a language borrowed from structural linguistics; and archaeology was a synchronic approach. However, although he did share the same 'epistemic' context, his archaeology was crucially different from structuralism: the 'structure' or 'set of relations' that determines discourse is not *a priori*. As in deconstruction, meanings are completely context-dependent, which places Foucault beside Derrida as a founder of 'poststructuralism'. Other differences include the non-continuous character of discourse, which was closely related to Foucault's opposition to the idea of a sovereign subject. That is why in *The Archaeology of Knowledge* he denied notions of tradition, influence, development, evolution, 'spirit' of an age and *mentalité*. *The Archaeology of Knowledge* submitted discourses (disciplines = bodies of knowledge) for scrutiny, with the aim of finding out how they constituted themselves as unities of discourse. That was one of his objectives in *The Order of Things*, which was to find out how political economy established itself as a discipline (discourse) at the end of the eighteenth century. Which set of conditions of possibility actually determined discourse on the economy? This is the question, which will be explored further in Chapters 3 and 5.

The study will be developed in two stages. Part I is a detailed critical reading of Foucault's writings on the archaeology. Chapter 2 outlines the nature of Foucault's project by considering him in his own context, dealing with his intellectual environment, background and philosophical historic project. Foucault believed that an author's work transcends the individual. Hence, an additional understanding may well be gained by considering Foucault in his own context. Chapter 3 introduces his project of the archaeology of knowledge and focuses especially on his *The Archaeology of Knowledge* and *The Order of Things*, given that these are his most important works for the main goals stated above. A conscientious account of his work will be carried out, which constitutes one of the major challenges of this book and which is considered to be absolutely necessary, in light of the complexity of his thought processes and because there have been very few studies carried out in economics regarding this matter.

Part II provides an analytical contribution in terms of his ideas and methods for the rethinking of economics following three major areas: the methodology of economics, the historiography of economic thought and the scholarship on Adam Smith's context, writings and method. It is thus subdivided into three chapters. Chapter 4 situates Foucault's project within economic methodology in order to develop a more comprehensive reading of his work and making it more suitable for application. As for historiography, the chapter focuses on the relations between his work and Thomas Kuhn's concept of 'paradigm'. Chapter 5 provides a case study applying Foucault's notion of 'episteme' to the history of economic thought, exploring the transition from pre-classical economics – 'mercantilism' and 'physiocracy' – to classical political economy. Much has been said about that important moment in the history of economic thought and this chapter intends to demonstrate another way of interpreting it, through Foucault's inquiry into the discursive formation of economics. His system provides a distinct account of the emergence of political economy when 'man' became an object of knowledge towards the end of the eighteenth century. His association of this event with the emergence of the human sciences is certainly an important aspect that deserves investigation. Chapter 6 focuses on Smith's writings on language and rhetoric, his epistemology and some other ideas regarding his work according to Foucault's genealogy of biopolitics. The aim of this chapter is to form a contribution to the debate concerning Smith's context, employing Foucault's archaeological project. Finally, Chapter 7 draws on some of the conclusions.

Although this book concentrates on Foucault's writings during the 1960s, given that this is the period that he dedicated to the archaeology, his lectures at the Collège de France in 1978–9 will also be considered when dealing with 'modern' economic thought and Smith's writings, due to the importance of these later reflections by Foucault. These open up a new range of investigations to do with our own epistemic context and shed light on the scholarship on Smith's works, demonstrating the connection between his early and late works.

Part I
Foucault's Archaeology

2
Foucault's Context

2.1 Introduction

The intention of this chapter is to outline the nature of Michel Foucault's project in his archaeology of political economy by examining his intellectual environment and background, and how his ideas place themselves in the history of philosophy. It is a firm belief that it is only through an understanding of some of the aspects of his context, his way of thinking and the main characteristics of his intellectual project that we can start to apprehend his ideas regarding political economy. This chapter will focus on his ideas regarding the history and philosophy of science and the methodological principles underlying his investigations, while addressing 'discourse', along with his commitment to the Enlightenment.

2.2 A biographical sketch and intellectual background

Foucault was born in Poitiers, France in 1926 and died in Paris in 1984. His books were mainly histories of medical, human and social sciences. In 1969, he was elected chair to the ultra-prestigious Collège de France, where he remained professor until his death, naming the chair 'The History of Systems of Thought'. He lectured in many other countries, particularly in the USA, where in 1983 he agreed to teach annually at the University of California at Berkeley.

Foucault's intellectual life has been divided into two phases, which are associated with two distinct methodological positions: archaeology and genealogy. However, his intellectual life can be seen as much more multifaceted. This led Dreyfus and Rabinow (1982) to define four stages: a Heideggerian stage, an archaeological or quasi-structuralist stage, a genealogical stage and finally an ethical stage.

At the beginning of his intellectual life, Foucault was strongly influenced by existential phenomenology, particularly that of Heidegger and Merleau-Ponty, having attended the lectures of Merleau-Ponty at the École Normale Supérieure. Hegel and Marx were also part of his studies through the influence of Jean Hyppolite and Louis Althusser, both teachers at the same school. As for existentialism, Jean-Paul Sartre played a very important part, although Foucault later openly distanced himself from Sartre's ideas. Foucault rejected what he defined as Sartre's 'centralization of the subject', calling it 'transcendental narcissism', and accused Sartre of playing a role as a 'universal intellectual' in the sense of 'judging a society in terms of transcendental principles' (Gutting, 2003, p. 2).

As for thought regarding the history and philosophy of science, Georges Canguilhem and Gaston Bachelard had a huge influence on Foucault's work. Canguilhem was famous in the French University because of his work in the history and philosophy of biology. He sponsored Foucault's doctoral thesis on the history of madness and was a great friend and supporter. Canguilhem's work on the history of science had a particular influence on Foucault's conception of discontinuities in scientific history and on his anti-subjectivist conviction, which placed Foucault in opposition to the phenomenologist idea of transcendental consciousness.

As for the theory of knowledge, Rorty (1986) provides a concise and very clarifying reflection of Foucault's place within the context of discussions in this subject. He argues that three lines of thought dominated Foucault's intellectual environment: the Cartesian, the Hegelian and the Nietzschean.

The Cartesian was concerned with epistemology, which included Carnap and Hempel. As Rorty made clear, beyond some non-cognitive, non-scientific areas (such as religion, morals and art), this trend divides knowledge into hard or mature sciences and softer or immature sciences. These latter sciences required the same objectivity and rationality as the former sciences and therefore needed to mirror themselves in those. Science should ensure that the representations corresponded to reality. Rationality was ahistorical and should someone wish to suggest that rationality was not the same thing in all ages, then Cartesians would argue that this implied an independence of thought from its object; hence it was 'idealistic' and 'relativistic' (Rorty, 1986, p. 44).

The Hegelian view took for granted that rationality progressed sociologically and historically throughout history (Dewey, Wittgenstein and Kuhn). Rorty notes that when accused of relativism, these Hegelians argued that the progress of thought should replace the Cartesian idea of 'correspondence'; since history could show the superiority of the present in relation to the past, it provided suggestions on how to catch up with the more progressive areas. The Hegelian historiography was therefore eschatological.

According to Rorty, Foucault thought of Hegelian historicism as simply a variation of Cartesianism. For Foucault, the Hegelian reaction against the Cartesian idea of epistemology had not gone far enough. Foucault did indeed have a Nietzschean attitude and presented genealogy as the alternative, given that it was a non-eschatological and non-edifying historiography. Introduced to philosophy by Nietzsche, genealogy was a search for the emergence and development of discourses through a field of forces. It was a critical method, in the sense that it did not accept absolute grounds and emphasised that things only emerged in relation to and in competition with other things. Foucault widely employed it, as he intended to rescue the emergence of certain historical events.

In Foucault's archaeological phase, among other essays and interviews, Foucault published *Madness and Civilization* (*Folie et Déraison*) in 1961, *The Birth of the Clinic: An Archaeology of Medical Perception* (*Naissance de la clinique: une archeologie du regard medical*) in 1963, *The Order of Things* (*Les Mots et les Choses: une archeologie des sciences humaines*) in 1966 and *The Archaeology of Knowledge* (*L'Archeologie du savoir*) in 1969. Archaeology was his search for the 'rules of formation' that shape and limit discourse. He declared (Foucault, 1971c) that he had actually borrowed the word 'archaeology' and its meaning from Kant's *Fortschritte der Metaphysik*, employing it like the German philosopher to mean the '*a priori* conditionings of perception'.

Foucault wrote *The Order of Discourse* (Foucault, 1970b) for his inaugural lecture at the Collège de France, which took place on 2 December 1970. This is considered to be the turning point of his shift from archaeology to genealogy. Another indication of this transition surfaces in *Discipline and Punish: The Birth of the Prison* (*Surveiller et punir: Naissance de la prison*), first published in 1975. The genealogical phase also includes the three volumes of *The History of Sexuality*: *The Will to Knowledge* (*Histoire de la sexualité, I: la volonte de savoir*) first published in 1976, and both *The Use of Pleasure* (*Histoire de la sexualité, II: l'usage des plaisirs*) and *The Care of the Self* (*Histoire de la sexualité, III: le souci de soi*), which were published in 1984.

Foucault's archaeological and genealogical stages of work were often regarded as being under the influence of structuralism and poststructuralism respectively. At least since the publication of *The Order of Things* in 1966, his association with such trends has been a matter for debate. It is not entirely possible to define or to clarify the connections or meanings between archaeology/genealogy and structuralism/poststructuralism coherently. Throughout all of Foucault's work, archaeology was part of genealogy. He later emphasised this in his lecture on 7 January 1976 at the Collège de France: 'Archaeology is the method specific to the analysis of local discursivities, and genealogy is the tactic which, once it has described these local discursivities, brings into play the desubjugated knowledges that have been released from them' (Foucault, 2003, pp. 10–11). He also demonstrated the connection between archaeology and genealogy in his article 'What is Enlightenment?', where he argued for a 'historical ontology' of ourselves, remarking that this should have a 'methodological coherence in the *at once archaeological and genealogical study* of practices' (Foucault, 1984c, p. 50, emphasis added). Archaeology is actually a genealogy of historical forms of rationality and knowledge. Foucault was concerned with the conditions of existence and the limits of discourse in both archaeology and genealogy; what changed in the genealogy was the fact that he overtly took into account the political and economic conditions. Whilst archaeology is the historical study of discursive formations, genealogy is considered to be the historical investigation of the practices by and through which the discursive formations are produced and reproduced. Although we cannot say that there was a 'break' or 'rigid division' between the earlier and later writings of Foucault, there was a clear change of emphasis, which occurred in the 1970s. In his later writings, he considered more explicitly the non-discursive practices, such as institutions, social practices and technologies of power. From a genealogical perspective, he took the discourse of knowledge, which was usually regarded as a neutral element, and analysed its power-knowledge fundamentals.

It was the publication of *The Order of Things* which revealed Foucault as one of the great thinkers of the twentieth century. It had a tremendous impact, becoming a fashionable book and a bestseller in France, despite being a very difficult read. Some months after its publication, Foucault appeared alongside Claude Lèvi-Strauss, Roland Barthes and Jacques Lacan (all sitting and dressed in jungle grass skirts) in the cartoon 'Le déjeuner des structuralistes' ('The structuralists' lunch party') by Maurice Henry. The cartoon was first published in the French literary periodical *La Quinzaine Littéraire,* later to become famous in its own right. This event demonstrated how quickly he could rise to stardom amongst the great intellectuals and how he too could be regarded as a 'thinker' on a par with Sartre, Freud and Marx. The cartoon also emphasised the way in which he was later to be perceived. As its title was to demonstrate, he was now regarded as part of the generation of structuralists.

The term 'structuralism' has been used to refer to a number of works of different thinkers in different countries. Nevertheless, it is most commonly associated with the intellectual movement present in France in the 1950s and 1960s, although at that time in France it was not clear what the movement was about, and to even call it a 'movement' could be considered controversial, as Barthes wrote in 1964: 'What is structuralism? Not a school, nor even a movement (at least, not yet), for most of the authors ordinarily labelled with this word are unaware of being united by any solidarity of doctrine or commitment' (Barthes, 1972, p. 213). Foucault (1983) declares that, except in some precise disciplines such as linguistics, which were applying structural methods, nobody, even those who were frequently designated 'structuralist', knew exactly what the movement related to.

There is, however, a consensus regarding the origins of the movement, which are identified in the work of Ferdinand de Saussure, specifically the transcription by his students from several courses in general linguistics that he provided in 1907–11, which was published posthumously in 1916 as *Course in General Linguistics*.

Saussure started considering two fundamental dimensions of language: *parole* and *langue*, more commonly translated as 'speech' and 'language' respectively. *Parole* refers to the combination of signs in the mind of a speaker and the psychophysical mechanisms by which they are externalised, while *langue* is the abstract system used by a speech community, which we call simply 'language' in English. In other words, *parole* is actual speech and *langue* is a transcendental structure of language (Robinson, 1997, p. 6). *Langue* or 'language' 'is the theoretical system or structure of a language, the corpus of linguistics rules which speakers of that language must obey if they are to communicate' and *parole* or 'speech' is 'the actual day-to-day use made of that system by individual speakers' (Sturrock, 1979, p. 8).

Saussure understood language (*langage*) as an object which was systematic, homogeneous and could be examined through logical theorising. He was not concerned with questions regarding the capacity of language to access or even to change reality. He made a distinction between the two approaches to language (*langage* or *langue*): synchronic and diachronic. The synchronic approach focuses on how a given system is at a specific moment and how each part fits into the system (structuralism is considered to rely on this type of approach). A diachronic approach searches for the history of the system, its origins and developments. To adopt an analogy, whilst the diachronic approach can be regarded as a film, the synchronic approach represented each frame or picture that constitutes it. Saussure himself proposed a synchronic study of language, as opposed to the work in historical linguistics carried out in the nineteenth century. As Schleifer (1997) describes, Saussure wanted to reduce the great variety of findings of historical linguistics to a manageable number of propositions based upon the formal relationships defining and existing between the elements of language, claiming that he had found a set of rules underlying language, being organised by binary oppositions, such as masculine and feminine, up and down, light and dark, right and wrong and so on.

Saussure saw language as a system of signs. In his 'theory of signs', 'sign' is a combination of a 'signifier' (or *signifiant*) and a 'signified' (or *signifié*). As Culler (1985, p. 19) explains, 'signifier' is a form that signifies and 'signified' is an idea signified, although they do not exist separately. Words are signs and noises can be signs if they express or communicate ideas. To communicate ideas, they must be part of a system of conventions, part of a system of signs. Concerning language, the 'signifier' is the material aspect of language: a 'meaningful sound' (spoken language) or a 'meaningful mark' on paper (written language). However, it was not only the physical thing (sound or mark). For Saussure, the signifier is also the psychological imprint of the sounds on our senses.

Following Saussure's linguistic model, other intellectuals engaged themselves in a kind of quest or inquisition on theory, predominantly concerned with the description of structures. Structure was understood as 'a system of transformations' that comprised laws, given that a system is 'not a mere collection of elements and their properties' (Piaget, 1971, p. 5). The structuralist approach was in the anthropology of Claude Lévi-Strauss, in the psychoanalytic model of Jacques Lacan and in the study of signs and their meanings (semiotics) of Roland Barthes. Piaget (ibid., pp. 4–5) argued that structuralism had an appeal for two basic reasons: the belief that structures were self-sufficient, which released investigations about 'extraneous' elements; and since structures were believed to have common and perhaps necessary properties, this would mean that if one succeeded in determining certain structures, then this in turn would provide an insight for others.

The structuralist approach in France was derived in particular from the concern to 'unmask things' (Mautner, 2000, p. 544). There was a conviction that things were not actually what they appeared to be and that psychological, social and political phenomena were indeed determined by some structures not yet apparent, which should be unveiled. Moreover, the French structuralists rebelled against the humanism of Marxism and the idea of the autonomy of a subject, which was present in existentialism. For structuralists, individuals were regarded as simple parts of structures and their decisions could not really have an impact on the social events.

Foucault refused to be given the label of 'structuralist'. He explicitly denied it in many interviews and especially in his Foreword to the English edition of *The Order of Things*. In a later interview, he openly stated 'I have never been a Freudian, I have never been a Marxist and I have never been a structuralist' (Foucault, 1983, p. 22). Indeed, he always refused to be associated with any determinate intellectual, ideological or political position.

He even appeared to indicate that he was beyond structuralism when he first thought about the use of the subtitle 'The Archaeology of Structuralism' in *The Order of Things*. As we know, he changed it to 'The Archaeology of Human Sciences', although the reason why he decided to change it is not known. Shumway (1989) suggests that if we understand that 'structuralism' is part of a new 'episteme', then Foucault would not be able to write its archaeology, since he stated that we are still in the modern episteme and *The Order of Things* could not present the description or foundations of a new one. One other factor to be considered is that Foucault saw structuralism as being related to the current of formal thought at the beginning of the twentieth century, which was not a particular focus of his investigation in *The Order of Things*. Indeed, he refrained from saying more than it was an interesting topic for investigation (Foucault, 1983).

Although he always refused to be called a 'structuralist', some writers continue to associate him with structuralism, arguing that he did indeed share many similar aspects in his work with this movement, the most important being the following:

1 Foucault shared the same mode of thought that took structural linguistics as a methodological model and he was interested in the deep structures that regulate human consciousness. Although he declared that he had never used the word 'structure' in *The Order of*

Things, he did employ some metaphors that did allude to 'structure', such as 'philosophical space', 'quadrilateral', 'volume', 'system' and '*trièdre*' (translated as 'three faces' in the English version), as noticed by Billouet (2003, pp. 65–6).

2   Foucault employed the same language as used by structuralists, that is, a terminology borrowed from structural linguistics. Barthes in his *Critical Essays* called this language the 'nomenclature of signification':

[W]hatever the case, it is probably the serious recourse to the nomenclature of signification [...] which we must ultimately take as structuralism's spoken sign: watch who uses signifier and signified, synchrony and diachrony, and you will know whether the structuralist vision is constituted. (Barthes, 1972, p. 214)

3   The synchronic character of archaeology would define it as structuralist. While in archaeology Foucault was developing a synchronic analysis, he turned his attention to a diacronic investigation of history in genealogy. In other words, while the primary aim of archaeology was a description (synchronic), genealogy searched for explanations. At the end of *The Archaeology of Knowledge* he acknowledged the synchronic character of archaeology in his discussion with an imaginary interlocutor, someone who was clearly a structuralist person. Foucault was in fact responding to his critics regarding the fact that archaeology did not explain the shifts between different 'epistemic' contexts. He admitted that he was not interested in this kind of diachronic consideration since this would mean seeing transcendence in discourse or referring to a sovereign subjectivity (*AK*, p. 220).

For instance, White (1973) argued that the designation of Foucault as a structuralist was fair comment, since he shared with Lévi-Strauss and Lacan an interest in the deep structures of human consciousness, together with a conviction that the study of such deep structures should start with an analysis of language and a conception of language, which had its own origins depicted in the work of Saussure.

Therefore, it could be said that Foucault, at least during the 1960s, was associated with the structuralist movement – that is, if structuralism were interpreted as a method of inquiry that was influenced greatly by the work of Saussurre and borrowed from it a 'nomenclature of signification' or, in other words, a language that was a semiotic system, understood as a system of signs. If this were the case, Foucault openly admits his connection to this movement:

> In a positive manner, we can say that structuralism investigates above all unconsciousness. It is the unconscious structures of language, of the literary work, and of knowledge that one is trying at this moment to illuminate. [...] I think that one can say that what one is essentially looking for are the forms, the system, that is to say that one tries to bring out the logical correlations that can exist among a great number of elements belonging to a language, to an ideology (as in the analyses of Althusser), to a society (as in Lévi-Strauss) or to different fields of knowledge; which is what I myself have studied [referring to *The Order of Things*]. One could describe structuralism roughly as the search for logical structures everywhere that they could occur. (Foucault, quoted in Davidson, 1997, pp. 6–7)

Foucault never denied that there was a close relationship between his project and structuralism. He reaffirmed it in the interview 'Michel Foucault explains his latest book', which was given soon after the publication of *The Archaeology of Knowledge* and published in *Dits et Ecrits*. However, refusing, once again, to be labelled a structuralist, he remarked that his method was alongside, not within, structuralism (Foucault, 2001, p. 807). For him it was termed 'aside' because it was beside the same transformation of knowledge as structuralism (the same 'episteme'). Following his own project about the existence of an underlying configuration of thought, he declared that he was quite aware of his own historical 'positive unconscious'. He indicated that in the Foreword to the English edition of *The Order of Things*:

> There may well be certain similarities between the works of the structuralists and my own work. It would hardly behove me, of all people, to claim that my discourse is independent of conditions and rules of which I am very largely unaware, and which determine other work that is being done today. But it is only too easy to avoid the trouble of analysing such work by giving it an admittedly impressive-sounding, but inaccurate, label. (*OT*, p. xiv)

Beyond sharing the same configuration of thought and even a conception of 'structure' underlying historical discourses (a 'set of relations'), Foucault's archaeology did exhibit some fundamental differences in relation to structuralism. In his work, he did not consider this 'set of relations' to be given, *a priori* or transcendental. In a structuralist language, signs in Foucault's work do not have atemporal signifiers. Perhaps it is possible to argue that Foucault analyses 'events' rather than 'structures'. Within structuralism, the singularity of an event seems to be shadowed by the meaning of a structure, while in Foucault's work it is the focal point, shown by archaeology as the analysis of 'statements', which are considered in their singularity, without evoking a structure. There is a regularity identified by the analysis of statements, although it alludes to a vicinity of modes of emergence and existence that make the statements possible.

If labels need to be applied, Foucault was much closer to 'poststructuralism'. He was considered, together with Jacques Derrida, to be one of the initiators of that 'movement'. As Rorty (1995, p. 166) writes, although 'poststructuralism' is a term that remains 'hopelessly vague', 'whatever sense it [acquired] had from a wave of the hand in the direction of Derrida and Michel Foucault'. Structuralism is seen as being superseded by Derrida's deconstruction and by the work of Foucault.

Deconstruction and 'poststructuralism' are thoroughly connected. Derrida is regarded as one of the first figures of 'poststructuralism', since deconstruction intends to demonstrate an underlying instability or play on the binary oppositions of language, as pointed out by Saussure. Derrida maintained that, contrary to what Saussure believed, those binary oppositions were unstable. Meanings became something completely context-dependent. A word needed to be placed within a context in order for its meaning to be understood. Diverging from what structuralists claimed, meaning could change historically. This broke the connection Saussure had made between the signifier and the signified, which was Derrida's essential critique on structuralism. The emergence of 'poststructuralism' can be precisely identified, according to Rorty (1995, p. 166), in Derrida's reading of a paper at a conference on structuralism at Johns Hopkins University in Baltimore in 1966.

Poststructuralists may be regarded as thinking in terms of underlying structures, conceiving the world as constructed through language. However, unlike their predecessors, poststructuralists do not believe that it is possible to map those structures, since they are not given and are not constituted of *a priori* elements and meanings. In opposition to structuralism, which did not give too much attention to 'the genetic or historical dimensions of the subject-matter' (Mautner, 2000, p. 544), poststructuralists believe that signs and meanings are historical.

Hence, Foucault's work produced some important differences in relation to 'structuralism'. For example, he mentioned in *Truth and Power* that the notion of discontinuity had indeed been excluded from structural analysis and that '[i]n that sense, I don't see who could be more of an anti-structuralist than myself' (Foucault, 1984a, p. 56). Foucault also declared that he understood that the transformation in thought which he and structuralists were experiencing was rather about the enquiry regarding the anthropological status and the sovereignty of man than the analysis of structures (Foucault, 2001, p. 807). As previously mentioned, this characteristic of anti-humanism or anti-subjectivism is sometimes considered as already being a part of structuralism. For example, O'Farrell (1989, p. 10) argues that structuralists were anti-humanists and anti-subjectivists. However, as Foucault suggests, this can be perceived as a weak belief amongst structuralists, although it is certainly present in the work of poststructuralists. Foucault was certainly an anti-humanist and anti-subjectivist. In *The Order of Things* he declared 'the end of man', that is, of the sovereign Kantian subject. Piaget (1971, p. 135) wrote: 'Foucault's ouster of the subject is more radical than any hitherto.' *The Order of Things* was written with the profound purpose of attacking the subject, which he considered the biggest problem in Western culture. In an interview in 1968, published as 'Foucault répond à Sartre' in *Dits et Ecrits*, he stated:

My work? You know, it is a work that is very limited. Very schematically, it is this: to try to recover in the history of science, of knowledges [*connaissances*] and of human knowledge [*savoir humain*] something that would be like the unconscious of it. If you wish, the working hypothesis is roughly this: the history of science, the history of knowledges does not obey simply the general law of the progress of reason, it is not human consciousness, it is not human reason that is in some way the keeper of the laws of its history. There is, beneath that which science knows of itself something that it does not know; and its history, its development, its episodes, its accidents obey a certain number of laws and of determinations. These laws and these determinations, it is these, that I have tried to bring to light. (Foucault, 2001, pp. 693–4)

The archaeology of the human sciences that Foucault developed in *The Order of Things* had as one of its main objectives the purpose of confronting the subject, suggesting that the figure of man, on which they focused, was a recent invention and one that was perhaps nearing the end of the importance that it had acquired in Western thought. Once again, we can see the foundation of archaeology and genealogy regarding this subject when he declared:

> And this is what I would call genealogy, that is, a form of history, which can account for the constitution of knowledges, discourses, domains of objects, etc., without having to make reference to a subject which is either transcendental in relation to the field of events or runs in its empty sameness throughout the course of history. (Foucault, 1984a, p. 59)

2.3 Foucault's strategies of thinking

Foucault described in *The Order of Discourse* (Foucault, 1970b) some methodological principles that he intended to follow in his investigations. Although this was written after the publication of *The Archaeology of Knowledge* and Foucault declared that those were the methodological principles that he would follow in his works in the years to come, they must be described here as strategies that seem to guide his work even before they were explicitly articulated by him. He mentioned four main principles:

1 *The principle of reversal.* In its simplified form, this means to establish the opposite interpretation usually given by traditional approaches. In Foucault's work, this governs the other three principles. Foucault intended to explore the implications of the reversed or opposite interpretations and called this principle the 'negative' activity of discourse, as opposed to the usual approach of philosophers and historians, who were concerned with the 'positive' role of discourse. Shumway (1989) identifies two kinds of reversal in Foucault's work. First, he reverses assumptions of continuity and non-contradiction. For example, with regards to the notion of the author, Foucault wrote 'What is an author?' (Foucault, 1984e), where he questioned this notion. The strategy of reversal considers discourse as authorless because to do otherwise would be to assume that there is continuity with the author's other writings and coherence with some clear goal that he or she has in mind. This would make us exclude other connections or contradictions that the author's work may have. Secondly, Foucault applied the 'reversal of value', as Shumway denoted it. For example, the traditional narrative of the history of the treatment of madness

usually assumes 'a positive value'. For example, according to Shumway, this would mean to look into history for a treatment that had failed to bring about a cure. Foucault suggests that we should look for unintended and overlooked consequences of different therapies.

2   *The principle of discontinuity*. As exemplified in the reversal principle, Foucault looks at history as if it were discontinuous. Therefore, we should look for discontinuities, 'events', without intending to explain them in terms of continuity. He claims: 'We must not imagine that there is a great unsaid or a great unthought, which runs throughout the world and intertwines with all its forms and all its events, and which we would have to articulate or to think at last' (Foucault, 1970b, p. 67). This is one reason why he does not discuss the causes of shifts between 'epistemes' and relates the notion of 'discontinuity' to the concept of 'event'. 'Events' for Foucault are moments of transformation. By using the term 'events', he not only wants to emphasise 'changes' but also the 'singularity' of historical moments. He stated that in this sense, he was looking for 'eventalisation' meaning 'making visible a *singularity* in places where there is a temptation to invoke a historical constant, an immediate anthropological trait, or an obviousness that imposes itself uniformly on all' (Foucault, 1987, p. 104, original emphasis). However, he is not suggesting that we should assume that there is always discontinuity; on the contrary, he suggests we should look at the continuities with suspicion. He declared in *Truth and Power* that he did not intend to proclaim discontinuity as an inherent/immanent characteristic of all human history, but that it was located in certain empirical forms of knowledge, like biology, political economy, psychiatry, medicine, etc., investigated by him (Foucault, 1984a, p. 54). He contrasted his view of 'discontinuity' with the dialectical and semiotic conception of history, since it was his belief, while following the view of Nietzsche, that history had no meaning and was governed by a relationship to force. Foucault states that this did not mean that 'history' was not intelligible. It can be interpreted through the 'genealogy' of conflicts. Furthermore, he argues that the Hegelian dialectic, as the 'logic of contradictions', and semiotics, 'as the structure of communication', are not able to deal with 'the intelligibility of struggles, of strategies and tactics' (Foucault, 1984a, pp. 56–7). Genealogy is the method for that.

3   *The principle of specificity*. Discourses must be approached in accordance with the particularity of their historical formation. As Shumway (1989, p. 21) writes, Foucault reverses the usual assumption that discourse is more or less an accurate representation of a non-discursive reality.

The world itself is not presumed to have its own expression, which we can then translate into our own language. Discourse is built and can change 'reality'. That is why Foucault says: 'We must conceive discourse as a violence which we do to things, or in any case a practice which we impose on them' (Foucault, 1970b, p. 67). Hence, discourse has to be regarded as a practice, in which case it is beyond language. In *The History of Sexuality*, Foucault refers to the 'repressive hypothesis' as the idea that human sexuality has been repressed since the Victorian era because it is a 'dark secret'. However, he argues that this hypothesis is a mistake, given that we have inexhaustibly been talking about sexuality in the twentieth century. Therefore, it is not an unspoken secret and the discourse surrounding it has not released us from the Victorian silence, while sexuality remains a topic for discussion and one that determines the way in which we consider it. The traditional approach to discourse adopts the view that once there was a transcendental conversation that led to what we think and speak today. But, for Foucault, discourses have to be considered within their own historical conditions. As Shumway (1989, p. 22) points out, this principle can also be called the strategy of 'alterity' or otherness, in the sense that we should assume that discourses of earlier historical periods are radically different from our own. For instance, the history of economic thought should not assume that discourse on wealth was the same during the seventeenth and the nineteenth centuries. Therefore, the concept of money, value, labour and so on was not the same during that period.

4 *The principle of exteriority.* This strategy simply rejects the idea that there are any deep meanings. Foucault does not look for a rational or irrational cause, that is, a fundamental nature of discourse. This does not mean that he is not concerned with the style or form of discourse. He actually looks for the conditions of possibility and the existence of discourse. As Shumway (1989, p. 23) explains, these conditions can be twofold. The first are the internal conditions which allow only some statements to be produced while within a system of discourse. Archaeology aims to find out these conditions. The other form of conditions are those that are external, in particular those being social conditions related to the relations of power. These conditions are the object of genealogy.

2.4   The history of systems of thought

Foucault's work emerged in France in the 1960s, when there was an intense discussion regarding how to write the history of ideas. The notion of continuous progress in both the human sciences and the natural sciences was placed under scrutiny. Two basic lines of historical thought were present in France at that time: the *Annales* historiography and the historical epistemology of Bachelard and Canguilhem (Kusch, 1991). The *Annales* School, represented by historians like Henri Berr, Lucien Febvre, Marc Bloch and Fernand Braudel, became dominant in French historical thought following the Second World War. The name of the School was derived from the review *Les Annales d'histoire économique et sociale*, founded by Lucien Febvre and Marc Bloch in 1929.

These points of view arose from the reaction to two basic lines of thought, derived from Hegel and Husserl. The Hegelian mainstream conceived that there was a form of universal reason beneath the surface of the forms of human knowledge. It was *continuist* and we could therefore discern the 'progress of reason' through the understanding of an ever-present *Geist* or spirit. Hegelianism had a great influence on Marxism, since it provided the basis of dialectical thought. The phenomenological tradition, stemming from Husserl's work, argued that the basic principle underlying historical change was not an abstract spirit but the freedom of individuals, given that human thought or consciousness was supreme and was therefore capable of transcending any apparently given or determining conditions. This was the view of history of Merleau-Ponty and of the existentialists, especially Sartre. Existentialism also had an impact on Marxism, especially the so-called 'humanistic' or 'cultural' Marxisms of the 1970s.

Foucault, influenced especially by Bachelard and Canguilhem, abandoned the conception of the history of thought as being a continuous and progressive journey. Bachelard emphasised revolutions, breaks and discontinuities in the history of the natural sciences with his model of scientific change built around four key epistemological categories: epistemological breaks, epistemological obstacles, epistemological profiles and epistemological acts. However, he maintained the belief in the progressiveness of science. Canguilhem, who was Bachelard's student, pursued many of his master's central arguments, defending the view that the history of science was the history of defeats in irrationalism, focusing on social factors, ideology and the interrelations between certain disciplines (Kusch, 1991, pp. 32–3). Canguilhem's history of concepts inspired Foucault, especially concerning *The Order of Things*.

In the Introduction to *The Archaeology of Knowledge*, Foucault positioned himself within a new movement on historical thought, which had been reconsidering the concept of 'great continuities of thought', in which Foucault particularly included Bachelard, Canguilhem and

Guéroult. He declared that he had 'decided to ignore no form of discontinuity, break, threshold, or limit' (*AK*, p. 34). In his project, the idea of thinking of history in terms of 'discontinuities' was related to or resulted from his criticism of the 'anthropologisation' of thought, which emerged in the modern episteme. According to him, the history of thought until then had been written as if there were a 'sovereign subject' that had 'consciously' made its own history in uninterrupted continuity. Foucault then proposed another way of thinking about our past. The subject, in his view, was decentred and history was written in terms of its discontinuities, displacements and transformations. Man was not the creative architect of his history and his 'cherished creativity was constrained by systems that antedate and would survive him' (Kermode, 1973, p. 9). It was not the sovereign subject that defined the course of history, but some 'rules of formation' through which 'groups of statements' form unities in terms of 'science', 'literature', 'philosophy', 'history', 'theory', 'discipline' and so on. Therefore, all notions derived from the assumption of a 'sovereign subject', such as 'tradition', 'development', 'influence', 'evolution' and 'spirit', or usual unities taken as central in the investigation, such as 'book', 'oeuvre' or even 'author', should be questioned. These notions perpetuated the concept of continuity and the belief in them as independent and, perhaps more than that, the idea that they were expressions of a conscious subject. Foucault writes:

> The frontiers of a book are never clear-cut [...] beyond its internal configuration and its autonomous form, it is caught up in a system of references to other books, other texts, other sentences: it is a node within a network. And this network of references is not the same in the case of a mathematical treatise, a textual commentary, a historical account, and an episode in a novel cycle. [...] its unity is variable and relative. As soon as one questions that unity, it loses its self-evidence; it indicates itself, constructs itself, only on the basis of a complex field of discourse. (*AK*, pp. 25–6)

Foucault intended to waken man from an 'anthropological slumber'. As such, he wanted to start the colossal task of dismantling the view that knowledge was an expression of ideas of some men (Macdonell, 1986, p. 86). In his archaeology, knowledge had to be regarded as if it were the result of a system of thought, that is, the modes of organisation of thought that lie beneath the formations of knowledge within a society in a particular age.

Foucault summarised these main problematic areas within the history of ideas as being 'genesis', 'continuity' and 'totalisation', in the sense that they were determining 'the choices of topics and the style of analysis of historians of ideas' (Kusch, 1991, p. 46). Foucault meant by 'history of ideas' the tendency thus far of studying the 'history' of 'what is consciously going on in the mind of scientists, philosophers, *et al*' (Gutting, 2005, p. 33), in opposition to his own archaeological project, which was looking for what was unconsciously underlying thought. 'Genesis' represented a problem, since the writing of history was conducted using a search for 'the origin'. The ideas of 'continuity' and 'totalisation' were also misleading historical research, in the sense that they assumed homogeneity between, amongst and within different periods of history. Therefore, this suggested the hypothesis that there was homogeneity between and amongst different ages and distinct fields of knowledge that belonged to a similar age. This resulted from the search for 'coherence', as Kusch (1991, p. 54) summarised, leading to the ideas of *Weltanschauung*, *mentalité* and *Zeitgeist*. For Foucault this coherence had its roots firmly established in the figure of a sovereign subject.

There were two basic steps to follow in order to change the thought on history. First, it would be necessary to undertake a 'negative', a critical work, or as Kusch (1991) referred to it, the analysis of those usual categories and units employed by historians *via negationis* or 'deconstruction'. Secondly, the archaeological enterprise should accomplish the 'positive', 'constructive', work of establishing a new set of questions, relations, concepts and notions for historical inquiry. As Foucault declared, 'there is a negative work to be carried out first: we must rid ourselves of a whole mass of notions, each of which, in its own way, diversifies the theme of continuity' (*AK*, p. 23). He listed the notions he had in mind: tradition, influence, development and evolution, and 'spirit' of an age. For him, it was also necessary to question the familiar 'divisions and groupings' of types of discourses, such as the 'forms or genres such as science, literature, philosophy, religion, history, fiction, etc.' (*AK*, p. 24). For example, 'literature' and 'politics' are recent categories and could only hypothetically be applied to analyse the medieval or classical cultures. However, Foucault declared that, above all, one should question the unity of the book and the oeuvre. Finally, one should abandon the search for origins and the idea that 'all manifest discourse is secretly based on an "already-said"', not forgetting that this 'already-said' was always assumed to be connected to that which was 'never-said' (*AK*, p. 28). Of course, there should not be a definite exclusion of these notions but 'the tranquillity with which they are accepted [should] be disturbed' (ibid.).

Keeping these notions in suspense, the next step would be to pursue a 'positive' work, in which the starting-point would be to take the already-given unities of discourse such as psychology, medicine or political economy. Instead of focusing on 'their internal configuration or their secret contradictions', the task would then be to subject them to further questions: what unities do they form? By what right can they claim their unity in time? According to what laws are they formed? Against the background of which discursive events do they stand out? Are their unities not only a surface effect of more firmly grounded unities? (*AK*, p. 29). Foucault declared that his final objective would be to see whether they could be 'legitimately reformed', 'whether other groupings should be made', and 'to construct a theory of them' (ibid.).

However, as Gutting (1989, pp. 218–19) observed, Foucault was not only searching for the way in which internal concepts were historically formed in different disciplines, but he was also looking for the conceptions that defined the conditions of possibility of formulating such concepts, which were therefore common to different domains of knowledge. Agamben (2002, p. 3) also states that Foucault's approaches to history may be distinguished in terms of metaphorical and metonymical figures of speech. He argues that Foucault's approach has been characterised by the searching of metaphorical contexts, instead of metonymical contexts which, he declares, refer to the approach of history in terms of chronological and geographical caesuras, for example, 'France in the 17th century'.

Cousins and Hussain (1984, p. 4) stressed two distinct characteristics in Foucault's approach. Firstly, Foucault was not concerned with reconstituting the past and so he developed case studies or case histories. This had one important consequence: the evidence could be managed in different ways. In a history that tries to reconstitute the past, the historian must exhaustively control the evidence. In other words, they must control the existence of other pieces of evidence which could change the narrative, the generalisations or the conclusions. However, in a case history, the evidence is restricted to the problem under investigation and it is thought of in terms of intelligibility. It does not necessarily need to be adequate in itself to certain canons of proof and demonstration. Cousins and Hussain identified a second point, which was that Foucault's analyses did not look for 'origins', which are usual in history since they provide a continuist view. Cousins and Hussain say that Foucault concentrated his researches in 'beginnings' instead of 'origins', in the sense that he looked for 'a configuration of elements', which marked the 'emergence' of an event.

In fact, the difference between 'origin' and 'emergence' constitutes a central aspect of Foucault's work. He denunciated the search for origins and emphasised his disagreement with such *modus operandi* in the article 'Nietzsche, genealogy, history', where he followed the distinction between 'origin' and 'emergence' in Nietzsche. Foucault draws attention to the fact that Nietzsche used different German terms to designate 'origin' – *entstehung, herkunft* and *ursprung* – and that the German philosopher challenged the pursuit of the origin (*ursprung*) whenever a genealogy was being developed (Foucault, 1971a, p. 78). *Entstehung* means 'emergence', 'the moment of arising', while *herkunft* is 'the equivalent of stock or descent'. These two German words are more exact than *ursprung*, declares Foucault, to refer to the true objective of genealogy:

> A genealogy of values, morality, asceticism, and knowledge will never confuse itself with a quest for their 'origins', will never neglect as inaccessible the vicissitudes of history. On the contrary, it will cultivate the details and accidents that accompany every beginning; it will be scrupulously attentive to their petty malice; it will await their emergence, once unmasked, as the face of the other [...]. *The genealogist needs history to dispel the chimeras of the origin* [...]. (Foucault, 1971a, p. 80, emphasis added)

Foucault argues that the problem with the search for 'origins' was that it assumed that things were of an essence. Genealogy is different from traditional history since it is conducted in order to dissolve the views of a continuous process. Genealogy intends to be a history of interpretations. As Habermas points out:

> [G]enealogy is not supposed to search for an *origin*, but to uncover the contingent *beginnings* of discourse formations, to analyze the multiplicity of factual histories of derivation, and to dissolve the illusion of identity, especially the putative identity of the history-writing subject himself and of his contemporaries. (Habermas 1987, p. 250, original emphasis)

Foucault was seeking to understand the facts of the past in terms of their own context. This is indeed what 'archaeology' is all about. It investigates the contexts in which events happened. It is an 'archaeological context', that is, an event in time which has been preserved in the archaeological record. The archaeologist investigates the several layers of contexts. Foucault concluded that there was no truth because what was considered truth in a certain spatiotemporal context was defined by the positivities of its own day.

This seems to be summed up in what Foucault called 'the history of the present', another very particular and influential notion that he introduced to historical studies. It was his intellectual project to perform a diagnosis of the past, with the objective of shedding light on the problems of the present.

Another important characteristic of Foucault's historical investigation during his archaeological phase (at least) was the fact that he was interested in the events that served as the index, though not as an explanation (Cousins and Hussain, 1984, p. 40). Differing from the ideas of other historians in his analysis of the theories and practices of an age, he tried to disclose the rules that defined knowledge in its entirety, although he was not looking for an explanation as to why those were the rules that applied at that moment. This synchronic characteristic of his archaeological investigations was one reason for it being called structuralist, as previously mentioned in this chapter.

Above all, Foucault had turned his attention to the conditions of possibility within the human sciences: psychology, sociology and analysis of the literature and the myths. As Dreyfus and Rabinow (1982) remarked, Foucault was always interested in how, in our culture, men could understand themselves. The general theme of his intellectual work was not the power, but the matter of the subject, as he himself tells us in *The Subject and the Power*. In particular, he believed that the study of human beings had changed radically by the end of the eighteenth century, when economics, biology and philology emerged as 'sciences', and these 'sciences' were only made possible on the foundation of a 'historical *a priori*' that took man as the subject and object of his own knowledge. Instead of looking for the rules of a good science, Foucault focused his study on how these rules were formulated and how they would change within certain empirical forms of knowledge.

2.5 Enlightenment, epistemology, ontology and discourse

What is Enlightenment? As Foucault (1984c) declared, this question has not only marked the dawn of modern philosophy, but its entire trajectory. From Hegel, Nietzsche and Marx, Weber to Horkheimer and Habermas, none could avoid raising it 'directly or indirectly' (ibid.). In what appears to be a paraphrasing of the well-known Kantian questions, Foucault put its persistent course down to the fact that this question defines 'what we are, what we think, and what we do today'. It is also in this sense that the question directly or indirectly traverses many of the studies in economic methodology. To understand the current state of affairs in economics involves thinking about the Enlightenment and the criticism of it.

The Enlightenment has been considered as the founding project of economics. One can understand the predominant current discourse in economics, derived from a historical project of rationality, first proposed by the Ancient Greeks and concluded by the philosophers and scientists of the modern age. It was a mathematical-rational project. The way the Greeks started questioning the mythological explanations of the world guided knowledge towards being an essentially rationalising activity, which called for an application of mathematical language. The mathematical approach in economics is considered coeval to its emergence, as Jevons stated in the Preface to the second edition of his *The Theory of Political Economy*. During a long period in the history of economics, the application of mathematics was limited to it being an instrument. By the end of the nineteenth century, the protagonists of the methodological revolution called the 'Marginalist Revolution' began to employ mathematics as a language in the formulation of theories. Although this process had not been continuous, as Mirowski (1991) argued, it was considered as being founded upon those basic characteristics attributed to the 'Enlightenment'.

Although the question about the nature of Enlightenment is highly disputed, the usual interpretation of the movement relates to the ideas of the French Enlightenment, such that they were not only the most influential at their time but they have also become dominant in the project concept up to the current day. Peter Hamilton, quoted by King (1999, p. 44), has summarised the main characteristic of Enlightenment thought as follows:

- The primacy of reason and rationality.
- Empiricism.
- Science became an important cultural and intellectual factor, promoting technological development.
- Universalism: the Enlightenment aimed at universal and unifying foundations, as the principle of rationality or a common human nature applicable to all human societies.
- The belief in a progressive history, today being the pinnacle of previous epochs.
- Individualism: the individual is the most essential of human society and history.

- The promotion of the value of tolerance of others with the development of notions about fundamental human rights, democratic political systems and the abolition of slavery.
- A rhetoric of freedom, including censure and the abolition of restrictions to trade, belief, social interaction, sexuality and ownership of property.
- The uniformity of human nature.
- Secularism: the total rejection of religious explanations within the world.

This was summed up by the Cartesian belief that man could understand and dominate the world surrounding him using reason, in particular, utilising scientific endeavour that comprises a mathematical language. The Enlightenment project subscribes to the idea that scientific knowledge leads progressively to a discovery of the truth about our universe. In mainstream economics at least, discourse was essentially determined by the aims attributed to the Enlightenment. At the same time, the criticism of the Enlightenment has been the basis for the emergence of a considerable variety of concepts, schools of thought and other approaches in economics.

In particular, criticism of the Enlightenment has been at the root of those perspectives in economic methodology that are similar to Foucault's archaeology, which is exemplified in Chapter 4, mentioning the 'radical' investigations about possible underlying configurations of thought (modes of thought, modernism, postmodernism and so on). For example, whatever the interpretation of 'modernism' and 'postmodernism' might be, the Enlightenment has often been considered as having drawn a line between the two of them. It is here that Foucault's perception relating to the project of Enlightenment becomes fundamental. The objective is not only to better understand his system, but also to grasp the intellectual resources he presented in order for man to achieve his freedom and, as Gutting (1989, p. 3) asserts, to dissolve 'contingent, historical constraints on thought'.

It would appear that Foucault never used the word 'Enlightenment' in *The Order of Things*, although if it was ever used, it would most likely have had a different meaning for him. He saw history as comprising different rationalities, not only in time but also in space. As he declared: 'It may be wise not to take as a whole the rationalisation of society or of culture, but to analyse this process in several fields, each of them grounded by a fundamental experience: madness, illness, death, crime, sexuality, etc.' (Foucault, 1988b, p. 59). While investigating the relationship between rationalism and power, he concluded that: 'After all, at least in this respect, political practices resemble scientific ones: it's not "reason in general" that is implemented, but always a very specific type of rationality' (ibid., p. 73). He summarised his work as follows: 'I believe, and developed a historical analysis of the forms of rationality and knowledge in a phenomenological perspective' (ibid., p. 23).

Foucault actually wrote an essay titled 'What is Enlightenment?' (Foucault, 1984c). In this article he analysed Kant's essay of the same title (Kant, 1963), written in 1784. In his essay, Kant defined Enlightenment as a process that releases us from the status of 'immaturity'. Kant started his essay by defining Enlightenment:

> Enlightenment is man's release from his self-incurred tutelage. Tutelage is man's inability to make use of his understanding without direction from another. Self-incurred is this tutelage when its cause lies not in lack of reason but in lack of resolution and courage to use it without direction from another. (Kant, 1963, p. 3)

Kant writes quoting Horace that the motto of Enlightenment is *Sapere aude!*, meaning 'Dare to know!', and regarding the question of 'Do we now live in an enlightened age?' Kant answered 'No' and added: 'but we do live in an age of enlightenment'. For Kant, the door had been opened for men to escape from their 'self-incurred tutelage'.

Foucault (1984c) agrees with Kant and argues that many of our historical experiences have demonstrated that we have not yet achieved an enlightened stage (of 'mature adults', as he defines it). Then he stresses that the question of 'what is Enlightenment?' marked the emergence of modern philosophy and remains unanswered (ibid., p. 32). He understood that 'modern philosophy',[1] in the sense of the historical point at which reason could appear in its 'adult' form, was initiated by Kant's question '*Was ist Aufklarung?*' (Foucault, 1988a, p. 25).

Foucault grasped in Kant's essay a *gaze*, a way of looking at history that had similarities and affinities to his own understanding. He emphasised that Kant approached the question looking for a difference, in other words 'what difference does today introduce with respect to yesterday?' (Foucault, 1984c, p. 34). The point here is that Kant was not seeing this event as an era or even as a moment of transition to another phase of the world. Kant was also not trying 'to decipher' its signs. What makes Kant's answer so special to Foucault was that he looked at the event in a negative way. Foucault saw in Kant's article an example of his own (Foucault's) principle of reversal.

According to Foucault and his own interpretation of Kant's understanding, Enlightenment was neither a historical phase nor an event that had already finished. For him, Enlightenment was a process, indeed an attitude, a philosophical life turned to 'a critical ontology of ourselves', to a 'historical ontology'. Enlightenment was 'the critique of what we are' and it consisted of 'the historical analysis of the limits that are imposed on us and an experiment with the possibility of going beyond them' (Foucault, 1984c, p. 50). Foucault certainly includes himself in the tradition of Enlightenment. More specifically, he understands that his work, his several inquiries through archaeological and genealogical studies, was part of the Enlightenment process, insofar as they were historical analyses of our limits. Foucault echoes Kant's concept of the Enlightenment as a 'way of philosophising'. It is an 'attitude', an 'ethos', a 'philosophical life', and cannot be understood as a theory, a doctrine or a progressive body of knowledge.

From the understanding of such a process derives a comprehension of the conditions of the possibility of knowledge. However, Foucault states that, although he was also working on the conditions of possibility of knowledge, he differed from Kant in two important aspects. First, while Kant concentrated on mathematics and physics, he turned to the human sciences, as these had established the constraints on human freedom. Secondly, Foucault's project also diverged from Kant's regarding the foundations of knowledge. Whilst Kant turned to the foundations of knowledge as the *a priori* forms and categories of the mind, Foucault related them to contingent events. Foucault departs from Kant's criticism related to the limits of reason, arguing that these limits were historical and contingent rather than universal and necessary, and hence open to change. Therefore, any criticism should use an historical approach, which is the main emphasis in genealogy. In Foucault's archaeology of human sciences, the 'episteme' was related to a certain perspective that determined that the ways in which to theorise, to speak, to read and so on are historical; that is, that in each historical moment, there are rules that define discourse of what can be and is said. Each 'episteme' was related to a particular way in which man considered the world together with his own character. Therefore, the 'episteme' is 'almost a historicised form of Kant's categories' (Merquior, 1991, p. 38). As Foucault declares in *The Birth of the Clinic*, his project was critical (meaning to unveil 'the conditions of possibility' as in Kant's critique) and historical:

The research that I am undertaking here therefore involves a project that is deliberately both historical and critical, in that it is concerned – outside all prescriptive intent – with determining the conditions of possibility of medical experience in modern times. (*BC*, p. xix)

Foucault referred to the relationship between his work and Kant's as follows:

> For Kant, the possibility and necessity of a critique were linked, through certain scientific contents, to the fact that there is such a thing as knowledge. In our time – Nietzsche the philologist testifies to it – they are linked to the fact that language exists and that, in the innumerable words spoken by man – whether they are reasonable or senseless, demonstrative or poetic – a meaning has taken shape that hangs over us, leading us forward in our blindness, but awaiting in the darkness for us to attain awareness before emerging into the light of day and speaking. We are doomed historically to history, to the patient construction of discourse about discourses, and to the task of hearing what has already been said. (*BC*, pp. xv–xvi)

For Foucault, the most important thing is to understand 'modernity' and, through it, to investigate how it led to opposite attitudes:

> rather than seeking to distinguish the 'modern era' from the 'pre-modern' or 'postmodern', I think it would be more useful to try to find out how the attitude of modernity, ever since its formation, has found itself struggling with attitudes of 'countermodernity'. (Foucault, 1984c, p. 39)

In light of Kant's essay, Foucault understands 'modernity' as man's attitude of trying to liberate himself from his immaturity. Mankind should be able to use its own reason instead of submitting it to other authorities, like Ancient authors, the church or even scientists.

Foucault follows Kant in respect of seeing modernity as a seeking for 'maturity', but disagrees with him in relation to the way to achieve it. As Norris (1994) remarks, Foucault follows Baudelaire rather than Kant in understanding modernity as a 'perpetual transformation'. What is at stake here is that, while in Kant we have the appeal to a transcendental subject, the source of knowledge and truth, configuring the humanism of the Western modern thought, Foucault sees man in perpetual self-transformation. Thus, he can see the end of humanism and the establishment of a perpetual criticism. His opposition to humanism was stronger in the sense that he did not believe in the 'progress of reason', that is, that there was a sovereign subject that consciously promoted this progress. For Foucault, there were unconscious laws and determinations that should be unveiled. This was his project in the archaeology.

This discussion regarding the position of Foucault on the Enlightenment project brings us to the usual view of Foucault, which is often adopted in economics. He has been considered as 'postmodern' (for example, by Hands, 2001 and Amariglio, 1988), although regardless of in which sense they were construed, Foucault always refused all labels. Clearly, this conception depends on what is understood by 'postmodernism'. Nonetheless, whatever that might be, Foucault did not abandon reason and never fell into nihilism. He did not succumb to the 'temptation' of 'romantic irrationalism', as Gutting (1989) remarks, referring to the alternative he had introduced, as understood by critics of the Enlightenment and commonly associated with 'postmodernism'. Considerately and reflectively, and within the tradition of the French Enlightenment, he made use of a rationality to formulate and pursue his project, which he understood to be part of the Enlightenment as a permanent critique. Gutting wrote: 'Foucault's philosophical project is rationalist, in the sense that it involves an acceptance of reason as the primary means of human liberation' (ibid., p. 265). Kusch (1991, p. 194) also states that Foucault 'never, neither directly nor implicitly, suggests that there is no knowledge, no progress, and no truth'. Most important of all, Foucault was not interested in this kind of investigation.

If a label had to be applied, then Foucault could indeed, at least regarding his archaeological investigations, be considered as a Kantian. He followed Kant's 'critical' project in the sense of looking for the conditions of possibility that established what we are today. Foucault actually historicised Kant's critical project. Hacking (2002, p. 3) declared that 'Foucault regularly historicised Kant'. It is certainly not extraordinary to couple the names of Foucault and Kant, since Foucault mentions this point in an interview, when he declares that he is in agreement with Habermas in saying that we should not abandon Kant or Weber, given that this would risk a lapse into irrationality (Foucault, 1994b, pp. 357–8). Foucault's questions, as he put it, were always: 'What is this Reason that we use? What are its historical effects? What are its limits, and what are its dangers? How can we exist as rational beings, fortunately committed to practicing a rationality that is unfortunately crisscrossed by intrinsic dangers?' (ibid., p. 358).

To answer questions of this kind, it was necessary that Foucault launched a new theory of discourse, providing a very distinctive theory in support of his archaeological inquiry into the history of economic thought. He inaugurated a new meaning for the term 'discourse' and helped to create a new kind of analysis. As White (1979, p. 82) noticed, 'discourse is the term under which he gathers all of the forms and categories of cultural life, including, apparently, his own efforts to submit this life to criticism'. In this sense, it may be more precise to say that he accomplished a 'metatheory of discourse', that is, a 'discourse about discourse', as he declared (*AK*, p. 226).

To address Foucault's theory of discourse requires at least a brief account of how discourse became an object of investigation and with a very singular character in French philosophy. The background of this event can be found within the emergence of the philosophy of language. The accomplishments made in this area were very influential on his thinking and will be explored further, since it is only then that it will be possible to address with rigour Foucault's theory, which was articulated in *The Archaeology of Knowledge* (and concisely summarised in *The Order of Discourse*).

The term 'discourse' has a natural connection to 'language'. Needless to say, the terms cannot be treated as synonymous. Studies, theories and approaches which emerged and developed during the twentieth century certainly disconnected both terms in some way. Macdonell (1986, p. 2), for example, defines discourse 'as a particular area of language use'. Throughout this book, we shall see the purpose of 'discourse', which can be treated as 'language' or 'knowledge'. The understanding of this is fundamental to apprehending Foucault's own theory, to improving our understanding of his proposal in *The Order of Things*, while situating it in relation to other studies within economics.

As Foucault pointed out, science has been 'looking in the science of language for something like a form or content of knowledge' since at least the eighteenth century (Foucault, 2001, p. 850).[2] However, Foucault's work was only possible because of a change in the way of thinking that has been known as the 'linguistic turn', as denominated by Rorty (1967). Rorty defines this revolution as being a change in philosophy that takes 'the view that philosophical problems are problems which may be solved (or dissolved) either by reforming language, or by understanding more about the language we presently use' (ibid., p. 3). This turn is usually understood as a change in philosophy, starting with Wittgenstein, which considers meanings intrinsic to language use. How this event took place in the history of philosophy was actually part of Foucault's investigation of the modern episteme in *The Order of Things*. He associated it with the end of the age of representation. The usual reading of this event is that, whilst the Ancient Greeks thought about 'reality', modern philosophy, beginning with Descartes, started thinking about our 'knowledge of reality', creating the subject-object duality. 'Method' became a central issue and later Hume concluded that knowledge was a well-justified true belief, and it became necessary to explain what 'truth' was and how beliefs could have a status of truth. Hume made Kant wake up from his 'dogmatic slumber'.

In his *Critique of Pure Reason*, first published in 1781, Kant investigates the conditions of possibility (*Critique*) of knowledge, more precisely of 'pure reason', that is, the *a priori* conditions of knowledge. This is depicted as one of the most important turning points in philosophy, called a 'Copernican Revolution', since Kant had promoted a similar revolution in philosophy to that of Copernicus's revolution in physics. For Kant, his predecessors were mistakenly focusing their attention on the 'wrong' centre. The case was not to investigate whether reality exists or whether it is rational. Instead, we should think about what 'reason' could or could not know. The main question would not be about 'reality' but about 'reason', which should hence be at the centre of our scrutiny. Kant argued that we have *a priori* knowledge, such as the notions of space and time, and we should distinguish between analytic and synthetic judgements. Regarding analytical judgements, nothing is added to the subject, such as in the statement 'all bodies are extended' (Kant, 1933, p. 48). Analytic judgements are always *a priori*. They are tautological. We cannot think about bodies without thinking about extensiveness. The predicate can be extracted from the subject of the sentence or proposition by analysis. In the case of synthetic judgements, the predicate adds something that is new to the subject. They are indeed what enhance our knowledge about the world. As an example, Kant mentions that all bodies are heavy (ibid., p. 49). They derive from our experience although they can be *a posteriori* and *a priori*. Mathematical propositions are examples of *a priori* synthetic judgements. For Kant, only the *a priori* synthetic judgements could enhance knowledge. Thus, Kant's critique led to the emergence of epistemology, the theory of knowledge, and much subsequent philosophy came to think about whether and how it was possible for man to know.

Subsequent developments in philosophy led to thinking about the importance of language. Is it possible for the mind to see reality and explore it without language? Language is not only an expression of thoughts, it is also the device, the apparatus that makes thought possible. Philosophers turned to language. Wittgenstein has been considered as the leading personage in this change. In his *Tractatus*

Logico-Philosophicus, which was first published in 1922, he proposed a new way of looking at the relations between the world, thought and language. The emphasis was not on ideas, but on the problematisation of the language in which they can or cannot be expressed. Since language expressed thought, it may be considered a critique of thought, through a critique of language. He was writing about the limits of language: what a logically constructed language could or could not say. This examination of what a logical language can properly express has been regarded as one of the major influences of his *Tractatus* on the members of the Vienna Circle when they formulated the principles of logical positivism. Later, Wittgenstein developed a very different philosophy in his posthumous book *Philosophical Investigations*, first published in 1969, where he rejected his earlier conclusions of the *Tractatus*. In his later philosophy, he saw language not as having a single basic pattern, whose character could be revealed through logical analysis. He contrasted the use of words in various practical situations with the abstract and uniform model of the *Tractatus*. He saw language as a mixture of a variety of practices that he called 'language-games', giving a list of examples, such as asking, thanking, giving orders and obeying them, and so on. He then contrasted 'meaning' and 'use', concluding that the meaning of a word is its use in the language.

The philosophy of language developed considerably in the twentieth century. Even a brief look at the modern philosophy of language now shows that it is very difficult to characterise it, such is the diversity of approaches. Perhaps the main strand is analytic philosophy, which originated with the works of Frege, Bertrand Russell, G.E. Moore and Wittgenstein. The main idea underlying the project could be summarised with the question regarding whether philosophy could have the same 'rigour' as science. This led (at least the first analytic) philosophers to try to reduce science to logic. It emerged as 'a descendant and voice of the Enlightenment Project', especially related to the epistemological belief in a continuity between human and physical nature: 'the same principles that explain physical nature are to be used to explain ourselves [and hence the knowing process]' (Capaldi, 1993, pp. 45–6). The movement gave rise to logical atomism, logical positivism, logical empiricism, logicism and ordinary language philosophy. Logical atomism, associated with Russell, Wittgenstein and Carnap, proposed that language, like other components of the world, was actually formed by ultimate logical elements (or 'atoms'). Therefore, to understand ordinary language implied 'analysing' it until these elemental components were found. Logical positivism, widely debated among economists nowadays, was associated in its early years with the principle of verification, with a distinction made between/among analytic, synthetic and 'meaningless' (basically metaphysical) propositions, and had as its main goal to link an empiricist conception of knowledge with the acknowledgement of the importance of logic in the elaboration of theories. The basic idea of the movement continued to be to reduce language to very simple statements. Physics was even thought of as a candidate to provide the model for that language. All languages should be reduced to simply one, which would make it possible to access reality. In *Wissenschaftliche Weltauffassung: Der Weiner Kreis*, a pamphlet that was written in 1926 and intended to be an announcement of the aims of the movement, Hans Hahn, Otto Neurath and Rudolf Carnap stated:

> We have characterised the scientific world-conception essentially by two features. First, it is empiricist and positivist: there is knowledge only from experience, which rests on what is immediately given. This sets the limits for the context of legitimate science. Secondly, the scientific world-conception was marked by the application of a certain method, namely logical analysis. The aim of scientific effort is to reach the goal, unified science, by applying logical analysis to the empirical material. (Hahn, Neurath and Carnap, quoted in Caldwell, 1994, p. 13)

Subsequent analytic philosophy, following the works of Gilbert Ryle, Willard Quine, John L. Austin and John Searle, became an active movement in many areas, including ethics, political philosophy, philosophy of religion and philosophy of the mind. Even distancing themselves from the first project of a strict logical analysis, analytic philosophers from the 1950s onwards kept an emphasis on a clear, precise approach to questions, since every question (and therefore every possible answer) had to be analysed, first through a scrutiny of language and then by looking at the terms and concepts used to formulate them. Two major strands are today associated with the analytical tradition. One approaches language through formal logic. It seeks to formalise the language used by philosophy. The other seeks to understand ideas through a close and careful examination of the natural, ordinary language used to express them, making use of common sense to deal with complex concepts. In economics, Uskali Maki would appear to be an example of a follower in this line of thought.

Foucault's work was consciously related to the developments in the philosophy of language. This was the case in relation to structuralism, as emphasised previously. He wrote about this context in the Introduction to *The Archaeology of Knowledge* and referred to it in many interviews and conferences, in particular with respect to analytic philosophy. Davidson (1997) provides a very clarifying text where he quotes Foucault:

> For a long time one has known that the role of philosophy is not to discover what is hidden but to make visible precisely what is visible, that is to say, to make evident what is so close, so immediate, so intimately linked to us, yet because of that we do not perceive it. Whereas the role of science is to reveal what we do not see, the role of philosophy is to let us see what we see. (Foucault, quoted in Davidson, 1997, p. 2)

Davidson (ibid., p. 2), quoting Wittgenstein, argues that what Foucault was saying here was identical to a statement in the *Philosophical Investigations*. Actually, Foucault states in the sequence that his genealogy had a very close relationship to Anglo-Saxon analytic philosophy:

> After all, Anglo-Saxon analytical philosophy does not give itself the task of considering the being of language or the deep structures of language; it considers the everyday use that one makes of language in different types of discourse. In Anglo-Saxon analytical philosophy, it was a critical analysis of thought, based on the way in which one says things. It could be imagined, in the same way, as in philosophy having to analyse the task of what happens every day in relationship to power. A philosophy that would try to establish what everything was about, in what forms they were and the stakes and objectives of these in relationship to power. [...] One could imagine, one should imagine something like an analytico-political philosophy. (Foucault, quoted in ibid., p. 3)

Davidson goes on to declare that Foucault is using 'the model of analytic philosophy of language, more specifically with the analysis of our everyday language games' that 'would show discourse to operate as a strategic field, discourse as a field of battle, not simply as a reflection of something already constituted and preexistent' (ibid., p. 4). However, Foucault's analyses differed from the earlier analyses of language in terms of laws and internal regularities. Foucault turned to a type of structural analysis in his archaeological investigations. As Davidson states, Foucault linked 'Russell, Wittgenstein, Lévi-Strauss, Lacan, Dumézil, Althusser, New Criticism, and linguistics as exemplifications of what he calls "analytic reason", and which he is opposes in human-ism, anthropology, and dialectical thought' (ibid., p. 6).

The understanding of this statement is fundamental to apprehending Foucault's place in all that followed the earlier investigations in philoso-phy of language and crucially explains the main aspects of his project of archaeology. For Foucault, according to Davidson (ibid., p. 6), human-ism, anthropology and dialectical thought, including existentialism and Marxist humanism, represented by Sartre's *Critique de la raison dialectique*, rejected the logic of analytic reason, insofar as they did not consider the concept of the unconscious, with its logical structures, which was actually the project of structuralism. Foucault unreservedly avowed his relation to structuralism and opposition to humanism, existentialism and dialectical reason.

The problem with dialectical reason was translated by Foucault in the notion that an episteme 'collapses, part by part, in unpredictable order; the movement is not dialectic, moves to no higher level' (Kermode, 1973, p. 12).

In relation to existentialism, Foucault disagrees with 'their corollary of freedom and causality' that is beneath the notions of consciousness and continuity (Foucault, 1970b, p. 50).

Summarising what Foucault pointed out in these texts as being his relationship with the philosophy of language, we can establish the following:

1 Foucault stated that his investigations were similar to those used by analytical philosophers in the sense of seeking 'to make visible what is visible'; as he stated in the interview 'Michel Foucault explains his latest book' in 1969: 'I try to make visible that which that is only invisible because it is too much in the surface of things' (Foucault, 2001, p. 800).
2 Foucault was not concerned with 'the being of language'; he was look-ing for 'the deep structures of language'. His approach was concerned with the everyday use of language in different types of discourse.
3 Although archaeology was not only descriptive, it was a critical anal-ysis, he affirms, 'on the basis of the way in which one says things'. He was treating 'statements in their functioning'.
4 Foucault stressed the distinction between what he called 'ana-lytic reason' (analytic philosophy, new criticism, linguistics and structuralism) and existentialism and Marxist humanism (Sartre, for example), saying that his project was related to the former. For him,

the problems with the latter were that they did not consider the 'unconscious' and logical structures, logical correlations.

'Language' and 'discourse' had become separated subjects in the whole of the philosophy of language since at least the 1960s and have frequently been associated with French philosophical thought, including Foucault's work of course. Indeed, discourse theory began with structuralism. As Macdonell remarks: 'Work on discourse both goes beyond and departs from structuralism' (Macdonell, 1986, p. 12). 'Discourse theory' sees 'discourse' as an act in a social context. The idea is that discourses differ according to who speaks and who is being addressed, as well as by the institutions and social practices in which they are shaped.

Nevertheless, Foucault's theory of discourse in his archaeology differs from other approaches to 'discourse' in the following terms:

1 Instead of considering 'context' as usually understood in social, cultural, political and economic terms, in Foucault's archaeology it means 'conditions of possibility of thought', 'conditions of emergence and existence' of knowledge. For Foucault, it was clear that when Petty stated that labour was the father and the active principle of wealth, as well as that the land was the mother, he was not interpreting the meaning of 'labour' in the same way as Ricardo. They were not talking about 'the same thing' at 'the same level', or at 'the same distance', or deploying 'the same conceptual field' (*AK*, p. 142). Foucault gave other examples, such as that we should rethink the idea that 'Petty's inventions are in continuity with Neumann's econometry' (*AK*, p. 34) or that 'Jevons [in some way] answers the Physiocrats' (*AK*, p. 142).

2 Foucault's theory of discourse is critical. McHoul and Grace (1995) classify their approaches to discourse into 'formalist', 'empirical' and 'critical'. In formal analyses, discourse is analysed in terms of text. This was the case for linguists. In this kind of approach, thinkers work either with variations of formal linguistic methods of analysis or with social functions of language and often use so-called 'naturally occurring' samples of linguistic usage as data. They are close to 'socio-linguistics' and 'ethnography of communication'. This formal approach is not always called 'discourse analyses', but 'text linguistics' (or 'text grammars'). Whilst formalist approaches are usually associated with linguistics, empirical approaches are usually sociological, taking 'discourse' as 'human conversation'. For McHoul and Grace, they are actually similar to Foucault's understanding of

the term, since they also take 'discourse' as knowledge. However, whilst Foucault was interested in the conditions (archaeology: conditions of possibility; genealogy: social, historical and political conditions) that enabled a certain discourse to emerge and exist, empirical approaches view 'discourse' as technical knowledge or know-how. Alternatively, Foucault had a critical and historical interest at heart, questioning how medical discourses produced a particular kind of social object in the twentieth century. The empirical approaches take empirical data as a 'corpus of materials', while Foucault takes them in order to understand how they are organised in terms of which set of rules established that the discourse would have a certain form and limit. This led to the distinction that Foucault made for the term 'archive' in his theory of discourse. An 'archive', as will be demonstrated in what follows, was in Foucault's archaeology not merely a collection of historical documents and conversations; an 'archive' meant the 'conditions' that made a discourse possible. Therefore, for McHoul and Grace (1995), Foucault's approach to 'discourse' is indeed classified in a third category: 'critical'. The Foucauldian approach is not 'formalist' in the sense that he is not interested in 'discourse' as a 'formal logical, linguistic, or even language-like system' (ibid., p. 29), as Foucault himself made perfectly clear in *The Archaeology of Knowledge* when he differentiated his notion of discourse from those of grammar, analytic philosophy or linguistic (see Chapter 3). It is not 'empirical' in the sense that he is looking for the conditions of its emergence and existence, it is 'critical' in the sense that 'it is geared towards a counter-reading of historical and social conditions and offering possibilities for social critique and renewal' (ibid., p. 27).

3   Discourse theory may be about discourse-as-language or discourse-as-knowledge, without implying that they are mutually exclusive. Dillon (1997) argues that 'discourse theorists' take 'discourse' not in the meaning of 'language', understanding it as 'a set of units and the rules for combining them to make well-formed sentences', but as 'a type of social action'. In the 'theory of discourse', 'discourse' is not the same as 'language' for linguistics and logicians. The theory of discourse also distinguishes from 'philosophical concerns with the truth of statements and the validity of arguments, substituting a concern for conditions under which one can be judged to have made a serious, sound, true, important, authoritative statement' (ibid.). This is clearly Foucault's proposal in *The Archaeology of Knowledge,* where 'discourse' does not refer to language in the sense of a linguistic system or grammar, and has not the sense of a text built to persuade, as it is conceived by rhetoric

analysis. Prior to Foucault, as he stated in *The Archaeology of Knowledge*, the work on 'discourse' was about techniques, structures and forms of how statements were produced and recognised. In his work, discourse is much more associated with the term 'discipline', which had two special meanings in his work. In the first instance, it refers to 'scholarly disciplines' or bodies of knowledge, such as science, economics, medicine and so on, which were the object of his archaeology in *The Order of Things*. Secondly, 'discipline' also means disciplinary institutions of social control, such as prison, university, hospital and so on, which were the object of genealogy.

4 Foucault was interested in how some social objects and practices became possible and pursued his research with the idea that every historical period had its own way of writing, speaking and thinking. In other words, according to Foucault, every age has its own way of producing the truth. Therefore, the truth is as a result of what can be written, spoken or thought. Foucault's concern was to identify the epistemic context where some bodies of knowledge became possible, that is to say, as Foucault denominated in *The Archaeology of Knowledge*, their 'discursive formations'. For him there was a strong nominalism in the human sciences, in the sense that their objects and what they discussed were not delimited before their emergence. They came into being only contemporaneously with their 'discursive formations'. It was their specific 'discursive formation' that made it possible to talk about those objects, that is, that there was not such a thing as 'wealth', 'money', 'value', 'labour' and so on. They emerged while being dealt with as an object of economic thought, in a specific way and due to some conditions of emergence, a 'discursive formation'.

5 For Foucault, discourse was a practice. He reverses the usual interpretation of discourse as being a result of the kinds of institutions and social practices in which they take shape. Indeed, for him, 'discourse' contributed to the way in which these institutions and social practices emerged and continued their existence. 'Discourse' is actually a practice that systematically forms the objects of which it speaks. 'To speak is to do something – something other than to express what one thinks; to translate what one knows, and something other than to play with the structures of language (*langue*)' (*AK*, p. 230). 'Discourse' is not only a group of signs or a spoken or written text. Indeed, 'discourses' produce 'discourses' and they do so by the elements of truth, power and knowledge. The archaeology 'describes discourses as practices specified in the element of discourse' (*AK*, p. 148). Economic discourses are discursive practices.

However, these factors are not merely transcendental; they are also produced. Truth, writes Foucault, 'is a thing of the world: it is produced only by virtue of multiple forms of constraints' and:

> In societies like ours, the 'political economy' of truth is characterised by five important traits. 'Truth' is centred on the form of scientific discourse and the institutions which produce it; it is subject to constant economic and political incitement (the demand for truth, as much for economic production as for political power); it is the object, under diverse forms, or immense diffusion and consumption (circulating through apparatuses of education and information whose extent is relatively broad in the social body, notwithstanding certain strict limitations); it is produced and transmitted under the control, dominant if not exclusive, of a few great political and economic apparatuses (university, army, writing, media); lastly, it is the issue of a whole political debate and social confrontation ('ideological' struggles). (Foucault, 1984a, p. 73)

The Foucault who is talking here is the late Foucault: the Foucault of the 'genealogy' of power-knowledge. However, though it can be said that in *The Order of Things*, and even in *The Archaeology of Knowledge*, Foucault was not fully aware of the importance of systems of power and knowledge, which for him were so fundamentally connected that he often wrote as a single hyphenated concept power-knowledge, this was certainly the underlying inquiry in the archaeology, as he made explicitly clear towards the end of *The Archaeology of Knowledge*.

When dealing with discourse-as-knowledge, Foucault made a very important distinction between *connaissance* and *savoir*, which both translate to 'knowledge' in English. He clarified this distinction in *The Archaeology of Knowledge*:

> By *connaissance* I mean the relation of the subject to the object and the formal rules that govern it. *Savoir* refers to the conditions that are necessary in a particular period for this or that type of object to be given to *connaissance* and for this or that enunciation to be formulated. (*AK*, p. 16)

Connaissance refers to a particular branch of knowledge, a particular discipline (such as economics, biology and philology, whose 'archaeology' he developed in *The Order of Things*, or rhetoric). *Savoir* is 'knowledge' in general, so to speak; it encompasses all branches, all domains of 'knowledge' (*les connaissances*).

This distinction has been attributed to Heidegger's influence on modern French philosophy (for example, by Descombes, 1980) and was depicted particularly in relation to Foucault by Dreyfus and Rabinow (1982). As Elden (2001) explains, it reflects Heidegger's distinction between ontic and ontological knowledge in *Being and Time*. For Heidegger, the question of being 'is an ontological question, which aims "at ascertaining the a priori conditions [...] for the possibility of the sciences which examine entities" – ontic knowledge' (ibid., p. 99). Therefore, Foucault's archaeology is not only 'theory of ontic' knowledge (an epistemology – *connaissance*), but also a theory of ontological knowledge ontology – *savoir*) and, for Foucault, ontology (in both meanings: 'what there is' and 'the study of what there is') is always historical.

We can follow Hacking (2002) and separate the objects that exist into two types: objects that are 'pre-constituted', 'the basic furniture of universe'; and objects that are brought into being by man in his everyday life, especially through scientific activity. Hacking understands that the second category of things correspond to that which is not 'from nature', in the sense that they are derived from man's practices. The subject matter of economic theory is certainly in the second category. In order to build theories about the economic activity, economists have to deal with phenomena that always entail man's practices. In this sense, the philosophy of economics must think about ontology according to the second category of 'things' and it is here that Foucault's work offers a fundamental insight to economics. Economics must study man, although it cannot be psychology, sociology or studies on literature and myths. Certainly, economics has its own object when referring to human activity. It has to recur to those human sciences. However, it is not a human science. So, how was the line drawn that separated the subject matter of economics from those of other sciences? Foucault investigated how the study of man together with human sciences emerged and what relationship they had with political economy in their origins.

3
The Archaeology of Knowledge

3.1 Introduction

In addition to the primary objective of this book, which has been to provide a conscientious study of Foucault's project of archaeology of knowledge and political economy, this chapter has two purposes. Primarily, it presents Foucault's theory of discourse through the review of *The Archaeology of Knowledge*. This is considered paramount, since he wrote it as a methodological addendum to his previous works, including *The Order of Things*. *The Archaeology of Knowledge*, first published in 1969, is regarded as a 'theoretical postscript to *The Order of Things*' (Sheridan, 1980). The analysis of this is therefore considered to be fundamental to an understanding of how he approached and analysed the history of economic discourse in *The Order of Things*. The chapter then carefully investigates *The Order of Things*, concluding with a review, comprising a brief summary of his main ideas and an assessment of the criticisms usually associated with his system.

3.2 *The Archaeology of Knowledge*

There are disagreements as to whether Foucault intended to provide a methodological treatise in *The Archaeology of Knowledge*. Lemert and Gillan (1982, pp. ix–x), for instance, suggested that the book should not be regarded as a methodological statement. However, Foucault was categorical when saying that he offered an alternative methodology for the history of science. In his introduction to *The Archaeology of Knowledge* he wrote: 'the theory that I am about to outline' (p. 17), declaring the book to be a 'general outline' (p. 127), a methodological exposition, of his previous works, including *The Order of Things*. He also intended to attend to some corrections and criticisms of his work: 'This work is not an exact description of what can be read in *Madness and Civilization, Naissance de la Clinique,* or *The Order of Things.* It is different on a great many points. It also includes a number of corrections and internal critiques' (p. 18).

In *The Archaeology of Knowledge,* Foucault details his new method and sketches a theory of discourse on which it was to be based. He declared that he intended to change the history of ideas by offering a new method and even appeared, as Rorty (1986, p. 43) remarks, 'to be unconsciously imitating Descartes'. Nevertheless, he did not intend to replace other methods. He proclaimed that we should of course definitely not abandon other methodologies, although, in his own words, we should disturb 'the tranquillity with which they are accepted' (*AK,* p. 28). He did not even claim that his method had no limitations (O'Farrell, 2005, p. 89).

The method he represents is archaeology, which is sometimes regarded as being somewhere between philosophy and history. As part of genealogy, it is a reference to a type of philosophical history. In this case, Foucault can be considered to be a historian-philosopher (O'Farrell, 1989). Hacking (1979, p. 40) defines 'archaeology' as 'a way of investigating the groundwork of bodies of knowledge'. It was a method that investigated the conditions that made it possible for different 'discourses' (discourse-as-knowledge) to emerge and become established in a particular way, within a certain moment and within our Western culture. It intends to find out how 'a set of relations' constituted the necessary and sufficient conditions to enable a certain discourse (for example, political economy) to become possible. The corollary of this was that for him, thought was not the expression of a truth but a practice in a complex set of relations.

Foucault utilised the expression 'set of relations' very often in his writings to describe the 'conditions of possibility' of those discourses that he was investigating. What were these relations that he was referring to? The archaeology, as he asserted (*AK,* p. 215), questions knowledge according to 'a set of relations'. A more attentive read of *The Order of Things* allows us to establish that these sets of relations could be uncovered using the following main conceptions:

1 The comprehension of the experience of language and representation that each period holds (language-representation relations).
2 The relationship of same-other in knowledge.
3 The place that time and space occupy in the structure of knowledge.

4 The distinct techniques of isolation within the subject matter of knowledge (resemblances, equalities and differences, leading to analogy or analysis).

5 The ontological conception that man historically held regarding his power or limitations to knowledge and the solution to the problems concerning his life, economic production and language (which were the main objects in biology, political economy and philology). This concept is investigated through the thought-unthought relationship.

These notions were specific to each moment in time and constituted the underlying structure that defined the way of thinking and, as a result, of speaking, writing and so on. Foucault never suggested that the set he described for each period of history he analysed (from the sixteenth century onwards) was a definitive tool for inquiry. Rather, he affirmed that he was only privileging some relations, while the limits were open (*AK*, pp. 32–3). Some may argue that he chose them 'arbitrarily' (for example, Kermode, 1973, p. 11). It is certain that he took those relations in accordance with his own strategies of thinking, as mentioned in the previous chapter.

Foucault believed that the investigation of those relations and how they historically changed would demonstrate how certain rhetoric, linguistic or methodological schemes emerged and were favoured above others in a special context of culture and time. This was what was meant when he claimed that his archaeology was looking for the conditions of the emergence and existence of certain discourses (the human sciences). Whilst pursuing this goal, Foucault accomplished a history of ontological conceptions and claimed (*AK*, p. 215) that he questioned the epistemologisation of discourses. The main intention of his enterprise was to suggest that 'what counts as reason, argument or evidence may itself be part of a system of thought, so that modes of "rationality" are topical and dated' (Hacking, 1979, p. 41). Foucault summarises the main focus of this type of inquiry:

I tried to explore scientific discourse not from the point of view of the individuals who are speaking, nor from the point of view of the formal structures of what they are saying, but from the point of view of the rules that come into play in the very existence of such discourse: what conditions did Linnaeus (or Petty, or Arnauld) have to fulfil, not to make his discourse coherent and true in general, but to give it, at the time when it was written and accepted, value and practical application as scientific discourse – or, more exactly, as naturalist, economic, or grammatical discourse? (*OT*, p. xiv)

For example, as will be explored further in Chapter 5, Foucault claims that the discourse present in the history of economic thought was about wealth during the eighteenth century, becoming a discourse on production and labour in the nineteenth century. In an interview, he explains what he had in mind when he was writing *The Order of Things*:

> In *The Order of Things*, I took as my starting-point some very manifest differences, the transformations of the empirical sciences around the end of the eighteenth century. It calls for a degree of ignorance [...] to fail to see that a treatise of medicine written in 1780 and a treatise of pathological anatomy written in 1820 belong to two different worlds. My problem was to ascertain the sets of transformations in the regime of discourses necessary and sufficient for people to use these words rather than those, a particular type of discourse rather than some other type, for people to be able to look at things from such and such an angle and not some other one. (Foucault, 1980, p. 211)

One important point that should be emphasised is whether archaeology analyses discourses in abstraction from the social practices and institutions in which they are embedded. Sometimes it is argued that Foucault provided 'a history of ideas' in his archaeological phase and especially in *The Order of Things*, and that only later, in what is called his genealogical phase, did practices and institutions become absorbed into the analyses of power-knowledge (for example, by Smart, 1985, pp. 41–2). Foucault was later to argue that the disciplines from which he had developed an archaeology (clinical medicine, the human sciences and political economy) were the 'means for disciplining human powers for the economic needs of modern industrial society' (Lemert and Gillan, 1982, p. 129).

It is true that in *The Order of Things* he used only the tools of discourse analysis, almost ignoring non-discursive practices. Explaining his choice in an interview, he argued that he believed that 'discursive domains did not always obey the structures that they share with their associated practical and institutional domains, but rather obey the structures shared with other epistemological domains' (Bellour, 1971, pp. 195–6). Therefore, in his archaeology, he decided to explore the relationship amongst different discourses, which he called an 'interdiscursive' domain or a 'region of interpositivities'.

Nevertheless, it is possible to argue that the history of reason that he developed in *The Order of Things* had already been initiated in his earlier works, at least since *Madness and Civilization* (Foucault, 1967), where he did consider other social practices. In Chapter 2 of this book, for instance, reference is made to his work on the notion of unreason in the classical age, associating it with documental analyses of social institutions during the seventeenth century, such as English workhouses and the German and French general hospitals. Foucault gathered documents (court records, census tabulations, letters, stories, clinical notes and so on) as discursive practices. Moreover, he took discourse as a practice in *The Order of Things*, for example, when referring to the practices of speaking, classifying and exchanging, while characterising the classical episteme.

Foucault may still be criticised for not considering social, economic and political events in the determination of the configuration of the epistemes. For example, how could he write a history of human sciences without considering such events as the French Revolution, the Industrial Revolution, civil wars, economic depressions, technological developments, climate change and so on? An answer to this question is that Foucault was looking for the intrinsic conditions of possibility within the discourse of the human sciences through an investigation of ontological and epistemological configurations. Although some of those events could have determined the content of the discourses, Foucault believed that to unveil those conditions, which were unconscious and resulted from the group of relations mentioned above, was only possible through a careful examination of the discursive practices of the period during their emergence.

The Archaeology of Knowledge is clearly a difficult read, something Foucault acknowledged himself (Foucault, 2001, p. 850), which could be regarded as one reason for it having been his least successful book. Rorty claimed that this point really struck him and that the book deserved more accurate attention, especially since Foucault intended to outline a 'successor subject' to epistemology (Rorty, 1986, p. 43). This is without doubt the case, but the reason for its lack of consideration can be explained. It is an extremely abstract book and Foucault struggled to compose the notions that conducted him in his investigations, a point noted by other writers. He spent a great deal of time emphasising what terms and notions were not about, instead of stating what they were about, even appearing to admit the vagueness when he declared that the book was related to 'theoretical problems' rather than 'questions of procedure' (Foucault, quoted in Shumway, 1989, p. 98). Some commentators argued that another problem was that Foucault seldom gave examples (for instance, Deleuze, 1988). In actual fact, Foucault did make an effort to present examples, but rarely took examples from his previous works, such as from *The Order of Things*, which might have been expected, since he was trying to explain the method that he had applied in that book. As Deleuze noticed, maybe he did not give examples because he believed that they were already there in his previous works. However, Foucault believed in this 'even if at the time [when he wrote his previous books] he was unaware that they were examples' (Deleuze, 1988, p. 2).

The Archaeology of Knowledge was also written with the objective of responding to his critics. One criticism was that he had been too ambitious in *The Order of Things*, the main intention of which was to find out the historical epistemic configurations of knowledge in general. He affirmed in his Foreword to the English edition that his intention was not 'to draw up a picture of a period or to reconstitute the spirit of century' and that '[it] was not an analysis of classicism in general, nor a search for a *Weltanschauung, but a strictly "regional study"'* (*OT*, p. x, emphasis added). However, as Gutting (1989, p. 178) argues, Foucault uses many expressions in *The Order of Things* that give us an impression to the contrary, such as 'Classical thought', 'modern thought', 'Western thought', or when he writes: 'In any given culture and at any given moment, there is always only one episteme that defines the conditions of possibility of all knowledge' (*OT*, p. 168). In the Introduction to *The Archaeology of Knowledge*, he again argues that in *The Order of Things* he was not speaking about 'cultural totalities' (*AK*, p. 18). He was eager to make it clear that he did not 'use the categories of cultural totalities (whether world-views, ideal types, the particular spirit of an age)' (*AK*, p. 17). He declared that he did not see what he called 'strategies' (themes and theories) of an age as an 'expression of a world-view that has been coined in the form of words' (*AK*, p. 77). He stressed that his archaeology of epistemes referred to a group of discourses *en bloc*, which he named 'interdiscursive practice' or a 'region of interpositivities'. In other words, and as will be highlighted in the following analysis of *The Order of Things*, Foucault wanted to unveil the conditions of possibility within the human sciences and, further to this, developed an archaeology of political economy, biology and linguistics which he believed all resulted from the same 'interdiscursive practice' and formed a 'region of interpositivities'.

3.2.1   Foucault's new conceptual network

In his archaeology, Foucault launched a new set of questions and in order to answer them, he deemed it necessary to introduce a series of new notions and to define a domain of analysis. The main discursive structures that he claimed to have used in *The Order of Things* were 'statement' and 'archive', which he explained in *The Archaeology of Knowledge*.

The archaeology analyses and describes discourses, and Foucault argues that the unity of discourses should be sought in the group of what he called 'the statements' (*l'énoncé*). In his words, the 'statement' is 'the atom of discourse' (*AK*, p. 90) and so is the object of archaeological inquiry. This fundamental element of analysis is a very singular and complex notion in *The Archaeology of Knowledge*. Kusch writes:

> a reconstruction of Foucault's notion of the statement is by no means an easy task. The 60-odd pages of The Archaeology of Knowledge [...] that elaborate on this concept are not only the most difficult part of the whole book, but they also contain some of the least transparent passages of Foucault's whole oeuvre. (Kusch, 1991, p. 60)

This is certainly one of those examples where Foucault defines the term much more in the sense of what it is not about than what it is actually about. He argues that a statement is not a proposition, a sentence or a speech act such as is taken, respectively, by logic, grammar or analytic philosophy. He proclaims that the same proposition, sentence or speech act can identify different statements, as in the example 'species evolve' quoted by Foucault:

> [A]t a certain scale of macro-history, one may consider that an affirmation like 'species evolve' forms the same statement in Darwin and in Simpson; at a finer level, and considering more limited fields of use ('neo-Darwinism' as opposed to the Darwinian system itself), we are presented with different statements. The constancy of the statement, the preservation of its identity through the unique events of the enunciations, its duplication through the identity of the forms is constituted by the function of the field of use in which it is placed. (*AK*, p. 117)

To understand the distinction between Foucault's notions of 'statement' and 'proposition', 'sentence' and 'speech act' requires an investigation into how these terms were conceived by logic, linguistics and analytic philosophy.

In modern philosophy, logic and linguistics, a proposition is the meaning of a sentence rather than the sentence itself. Different sentences express the same proposition when they have the same meaning. These sentences can be in different languages (such as French and English) or in the same language. For example, *I love you* and *Je t'aime* is the same proposition, or *I love you* and *I adore you* may be the same proposition in English. In logic, a proposition is a particular kind of sentence, one which affirms or denies a predicate of a subject, as in the Aristotelian syllogism *All men are mortal* and *Socrates is a man.* However, Foucault alludes to the relation of a proposition to its 'referent', which in Frege and Russell's theories meant the thing in the real world.

The Speech Act Theory is based on J.L. Austin's *How to Do Things with Words* (Austin, 1975). This theory addressed the issue as to whether language should be conceived as essentially a system of structures and meanings or as a set of acts and practices. Is language an inert transcendental structure? Or is it a creative human action? Wittgenstein had formulated his theory of ordinary language in his *Philosophical Investigations*, saying that the meaning of a word was its use in language. Austin's speech-act theory distinguished 'constative' (stating things) from 'performative' (doing things, performing acts) utterances.

Foucault's 'statements' differ from those linguistics elements in the following terms:

1 The relationship of a statement to what it states (Foucault calls it the 'correlate' of a statement) is different from the relationship between a linguistic element and what it designates or signifies. It is different from the relationship between a signifier and the signified, a noun and that which it designates, a sentence and its meaning or a proposition and its referent. The 'correlate' of statements is always 'a group of domains' (*AK*, p. 102). These domains can be either a domain of objects or a state of affairs, which can be material or fictitious. They are not *a priori* entities. They are indeed made possible by the 'referential' to the statement. The 'referential' of the statement comprises all the conditions of possibility of the correlate of the statement (domains). Whilst the relationship of the statement to what it states 'is anterior to' the relations between the other linguistic elements and what they designate or signify (*AK*, p. 101), the 'referential' of the statement is anterior to the correlate of the statement. Foucault mentioned some examples: for a logician the 'proposition' 'the golden mountain is in California' cannot be said to be true or false if it has no 'referent'. The sentence 'colourless green ideas sleep furiously' may not have meaning in a linguistic analysis in spite of its perfect grammatical structure. The 'statement' as 'an enunciative

function' refers to 'domains of possibility' that make that proposition or that sentence possible.

2 'Statements' have 'a particular relation with a subject' (*AK*, p. 103). A 'proposition' (logic), a 'sentence' (grammar) and a 'speech act' (analytic philosophy) may all be 'statements'. However, the 'statement' actually has no defined subject. As Kusch states, 'each statement [in Foucault's sense] prescribes certain conditions that a speaker/writer must perform in order to qualify himself or herself as the "author" of that statement' (Kusch, 1991, p. 62). According to Kusch, this point in Foucault's definition of 'statement' can be understood by the distinction between 'modalities' in Latour and Woolgar's theory (Latour and Woolgar, 1986). As these authors (ibid., p. 90) explain, quoting the *Oxford Dictionary*, 'modality' in the Aristotelian meaning is 'a proposition in which the predicate is affirmed or denied of the subject with any kind of qualification' or, as they continued to suggest, in a more modern sense, 'modality' means 'any statement about another statement' (notice that the term 'statement' is now being used in a different sense from that of Foucault). In their analysis of scientific texts, Latour and Woolgar argue that there are five modalities of statement, which Kusch (1991, p. 62) summarises as: (1) wild speculation, (2) plausible suggestion, (3) reporting the finding of the others, (4) fact-stating, and (5) taking-for-granted. Latour and Woolgar analysed how these modalities were modified by scientists who were mentioning the same statement in different works. This would appear to be the point that Foucault was making when he stated that:

If a proposition, a sentence, a group of signs can be called statement, it is not because, one day, someone happened to speak of them or put them into some concrete form of writing; it is because the position of the subject can be assigned. To describe a formulation qua statement does not consist in analysing the relations between the author and what he says (or wanted to say, or said without wanting to); but in determining what position can and must be occupied by any individual if he is to be the subject of it. (*AK*, p. 107)

3 'The statement Arent cannot operate without the existence of an associated domain' (*AK*, p. 108). Whilst it is both necessary and sufficient that sentences and propositions obey some basic rules in order to be constructed, the statement has to be associated with another statement. For example, 'Peter arrived yesterday' forms a sentence, but

'yesterday arrived Peter' does not; A + B = C + D constitutes a proposition, but ABC + = D does not. Hence, an accumulation of signs *per se* does not constitute a sentence or proposition without reference to a system – natural or artificial – of language (*langue*).[1] They do not even need to be in context to be recognised as a sentence or proposition. A sentence and a proposition remain so, even if they do not have meaning or are untrue. However, in order to exist, a statement has to be related to an 'adjacent field' (*AK*, p. 109) or an 'associated domain'. The first impression is that Foucault is referring to 'context', but he soon states that this is not the usual understanding of 'context' and that actually the 'associated domain' is what provides 'context' to a sentence or a 'series of signs'. It forms an 'enunciative network', which is the background of 'the grammatical relations between sentences, the logical relationship between propositions, the metalinguistics relations between an object language and one that defines the rules, the rhetorical relations between groups (or elements) of sentences' (*AK*, p. 112). Kusch (1991) writes that what Foucault means by this is that:

what counts as a possible context of some statement is determined by the rules and the structure of its associated domain, for example, restrictions on context work differently in poetry and mathematics: whereas the two statements 'I love Ronny' and '2 + 2 = 4' can immediately follow each other in a poetic text, they can hardly do so in a mathematical treatise. (Kusch, 1991, p. 62)

4   A sequence of linguistic elements can only be analysed and described as a statement if it has a material existence. It cannot be 'ideal' or 'silent'. It is not that propositions, sentences or other sequences of signs do not have to have a material status, declares Foucault. The case is that the materiality is a constitutive element of the statement, but this 'materiality' is 'not defined by the space occupied or the date of its formulation, but rather by its status as a thing or object' (*AK*, p. 115). Rather than a spatio-temporal localisation, this 'materiality' is 'of the order of institution' (*AK*, p. 116). '[I]ts identity varies with a complex of set of material institutions' (*AK*, p. 115).

Foucault writes that, unlike in analytic philosophy, he does not regard the 'statement' in order to establish claims to its conditions of truth. He was not even interested in the contents of the statements, their meaning, intention or the moment of their origin. The archaeological study is a description of the 'statement' 'in its actual practice, its conditions, the rules that govern it, and the field in which it operates' (*AK*, p. 98). Archaeology is 'the analysis of statements':

> The analysis of statements [archaeology], then, is a historical analysis, but one that avoids all interpretation: it does not question things said as to what they are hiding, what they were 'really' saying, in spite of themselves, the unspoken element that they contain, the proliferation of thoughts, images, or fantasies that inhabit them; but, on the contrary, it questions them as to their mode of existence, what it means to them to have come into existence, to have left traces, and perhaps to remain there, awaiting the moment when they might be of use once more; what it means to them to have appeared when and where they did – they and no others. From this point of view, there is no such thing as a latent statement: for what one is concerned with is the fact of language (*langage*). (*AK*, p. 123)

Archaeology is distinguished from hermeneutics, semantic analysis or rhetorical studies, since its motto is not the idea 'that in one way or another, things said say more than themselves', that there is something called polysemia or that suppression may exist in what is said (*AK*, p. 123). It is worth quoting Foucault himself:

> In particular, [the analysis of statements] does not replace a logical analysis of propositions, a grammatical analysis of sentences, a psychological or contextual analysis of formulations; it is another way of attacking verbal performances, of dissociating their complexity, of isolating the terms that are entangled in its web, and of locating the various regularities that they obey. (*AK*, p. 121)

Foucault's main concept in *The Order of Things*, the 'episteme', is built in accordance with sets of statements (*énoncés*) grouped into different discourses or discursive frameworks.

Finally, Foucault defines 'statement' as follows:

> [I]t is a function of existence that properly belongs to signs and on the basis of which one may then decide, through analysis or intuition, whether or not they 'make sense', according to what rule they follow one another or are juxtaposed, of what they are the sign, and what sort of act is carried out by their formulation (oral or written). (*AK*, p. 97)

As for the notion of 'archive', Foucault defined 'archaeology' as the 'description of the archive' (*AK*, p. 7) and for that reason, Deleuze (1988, p. 1) referred to Foucault as 'a new archivist' who 'proclaims that henceforth he will deal only with statements'.

Foucault differed once again in his notion of 'archive' from what is normally understood by the term. He declared that he established the notion of 'archive' as neither a set of documents nor the totality of documents collected by a culture within a certain moment. He also declared that 'archive' did not mean a group of institutions that made those documents possible:

> by [archive] I do not mean the sum of all the texts that a culture has kept upon its person as documents attesting to its past, or as evidence of a continuing identity; nor do I mean the institutions, which, in a given society, make it possible to record and preserve those discourses that one wishes to remember and keep in circulation. (*AK*, p. 145)

In this regard, Foucault distinguishes his archaeology from the history of ideas, since archaeology is not an interpretative tool. Archaeology does not intend to deal with documents as signs of other things; it takes documents as practices.

In an interview, 'Michel Foucault explains his latest book', in 1969, Foucault appeared to have added some more elements to the difficult task of understanding his new notion of 'archive'. He continues to list different meanings to the word:

1 He declares: 'By archive, I understand the set of discourses effectively pronounced' (Foucault, 2001, p. 800).
2 He also states that the 'archive' is the group of regularising rules, a 'set of relations that are peculiar to the discursive level [...] the law of what can be said, the system that governs the appearance of statements as unique events' (*AK*, p. 145).
3 The 'archive' is what defines 'the system of enunciability' of the 'statement' (*AK*, p. 146). '*It is the general system of the formation and transformation of statements*' (ibid., original emphasis). It cannot 'be described exhaustively' because, with regards to the episteme, the archive cannot be described when we are under its auspices, since it is also part of the unconsciousness of knowledge.
4 Since it is from within the rules established by the 'archive' that we speak, the 'archive' is therefore 'that which gives to what we can say – and to itself, the object of our discourse – its mode of appearance, its

forms of existence and coexistence, its system of accumulation, historicity, and disappearance' (*AK*, p. 146). The 'archive' is a historical *a priori* and has a very close relationship to the episteme.

Therefore, it is clear by these declarations that the notion of 'archive' cannot be fully understood. Foucault defined it as the group of the discourses (for example, human sciences, political economy, biology and linguistics) and the rules that govern them, which are unconscious and are confused within the episteme itself.

3.2.2 The unity of discourse and discursive formation

Foucault argues that the foundation of the unity of the 'group of statements' that form 'discourses', such as 'political economy', 'medicine', 'grammar' and so on, is not a common object, a style, a group of concepts or even a choice of themes. According to him, their unity falls instead under a systematic 'dispersion' of elements. We should look for what makes a discourse and maintains its unity in time within a 'system of dispersion'. Nevertheless, Foucault does not appear to make a consistent effort in providing a clear definition for this expression. One thing is for certain: he employs this expression for arguing the point that the unity of discourses is not due to their objects, axioms, principles, origins, essences or meanings, highlighting once again what it is not about. For him, these elements would not explain why and how the discourse of political economy maintained its unity during certain periods of time. He claims that the unity of dispersion is at a prediscursive level and consists of a system of rules and relations, which should then be established through an investigation of the episteme. The 'prediscursive level' constitutes the conditions that allow a discourse to be made possible.

Foucault ruled out the anthropological notion of choice. He refused to accept the idea that decisions about what constitutes a certain discourse are taken by 'man' (as for Sartre) or by 'being' (as for Heidegger) (Billouet, 2003, p. 109). In *The Order of Things*, Foucault was determined to exclude the conception of a subject that decides. There is no such transcendental subject. For him, the discursive formation occurred by chance. Structures combine accidentally, giving rise to discourses. Discursive practices follow an accidental combination of relations and that is one of the reasons for him not attempting to explain the shifts between different structures of relations (epistemes).

More emphatically, Foucault ruled out the following hypotheses usually adopted as an explanation into the unity of discourses:

1 The object to which the 'statements' refer. The hypothesis has been that 'statements' form a unitary discourse, such that they refer to one and the same object. Foucault disagrees, for two basic reasons: i) the being of the object is constituted by what is said by the 'statements'; ii) there is no one permanent and true object of discourse, since it changes over time. For example, he argues in *The Order of Things* that the object dealt with in economic thought during the seventeenth and the eighteenth centuries (wealth) was not the same as during the nineteenth century (production). Instead of the object, the unity of discourse is given by the interplay of the rules that enable the appearance and the transformations of objects during a given period of time (*AK*, p. 36). A corollary of this argument is that Foucault's archaeology is not only anti the *subject*, but also 'the correlative category, the *object*', as pointed out by Lecourt (1975, p. 192). 'An archaeology is suspicious of objects' (Major-Poetzl, 1983, p. 5). This is intimately linked to the idea of 'rupture' in archaeology. It undermines the concept of unity in a 'science', a 'discourse', based on its *object*. There is no such thing as a defined object with which economics can deal in any period of history. The archaeology shifts the attention from the subject and object to the structure of a 'discourse' as an organised body of knowledge within its specific spatiotemporal articulations (ibid.). As Rorty points out, this conviction by Foucault certainly echoes Wittgenstein and reminds us that 'the way people talk can "create objects", in the sense that there are lots of things which wouldn't exist unless people had come to talk in certain ways' (Rorty, 1986, p. 42).

2 The form and type of connection of 'statements', hence the hypothesis that the unifying principle of discourses is in their 'style', such as the way in which we look at and describe things, the attention to either the visible or to what is in the 'deepness' of an object, and 'the system of transcribing what one perceived in what one said (same vocabulary, same play of metaphor)' (*AK*, pp. 36–7). Foucault states that he also had to abandon this hypothesis. He provides the example of his archaeology of medical discourse, since it had demonstrated to him that the system of description of 'statements' had changed constantly. Scales, guidelines, the lexicon of signs and their decipherment, along with the role of doctors in the process, have all

changed. Foucault elaborates on this, emphasising what should be considered, stating a need to know how these different and dispersed statements are kept under the same unity of discourse.

3 The system of permanent and coherent concepts. Foucault denied that discourses are unified by a group of concepts established once and for all. He wrote in *The Order of Things*, for example, that the concepts of value, price, trade, circulation, income and interest could only be thought of in the context of 'their positivity' (*OT*, p. 166).[2] In the classical age, these concepts had a different meaning from that of the modern era. These 'names', although perpetuated over time, referred to 'the analysis of wealth' (which is how Foucault denominated economic thought in the classical episteme) during the seventeenth and eighteenth centuries, before turning to a theory of production and labour during the period of modern history of economic thought (from the end of the eighteenth century onwards).

4 The identity and persistence of themes. For Foucault, the unity of discourses, such as is found in economics, could not be based on the permanence of a theme. He observed that the same theme may either be part of different discourses or various theories within one discourse may refer to incompatible themes (*AK*, p. 41). For example, he mentions that the theme 'evolutionism' in the discourse of living beings was different in the eighteenth century from that of the nineteenth century. 'Evolutionism' in the eighteenth century had been regarded in terms of a 'continuum' between species that had been built up over a period of time. The main intention was to consider continuum in terms of a 'table' of species in which 'the space', especially the kinship of species, was privileged. In the nineteenth century, this changed and 'evolutionism' started to become regarded as the 'discontinuous' groups of species in time. In economics, the physiocrats and some 'utilitarians' of the eighteenth century (Condillac, Galliani, Graslin and Destutt de Tracy) dealt with the formation of value in a different manner. They fell under the same unity of discourse, 'the analysis of wealth' and shared a 'relatively limited set of concepts (what money was, how prices were determined, how labour costs should be calculated), but, whilst physiocrats explained value according to the remuneration of labour, these utilitarians saw it on the basis of exchange' (*AK*, p. 40).[3] In other words, the discourse regarding value at that time admitted two distinct themes. Instead of looking for the individualisation of discourses in the themes, the archaeology should consider the 'systems of dispersions'. For instance, the archaeology should describe how it was possible for

the discourse on wealth 'to play different games' with the same set of determined concepts.

Therefore, Foucault's intention was to approach political economy as 'a group of statements' and in order to understand how they formed this 'unity' (this 'regularity' called 'political economy'), its 'discursive formation' should be considered, that is, we should investigate how the statements were ordered, correlated, positioned and transformed. He uses the expression 'discursive formation' in a manner synonymous with 'science', 'ideology' and even 'theory'. He explains that, by using 'discursive formation', he wanted to avoid the conditions and consequences that these words ('science', 'ideology' and 'theory') were already carrying. Archaeology was indeed an investigation of the 'rules of formation' of discourses, which he defined as 'the conditions of existence (but also coexistence, maintenance, modification, and disappearance) in a given discursive division', the intention being 'to determine the possible points of dispersion of the discourse' and to describe the relations that determined that certain statements were included in, or excluded from, a given discourse (*AK*, p. 42).

In *The Archaeology of Knowledge*, he also declares:

> I would like to show with precise examples that in analysing discourses themselves, one sees the loosening of the embrace, apparently so tight, of words and things, and the emergence of a group of rules proper to discursive practice. These rules define not the dumb existence of a reality, nor the canonical use of a vocabulary, but the ordering of objects. 'Words and things' is the entirely serious title of a problem; it is the ironic title of a work that modifies its own form, displaces its own data, and reveals, at the end of the day, a quite different task. A task that consists of not – of no longer – treating discourses as groups of signs (signifying elements referring to contents representations) but as practices that systematically form the objects of which they speak. Of course, discourses are composed of signs; but, what they do is more than use these signs to designate things. It is *more* that renders them irreducible to the language (*langue*) and to speech. It is this 'more' that we must reveal and describe. (*AK*, p. 54, original emphasis)

3.2.3   Science and knowledge: thresholds

Foucault writes that one of the consequences of considering continuities in the history of knowledge or believing in the 'progress' of reason ('accumulation of truths' or 'the orthogenesis of reason') is that of analysing knowledge only in terms of what is, or is not 'science'. These examinations fail to recognise that 'a discursive practice [...] has its own levels, its own thresholds, its own various ruptures' (*AK*, p. 207). He then distinguishes four thresholds in knowledge (*savoir*) which characterise the distinctive emergences and changes that occur within a discursive formation:

1 Positivity: when a discursive practice achieves individuality and autonomy; when a system for the formation of statements emerges or is transformed; the 'positivity' of a discourse 'reveals that within a discourse, reference is being made to the same thing within the same conceptual field, at the same level' (Smart, 1985, p. 40).
2 Epistemologisation: when the group of statements in a discursive formation is articulated, with the intention of validating it through norms of verification and coherence.
3 Scientificity: when a knowledge (that has already crossed the threshold of epistemologisation) follows some formal criteria in the construction of propositions.
4 Formalisation: when a scientific discourse is able to define its necessary axioms.

Foucault writes that some major concerns of archaeology are: a) to investigate how these thresholds occurred over time; b) to analyse if there are overlaps between/among the thresholds or, alternatively, if one of them governs another during a certain period in the history of that discourse; c) to find out the conditions of their emergence and establishment. He stresses that these thresholds are neither successive nor evolutive and states, for example, that 'in some cases, the threshold of positivity is crossed well before that of epistemologisation' (*AK*, p. 206) and even continues to mention political economy as an example. He argues that there are cases when they may occur simultaneously: 'the establishment of positivity evolves at the same time as the emergence of an epistemological figure' (*AK*, p. 207). The threshold of scientificity may occur during a transition from one 'positivity' to another, as for example during the transition from natural history to biology, which Foucault explored in *The Order of Things*, as they had different formal criteria (classification of beings in natural history and specific correlations of different organisms in biology). Some regions of knowledge (*connaissances*) may never achieve some of these thresholds, but that does not mean that they are not 'sciences'. A 'positivity' is not a science, although it does not exclude it.

Foucault describes the case of economics and this is one more example of his reflections that would deserve a more careful consideration by economists interested in methodology and historiography of economics:

> In the case of economics the disconnexions are particularly numerous. In the seventeenth century, one can recognize a threshold of positivity: it almost coincides with the practice and theory of mercantilism; but its epistemologisation did not occur until later, at the very end of the century, or the beginning of the next century, with Locke and Cantillon. However, the nineteenth century, with Ricardo, marks both a new type of positivity, a new form of epistemologisation, which was later to be modified in turn by Cournot and Jevons, at the very time that Marx was to reveal an entirely new discursive practice on the basis of political economy. (*AK*, p. 207)

Foucault identifies mathematics as being 'the only discursive practice to have crossed at one and the same time' all those thresholds (*AK*, p. 208). That is why it has been taken as a prototype for the emergence and development of all other sciences. However, Foucault refuses to take it as his model, since this would reproduce a 'historico-transcendental analysis'. According to him, the historian of science who follows this kind of analysis would fail to notice that mathematics might well serve as a model for the discursive practices that seek formal rigour, while it cannot be a model for other 'sciences', such as those he analysed in *The Order of Things*, including economics.

For Foucault, these different thresholds have given rise to different possible forms of historical analysis:

1 Analysis at the level of formalisation. In this kind of analysis, the past 'is revealed as a particular case, a naïve model, a partial and insufficiently generalized sketch, of a more abstract, or more powerful theory, or one existing at a higher level' and 'each historical event has its own formal level and localization' (*AK*, p. 209). It is the history of mathematics itself and the histories that take mathematics as a model.
2 Analysis at the threshold of scientificity. The aim is to investigate how a discourse acquired the status of a 'scientific domain'. It is an epistemological history of sciences, such as those accomplished by Bachelard and Canguilhem.
3 Archaeological history. This analysis does not take scientificity as the norm. It tries to unveil discursive practices in as far as they gave rise

to a corpus of knowledge. It is a description of discursive practices, attempting to identify those thresholds (positivity, epistemologisation, scientificity and formalisation), keeping in mind that they may not even occur, and reveal 'a role set of differences, relations, gaps, shifts, independences, autonomies, and the way in which they articulate their own historicities on one another' (*AK*, p. 210). This is indeed the analysis of the 'episteme', writes Foucault (*AK*, p. 211).

3.2.4 The episteme

Foucault defined 'episteme' at the end of *The Archaeology of Knowledge*. It is only after the inquiry into his particular theory of discourse and the review of *The Archaeology of Knowledge* that we can fully address his definition. He writes that episteme is:

> the total set of relations that unite, at a given period, the discursive practices that give rise to epistemological figures, sciences, and possibly formalized systems; the way in which, in each of these discursive formations, the transitions to epistemologisation, scientificity, and formalization are situated and operate; the distribution of these thresholds, which may coincide, be subordinated to one another, or be separated by shifts in time; the lateral relations that may exist between epistemological figures or sciences in so far as they belong to neighbouring, but distinct, discursive practices. The episteme is not a form of knowledge (*connaissance*) or type of rationality which, crossing the boundaries of the most varied sciences, manifests the sovereign unity of a subject, a spirit, or a period; it is the totality of relations that can be discovered, for a given period, between the sciences when one analyses them at the level of discursive regularities. (*AK*, p. 211)

In this definition, Foucault described episteme as an arrangement of certain relations which comprise the conditions of emergence (as well as the conditions of existence, coexistence, modification and disappearance) of particular practices in the discourse of knowledge of a certain age. Therefore, the episteme for him also delineates the thresholds of knowledge (positivity, epistemologisation, scientificity and formalisation) and how they occur within the forms of knowledge. He emphasises that episteme is not a type of rationality or a form of knowledge. Episteme defines some forms of knowledge, although this does not suggest that it will establish a type of rationality within a period of time. Foucault stressed that in *The Order of Things* he was approaching a group of discourses in knowledge that had obeyed the same regularities and hence formed the same interdiscursive practice. The content of the discourses are different (political economy, biology and linguistics), but what is of concern to an archaeological investigation is that they belong to the same epistemic configuration, which was defined by the same composition of some relations (language-representation, same-other, time-space, thought-unthought).

In the Foreword to the English edition of *The Order of Things*, Foucault expressed another characteristic of the episteme. He stated that he was looking for the episteme as the 'positive unconscious of knowledge'. He affirmed again in the last pages of *The Order of Things* that the episteme is 'the positive ground of our knowledge' (p. 385). He claimed that the unconsciousness of knowledge had usually been thought of in terms of the 'negative' role that it plays in the development of science, although he was rather more interested in finding out the 'positive' unconscious, that is, those conditions which promote and conduct thought in a certain time and culture.

It is assumed in the archaeology that there is a set of notions and conceptions that are united as the 'positive unconscious of knowledge'. This 'positive ground of our knowledge' formed the conditions for the emergence and existence of a group of fields of knowledge in a certain spatiotemporal context. In particular, Foucault identified these relations as being the conditions of possibility of the human sciences of Western culture: psychology, sociology and the analysis of literature and myths. He believed that the study of human beings had radically changed towards the end of the eighteenth century, when economics, biology and philology emerged as 'positivities'. Therefore, in order to address the emergence of the human sciences, he also had to produce the archaeology for these *connaissances*, which he called 'empiricities'. He uses terms like 'empiricity', 'positivity' and even the expression 'epistemological regions' (*OT*, p. 355) to address political economy, biology and linguistics (as well as their counterparts in the previous epistemes), since he refuses to employ the term 'science' to designate them. Although 'empiricity' and 'positivity' have a slightly different meaning, they both refer to knowledge, in the sense of 'representation-as-effects', within that episteme and differ principally in terms of method. 'Empiricity' means that each science 'is conceived to have its own peculiar objects of study' and 'positivity' means that each science has 'its own unique strategy for determining the relationships existing among the objects inhabiting its domain' (White, 1973, p. 27). As depicted above, 'positivity' was actually defined by Foucault as one of the thresholds of knowledge. It is also worth mentioning that the problem of demarcation, between a 'science' and 'not science', 'science' and ideology', 'exact' and 'inexact' science and so on, was not a concern for him. His description is not concerned with legitimating 'science'. For example, he differentiates physics from psychology, although he does this in terms of features and conditions. Even when he uses the expression 'human sciences', he does not really mean that they are 'sciences'. Indeed, the 'human sciences' are not 'sciences' for Foucault. As Cousins and Hussain (1984, p. 66) argue, this does not mean that they are 'a monument to error' or 'merely phantasmagorical elaborations of political interests'; they are in the vicinity of the sciences, but they cannot be sciences as their conditions fall within the figure of man, in the sense that they are organised 'by a complex scheme of producing a knowledge of Man'. Foucault (1994b, p. 364) writes that he was interested in what the Greeks called the *tekhne*, that is, 'a practical rationality governed by a conscious goal'.

3.3   *The Order of Things*

Foucault declared that his inspiration for *The Order of Things* was a reference by Borges to 'a certain Chinese encyclopaedia':

> [A]nimals are divided into: a) belonging to the Emperor; b) embalmed; c) tame; d) sucking pigs; e) sirens; f) fabulous, g) stray dogs; h) included in the present classification; I) frenzied; j) innumerable; k) drawn with a very fine camelhair brush; l) *et cetera*; m) having just broken the water pitcher; n) that from a long way off look like flies. (Borges, quoted in *OT*, p. xv)

In the careful words of Foucault, his *The Order of Things* arose out of that passage:

> out of the laughter that shattered [...] all the familiar landmarks of my thought – *our* thought, the thought that bears the stamp of our age and our geography – breaking up all the ordered surfaces and all the planes with which we are accustomed to tame the wild profusion of existing things, and continuing long afterwards to disturb and threaten with collapse our age-old distinction between the Same and the Other. (*OT*, p. XV, original emphasis)

Borges's text was an inspiration to Foucault, to wonder about the frontiers of our way of thinking and the way in which we order events. Why is it not possible for us to consider that enumeration? When we reflect on the question, our intuition suggests that there are some conditions of possibility of thought, but what are they? Are they historical or timeless? Are they cultural? How could we understand them? We could still question whether it is possible to consider them from the outside. Do the necessary transcendental *a priori* notions and categories of mind define them, as in Kant's system, or are they historical and cultural, as for Foucault? Foucault concludes that there is a configuration of relations that defines what has been considered as the modes of thought, modern/postmodern matrices, paradigms, conceptions of closed/open systems and so on. These are like epiphenomena of an underlying arrangement that allows us to think what we think, which he went on to investigate in *The Order of Things*.

In an interview to the *Magazine Littéraire* in 1969, entitled 'Michel Foucault explains his latest book' (that is, *The Archaeology of Knowledge*), Foucault emphasised that the title *The Order of Things* (originally *Les Mots et Les Choses* in French) was actually ironic and explains the main purpose of *The Archaeology of Knowledge* as follows:

The title *Les Mots et les Choses* was completely ironic. [...] There is a problem: how is it possible that real things, and perceived ones, can be articulated by words within a discourse? Is it words which impose our definition of things or is it things themselves that, for some interference of a subject, transcribe themselves on the surface of words? It was absolutely not this old problem that I wanted to deal with in *Les Mots et les Choses*. I tried to invert it: to analyse the discourses themselves, that is, the discursive practices that are in between words and things. [...] I try to do another thing and to show that there were [...] rules for the formation of objects (which are the rules of use of words), rules for the formation of concepts (which are the rules of syntax), rules for the formation of theories (which are neither rules of deduction nor rhetorical rules). It is these rules, which are put in action by a discursive practice at a given moment, that explain that things are seen (or omitted), that they are focused on according to some aspect and analysed at a certain level; that a certain word is employed, with a certain signification, and in a certain kind of sentence. (Foucault, 2001, p. 804)

Further to Foucault's archaeological project, he turns in *The Order of Things* to the conditions of possibility of the human sciences. In particular, he believed that they were only possible on the foundation of a certain epistemic configuration, which he named a 'historical *a priori*', that took man as the subject and object of his own knowledge.

As mentioned previously, the episteme is a structure that comprises same-other relations, conceptions of language, representation, time (history) and space as the variable (foreground or background) to consider the subject matter,[4] and man-finitude (thought-unthought). Structure is identified under the notions of representation and historicity, which are the basis/ground of thought within a certain spatiotemporal context. Representation corresponds to the relations between subject (through words, that is, language) and object (things).

Foucault identified three historical periods marked by different epistemes: 'the age of resemblance' until the end of the sixteenth century (pre-classic); 'the age of representation', or classical episteme, which included the period from the early seventeenth century to the second half of the eighteenth century; and 'the age of history' or modern era from the end of the eighteenth century until the present time. Foucault declared that we are clearly still in the modern episteme. For instance, he declared that 'the entire modern episteme [...] still serves as the positive ground of our knowledge' (*OT*, p. 385). Table 3.1 summarises the main characteristics of the three epistemes, which are explained in the following sections.

3.3.1   The pre-classical episteme: the age of resemblance

Foucault characterised the period 'up to the end of the 16th century' as 'the age of resemblance'. Although regarded as the period of Renaissance, he was to depict its conception in a very different way.

Foucault stated that at that time, knowledge was a kind of 'mirror of nature', since words and things were combined, so to speak. Words mirrored things. 'Seeing and saying [were] still one' (*BC*, p. xi). Language could express the meanings of things. There was no difference between what was read and what was seen. 'Language partakes in the world-wide dissemination of similitudes and signatures' (*OT*, p. 35).

The meanings of 'things' had been given by a superior entity and could be known by the search for the resemblances. In other words, everything could be known through a set of connections of similitudes, which were printed on the world by God. Indeed, resemblances were God's signature. The task for man was to find them by detecting signs and finding analogies. Analogy was the main procedure of knowing and man was included in this web of analogies. Everything could be explained in relation to God and man, and man could be explained in relation to everything else:

Table 3.1   The three epistemes – main characteristics: *savoir*

	Episteme – *Savoir*		
	---	---	---
Main *Notions/Relations*	**Pre-classical** Until the end of the 16th century	**Classical** The 17th and 18th centuries	**Modern** From the end of the 18th century until the present day
General Character	*Age of Resemblance*	*Age of Representation*	*Age of History*
Object of Knowledge	*God*	*Nature*	*Man*
Mode of Savoir	Interpretation: Signs are given by God	Representation: Signs constitute themselves during the process of *connaissance*	Interpretation: Signs created by Man
Main Procedure	Analogy	Analysis & Order	Analogy & Succession
Visibility/Deepness	Visible	Visible	Invisible/Unconscious; 'Organic Structures': 'Vertical' investigation
Orientation	Time and Space had no significance	Spacialisation of the object; Timeless table	Temporal: The object has a history
'Things' mode of being	Resemblance	Order	History
Words & Things	They were combined	They separated, while representation through language occupied the gap	Representation can no longer occupy the gap. 'Man' is responsible for representation (he became the Subject and Object of Knowledge). Self-representation
Same & Other	Same	Same/Other. The Other is the Different. *Cogito*: There was no 'Unthought'	Same/Other. 'The Other' is the 'unthought', which includes the 'unconscious' (object of the human sciences) and the hidden meanings

Epistemology — *General Character, Object of Knowledge, Mode of Savoir, Main Procedure, Visibility/Deepness, Orientation*

Ontology — *'Things' mode of being, Words & Things, Same & Other*

(*Continued*)

Table 3.1 Continued

Ontology	***Nature/Human Nature***	Man is part of Nature	Nature and Human nature were defined under a similar plan	Nature and human nature are not on the same level. There is something 'External' to Man; there is something unconscious that has to be thought. Unthought: Something that has not or cannot be thought
	Finitude			It is only in the modern episteme that 'Man' established his limitations in *savoir* and *connaissance*
	Perception of Things		Continuity	Discontinuity; if there is continuity, it should be within things
Philosophy		Theology	Rationalism; Knowledge is unified: *mathesis universalis*	Philosophy is fragmented: science & metaphysics; epistemology & science
Language		'Transparent'	'Discourse' as a sequence of verbal signs was studied. It is still 'transparent' although it has to be constructed. Grammar therefore became necessary, Latin being the best language	Lost its transparency. Language has a historical nature and it is the means to express a subject. 'Language' became object of knowledge (*connaissance*): Philosophy & Linguistics

Source: Author's own work based upon Foucault (1970a).

The space occupied by analogies is really a space of radiation. Man is surrounded by it on every side; but, inversely, he transmits these resemblances back into the world from which he receives them. He is the great fulcrum of proportions – the centre upon which relations are concentrated and from which they once again reflected. (*OT*, p. 23)

Thus, knowledge was possible through a realisation of 'the same', such that 'the same' is that which is 'both dispersed and related, therefore to be distinguished by kinds and to be collected together into identities' (Foucault's definition for 'the same' – *OT*, p. xxiv). For knowledge, man had to become fully aware of the same, since it was already there to be explored.

Resemblance was determined by the figures of *convenientia* (there is a kinship between things – a neighbourhood), *aemulatio* (there is a force of reflection, or a mirror image, of one thing upon another), *analogy* (in which *convenientia* and *aemulatio* are superposed) and *sympathy*. Sympathy and antipathy were twins. 'Antipathy maintains the isola tion of things and prevents their assimilation; it encloses every species within its impenetrable difference and its propensity to continue being what it is' (*OT*, p. 24). To know was to gather things together. Man was never to become conscious of the other, since there was not a sense of differentiation. The 'other' was not an agent for knowledge. The world was like a book that should be read and interpreted. For example, there were resemblances between the sky and the earth, a relationship between the composition of sky and of plants and equality between money (precious metals) and wealth, and so on. There was nothing scattered in the world – things were linked one to another through kinship and analogies.

To know is not to analyse, but to interpret and, because of that, divination and erudition were not different forms of knowledge (Cousins and Hussain, 1984, p. 34).

The interplay of similitudes was infinite, it always being possible to discover new ones. The limit of this was the proper order of things, given that the world was finite. Knowledge was limitless in as much as resemblance reproduced itself. Similitude needed another similitude in order to exist and there was an 'accumulation of confirmations', which enabled certainty. However, at the same time, knowledge was 'a thing of sand', since man was condemned 'to never knowing anything but the same thing and to knowing that thing only at the unattainable end of an endless journey' (*OT*, p. 30). Thought in the age of resemblance 'had not yet achieved the age of reason' (*OT*, p. 51).

3.3.2 The classical episteme: the age of representation

Foucault describes the classical episteme (from the beginning of the seventeenth century up until the end of the eighteenth century) as being 'the age of representation', where the space occupied by things and their visibility (their surface) were privileged. To know was mainly to name the visible surface of things.[5] Referring to natural scientists of that period, Foucault observed that 'they didn't even want to use a microscope' (Foucault, 1994b, p. 363).

At the beginning of the seventeenth century, Foucault wrote, 'thought ceases to move in the element of resemblance' (*OT*, p. 51). Similitude, which was a fundamental category of knowledge during the sixteenth century, did not disappear, although from that time on, it was regarded not only with suspicion but as being on the edge of visionary or a sign of madness.

Foucault identifies the transition between these two epistemes in *Don Quixote*, first published in 1605. This personage was on the bridge between the two epistemes since he wondered about the relationship between words and things. He 'marks the point where resemblance enters an age which is, from the point of view of resemblance, one of madness and imagination' (*OT*, p. 49).

Foucault writes that words and things separated, and that something occupied the gap: representation. Representation brought words and things back together through language. The act of knowing became the search for a well-constructed language. Although 'the written word and things no longer resemble one another [...] language has not become entirely impotent' (*OT*, p. 48).

Usually, 'representation' has the meaning of 'correspond to'. In the philosophical meaning, as Lalande (1999, p. 953) defines it, 'representation' is 'what is present to the spirit: what someone "represents to him/herself"; what makes the concrete content of an act of thinking'. Lalande informs us that we can suppose that the philosophical meaning of the word 'representation' arose from the French verb *représenter*, which traditionally had the meaning of 'imagination'. Another supposition is that it could have originated from Leibniz's writings, to the extent that he used the term to designate 'correspondence'. Clare O'Farrell (1996) has a definition for 'representation', which corresponds to the meaning given to it by Foucault in *The Order of Things*. O'Farrell sees 'representation' as the interrelation amongst 'the rules governing language, the rules governing imagination and thought and the rules governing material existence'. This is the meaning of 'representation' that Foucault employs as his *central notion* in *The Order of Things*, given that the classical episteme's configuration is the axis of the book. In what could be considered to be one of his most famous passages in the book, he discussed Velázquez's *Las Meninas* ('Maids of Honour') in order to illustrate the main claim of his work and to represent the limits of the classical episteme.

In *Las Meninas*, Velázquez depicted himself in the act of painting two figures: King Philip IV and his wife, Mariana. Whereas the couple appear reflected in a mirror on the wall behind the central scene, everybody in the picture is looking to the couple 'represented' in the mirror; no one is actually looking towards the mirror. The central scene shows their daughter, Infanta Margarita – as if she had come to watch the act of painting – accompanied by her maids of honour, courtiers and dwarfs. Velázquez is on the left side of the picture holding a brush together with a palette and standing a little back from his canvas, as if taking a pause from his work. He is looking at the couple as if they were an invisible point outside the picture, which can be represented as the couple and us – the spectators. We, the spectators, cannot see what is in front of the canvas; all we can see is the back. Foucault states that because of this 'we do not know who we are, or what we are doing' (*OT*, p. 5). It would appear that he is referring to his idea of the 'unconscious' character of epistemes, or to the detail in the painting as a suggestion of the impossibility of going outside to look at the act of representation. Foucault scrutinised each detail of the painting in a long description and characterised it by 'spectacle-as-observation' (*spectacle-en-regard*, which could be better translated as 'spectacle of gazes'). Velázquez is seen to be in such a position that, whenever he is 'representing', he is not 'represented' in the picture. Thus, the act of 'representing' cannot be 'represented'. As Foucault remarks, 'we are looking at a picture in which the painter is in turn looking out at us', but 'only insofar as we happen to occupy the same position as his subject' (*OT*, p. 4). Since the spectators can be the models, there are as many models as there are spectators. 'No gaze is stable', Foucault writes. This statement suggests 'instability' of the roles of the subject and the object, both the spectator and the model. Whoever is represented is looking at a place that can change constantly. At the same time, the spectators are included in the 'representation' of the picture. There is also a man who is in the background, with one foot on a step, as if to about to go upstairs or ready to enter a room. As with all the others 'represented' in the painting, he is looking at the couple, who are 'represented' only in the mirror but, like all the others, he 'cannot be given a place in the mirror' (*OT*, p. 15).

Las Meninas illustrated the threshold of this episteme, demonstrating its contradictions and the reason for its collapse, giving rise to a new one: the modern age. In the painting, all the functions of representation (the representor, the represented and the representee) are depicted, except for the proper act of representing; that is, that what is not represented is 'a unified and unifying subject who posits these representations and who makes them objects for himself' (Dreyfus and Rabinow, 1982, p. 25).

In *The Order of Things*, Foucault's system of 'representation' refers to the relations between words and things or what is in the gap between them. Hence, how man can represent the world to himself? In this case, given that it is through language that man can know, language provides the most important signs to knowledge.

When the idea of resemblance started to be regarded with suspicion, the views of Bacon and Descartes became an alternative option. Bacon criticised resemblance through the description of idols and Descartes saw resemblance as 'a confused mixture that must be analysed in terms of *identity, difference, measurement* and *order*' (*OT*, p. 52, emphasis added).

During the classical period, order and analysis replaced interpretation, while representation replaced resemblance. Discrimination brought the space occupied by things to the forefront of knowledge. Things were now regarded as within a plan and to know was to organise them within a kind of table, in which identities and differences (the relations between the same and the other) could be identified. Foucault saw Descartes's general science of order, the *mathesis universalis*, as an expression of that episteme. It is here that Foucault refers to Descartes's dream of founding a universal science with the help of mathematics. *Mathesis universalis* was Descartes's designation to the science that would result in an application of a unified mathematical method. He already pronounced this idea in rule four of the *Regulae*: 'there must be a general science which explains all the points that can be raised concerning order and measure irrespective of the subject-matter, and that this science should be termed *mathesis universalis*' (Descartes, 1985a, p. 19). The basic proposal was that knowledge should follow a schedule from the ideas to the reality of things, the first step being to establish a unique certainty, a 'clear' and 'distinct' idea ('innate'), from which it would be possible to derive, by deduction, all knowledge. In his own philosophical project, this idea – axiom – was the *Cogito*. Therefore, the procedure should mirror itself on the sciences of mathematics. Descartes declared in the *Discourse on Method*: 'Those long chains composed of very simple and easy reasoning, which geometers customarily use to arrive at their most difficult demonstrations, had given me occasion to suppose that all the things which can fall under human knowledge are interconnected in the same way' (Descartes, 1985b, p. 120).

Knowing was no longer a case of trying to connect things, but instead 'to discriminate' and to order representations correctly. To know is to tabulate. Whereas in the previous episteme to know was 'to draw things together' or to bring things together by comparison, in the classical age to know was 'to discriminate' them. It is therefore necessary to compare things while looking for their differences.

Despite the unity of knowledge projected in a *mathesis universalis*, there were, according to Foucault, two basic ways to pursue knowledge: *mathesis* or *taxonomia*. *Mathesis* was the science of calculable order; Foucault states that *mathesis* was applied when dealing with 'simple natures', aspects of reality susceptible to a quantitative, mathematical treatment. In the case of 'complex natures', like the empirical domains of knowledge he was investigating (economic thought, natural history and grammar), a *taxonomia* was pursued. Unlike *mathesis* (whose method was algebra), *taxonomia* did not have a pre-established method and had to create a system of signs (*OT*, p. 72). 'What algebra is to *mathesis*, signs and words in particular, are to *taxonomia*: a constitution and evident manifestation of the order of things' (*OT*, p. 203). The empirical domains of knowledge of general grammar, natural history and analysis of wealth pursued a *taxonomia* of their objects. Therefore, Foucault writes, although following a *taxonomia*, these 'empirical analyses are not in opposition to the project of a universal mathesis, in the sense that scepticism is to rationalism' (*OT*, p. 73).

Thus, economic analysis was a *taxonomia* and Foucault argues that 'mercantilism', chronologically delimited by Scipion de Grammont and Nicolas Barbon, provided the necessary system of signs.

'Order' is the 'mode of being' of things in the classical age (*OT*, p. 219). For example, in relation to the study of living beings (natural history), knowing consisted of describing them, ordering them and putting them in a table, which was in accordance with their *structure* and *character*. Moreover, there was a visible 'continuity' between/among things, which allowed one to 'order' them.

Although resemblance was no longer the central category of knowledge, it was maintained as 'an indispensable border of knowledge' (*OT*, p. 67). Ordering could not be possible if it were not for the possibility of grouping some of the perceptions according to the resemblances between them. Resemblance could only be established by imagination, given that '[w]ithout imagination, there would be no resemblance between things' (*OT*, p. 69). Resemblance and imagination formed the fundamental pair that allowed the discrimination of identities and differences.

In the project of comparing and ordering things, the thought of the classical episteme essentially had two main aspects. In the first instance, it had to deal with a confused mixture of things. Secondly, although the order of things was confused, it could be considered in the form of 'resemblances'. Imagination determined the ordering by bringing to mind, even if involuntarily, a reverberation that could form a table of comparisons.

As Major-Poetzl (1983, p. 181) points out, 'time' was in the background, while 'space' was in the foreground in the classical tabular form of knowledge. The relation to time resulted from the fact that mixed up things involved other things that occurred or were presented to the mind linearly over time. It is clear that during the construction of such a table, it would be necessary to bring them all together and at the same moment in time, which could be directly influenced by the imagination itself. Foucault evokes Hume in order to stress the role of imagination for knowledge. Imagination was the operation of mind that allowed one to deal with certain 'mechanics of the image in time' (*OT*, p. 69). According to Norton (1993), imagination for Hume is a faculty that allows 'compounding' impressions with the abstract 'ideas' of time and space. Hume argued that although we have 'ideas' of space and time, we have no impression of space and time. For Hume, imagination was what allowed us to compound impressions in time and space since, as noted by Norton, it 'achieves what neither the senses nor reason can achieve' (ibid., p. 9).

Resemblance and imagination were the combined underlying configuration of the science of order. Foucault denominated *genesis* the process by which imagination connects and orders impressions. 'Genesis' linked two types of analysis: the *analysis of nature* and the *analytic of imagination*. The *analysis of nature* is summarised as the process of perceiving the resemblance between things, before putting them in order. The *analytic of imagination* is related to how imagination allows us to order the confused flux of impressions. Both the *analysis of nature* and the *analytic of imagination* provided an account of how *taxonomia* and *mathesis* could order things.

Foucault's argument certainly reminds us of Adam Smith's *The History of Astronomy*. The similarity between Foucault's 'genesis' and Smith's explorations of the principles that conduct human nature to knowledge are striking similar, although we cannot be certain as to whether Foucault had read it. Referring to the sentiment of 'wonder', the feeling provoked in man by something unknown to him so far, as 'new and singular', Smith investigated the role of resemblance and imagination. There is also an impressive similarity, in the same essay, to Foucault's description of that episteme as an analysis of equalities and differences.

There was a fundamental change concerning the nature of the sign at the beginning of the seventeenth century. Up until then, it was considered that God had created all things and put his signature on them. Since then, the sign was to be conceived as being constituted as such only during the process of knowledge. 'Now signs are knowledge, tools of analysis and means of representing order' (Cousins and Hussain, 1984, p. 33). As Cousins and Hussain note, during the Renaissance, sign was ternary: there was that which signifies, that which was signified and that which allowed us to see the mark of the second within the first element. Now, in the classical episteme, the sign will be binary: a signifier and a signified. 'Signs are modes of representation not properties of things' (ibid., p. 35).

According to Foucault, this fact and its consequences concerning the relation between a sign and that which it signifies must be analysed in accordance with three variables, which again clearly refer to Hume's philosophy. In the first instance, there is the certainty of the relation: a sign became certain or probable. Since the signifying function of a sign only took place in the process of knowledge, it could be certain or probable. The connection of significations does not necessarily correspond to a relationship between cause and effect, but rather to an indication and to the relation of a sign to what it signifies. Hence, the relationship of cause can be questionable, as clearly mentioned in Hume's problem of causation. Secondly, there is the issue of the type of relation: a sign may belong to the whole of what it denotes or could be separate from it. It is only through analysis that a sign can become apparent. Foucault writes that because the mind analyses, the sign appears (*OT*, p. 61) and, at the same time, a sign plays the role of an instrument of analysis. Having established it as such, a sign could be deployed in other impressions, such as if it were in a grid. Thirdly, there is the origin of the relation: a sign may be natural or conventional. Although this had already been mentioned in Plato, for example, as Foucault reminds us, what changed at that moment in history was that now an artificial sign need not keep its fidelity to a natural sign in order to be believable in knowledge. One other difference was that 'man-made signs' were thought to be superior. This idea of creating an ideal, of conventional signs during that period in history led to the ambition of creating a transparent language.

Knowing was understood to be the building of a taxonomy, given that knowledge was synonymous with a 'well-constructed language'.

Therefore, at the level of the most elementary conditions of possibility, Foucault argues that this change in the organisation of a sign that occurred in the beginning of the seventeenth century was due to the breaking off from *divinatio*:

> the dissociation of the sign and resemblance in the early seventeenth century caused these new forms – probability, analysis, combination, and universal language system – to emerge, not as successive themes engendering one another or driving one another out, but as a single network of necessities. And it was this network that made possible the individuals we term Hobbes, Berkeley, Hume, or Condillac. (*OT*, p. 63)

Foucault also writes: 'The knowledge that divided, *at random*, signs that were absolute and older than itself has been replaced by a network of signs built up step by step in accordance with a knowledge of what is probable. Hume has become possible' (*OT*, p. 60).

The age of a secular knowledge had emerged. Knowledge in the classical age was to represent the unveiling of a natural order.

Insofar as knowledge can be uncertain, Hume introduced the case of probability. Russell (1946) explains Hume's understanding of probability:

> Hume does not mean by 'probability' the sort of knowledge contained in the mathematical theory of probability, such as that the chance of throwing double sixes with two dice is one thirty-sixth. [...] What Hume is concerned with is uncertain knowledge, such as is obtained from empirical data by inferences that are not demonstrative. This includes all our knowledge as to the future, and as to unobserved portions of the past and present. In fact, it includes everything except, on the one hand, direct observation, and, on the other, logic and mathematics. (Russell, 1946, p. 689)

Foucault then analysed what he called the empirical sciences: analysis of wealth, natural history and general grammar. For him, these domains of classical knowledge were subdomains of *taxonomia*, because 'they undertake qualitative orderings of the complex representations belonging to specific regions of our experience of the world' and 'in this sense, they are empirical rather than mathematical disciplines' (Gutting, 1989, p. 156).

Representation in the seventeenth and eighteenth centuries was what resemblance was in the sixteenth century. However, representation was no longer a mirror of nature, since it was language that provided the signs for representations. So the issue became a question of how to build the right language. Representation was not questioned and was therefore conceived as something similar to a map. The ability of the map to represent was also not questioned. The only question was related to the accuracy of the map. The classical episteme did not question the ability of representation to represent, but merely its acuity (Cousins and Hussain, 1984, p. 47).

The separation between words and things led to two major consequences: a) the gap was filled by representation; and b) a theory of language became possible and necessary. Knowledge is like a language where every word had been examined and every relationship had been verified. To know is to speak correctly. 'The sciences are well-made languages' (*OT*, p. 87). That is why 'language' could and should be studied, and a theory of language emerged (grammar). Foucault summarises the changes in the conception of language since the Renaissance as follows:

The profound vocation of Classical language has always been to create a table – a 'picture': whether it be in form of natural discourse, the accumulation of truth, descriptions of things, a body of exact knowledge, or an encyclopaedic dictionary. It exists, therefore, only in order to be transparent; it has lost that secret consistency which, in the 16th century, inspissated it into a word to be deciphered, and interwove it with all the things of the world; it has not yet acquired the multiple existence about which we question ourselves today. (*OT*, p. 311)

Language was 'transparent' in the age of resemblance insofar as it was a sign, like all the others, left by a superior entity, which could be interpreted. In the classical age, it still had 'transparency', although the 'discourse' had to be studied in order to build a well-made language (grammar) to provide the knowledge of nature. Indeed, it was not the 'language' that was studied but the 'discourse'. Discourse was studied as a verbal performance of language, as the first representation of thought. Until then, language was able to represent and there was no thought in terms of the limitations. 'Critiques' in the classical episteme simply analysed language 'in terms of truth, precision, appropriateness, or expressive value' (*OT*, p. 80). As regards to what follows in this chapter, within the modern age, language was studied instead of discourse. When philology and linguistics emerged in the modern age, language was conceived not only as a representation of thought but as an expression of a subject, since it is man who gave meaning to things.

In the classical age, there was a split between science and history, as the relationship between them had only led to obscurity, confusion and disagreements. For example, it was considered that Plato and Aristotle should no longer be studied since they were considered to be something of the past that had only led to differences in opinion. 'History' in the classical episteme acquired new meaning, a history of the object. Foucault proclaims: 'The classical age gives history a quite different meaning; that of undertaking a meticulous examination of things themselves for the first time' (*OT*, p. 131). This concept of history, in the classical episteme, reinforces his argument regarding the 'history of the present', where he states:

> The history of knowledge can be written only on the basis of what was contemporaneous with it, and certainly not in terms of reciprocal influence, but in terms of conditions and *a priori* established in time. It is in this sense that archaeology can give account of the *existence* of a general grammar, a natural history, and an analysis of wealth, and thus open up a free, undivided area in which the history of the sciences, the history of ideas, and the history of opinions can, if they wish, frolic at ease. (*OT*, p. 208, original emphasis)

Foucault's statement regarding history in the classical age raises a number of doubts relating to the thinkers of that time. For example, Hume, who had a great interest in history resulting from his empiricism, was indeed recognised, for a long time, for his work on the *History of England* and his frequent use of historical data to support his theories. Foucault meant that the 'history of knowledge' was neglected during that period and that knowledge should restart everything, while focusing on the visibilities of things. It can also be argued that Hume, while following a tendency of the Scottish Enlightenment, studied many past thinkers and would undoubtedly have taken his influence from them, while often using historical sources of data to inspire his investigations and support his conclusions. The same was apparent for Smith's interest in history, which was replicated in his approach to economy through a frequent use of historical examples.

3.3.2.1   *Foucault's epistemological model for the classical episteme: general grammar*

Foucault argued that general grammar was the most fundamental of the empiricities that he analysed in *The Order of Things*, since he believed that it was possible to understand the other empiricities through what was thought of in relation to language. In this sense, he developed an epistemological view, arguing that through the theory of language of that age it would be possible to understand the thought regarding the empirical sciences. He writes:

> In the Classical age, knowing and speaking are interwoven into the same fabric; in the case of both knowledge and language, it is a question of providing representation with the signs, by the means of which, it can then unfold itself in obedience to a necessary and visible order. Even when stated, knowledge in the sixteenth century was still a secret, albeit a shared one. Even when hidden, knowledge in the seventeenth and eighteenth centuries is discourse with a veil drawn over it. This is because it is of the very nature of science to enter into the system of verbal communications, and of the very nature of language to be knowledge from its very first word. Speaking, enlightening, and knowing are, in the strict sense of the term, of the same order. (*OT*, pp. 88–9)

As Cousins and Hussain (1984) remark, *The Order of Things* seems to be built in accordance with Foucault's interpretation of the *Port-Royal Grammar*. The *Port-Royal Grammar* was written by Antoine Arnauld and Claude Lancelot. A first edition of the book appeared on 28 April 1660 and became a referential work. However, Foucault also studied other works on language and rhetoric, which constituted the 'sciences of language' at that time. He read what Locke, Condillac, Destutt de Tracy and Adam Smith wrote about it. Of particular interest is the frequency and the way in which he uses Adam Smith's *Considerations Concerning the First Formation of Languages*. Foucault explained the classical system of thought through a diagram, a General Table, in which the theory of language was used to map out the analogies among the empirical spheres of knowledge.

For Foucault, there was a pattern of ordering which could be understood in terms of four linguistic categories or 'theoretical segments': attribution, articulation, designation and derivation. In the classical age, thought occurred within the periphery of a rectangle whose vertices were those four linguistic categories. Foucault divulged his method as follows:

> Our step-by-step analysis of these segments [the theoretical seg-ments: attribution, articulation, designation and derivation] was not undertaken in order to provide a history of grammatical conceptions in the seventeenth and eighteenth centuries, or to establish the gen-eral outline of what men might have thought about language at that time. The intention was to determine in what *conditions* language could become the object of a period's knowledge, and between what limits this epistemological domain developed. Not to calculate the common denominator of men's opinions, but to define what made it possible for opinions about language – whatever the opinions may have been – to exist at all. (*OT*, p. 119, emphasis added)

Arnauld and Lancelot (1975, p. 41) start the *Port-Royal Grammar* by arguing that grammar is the art of speaking, which is the explanation of one's thought by means of signs. Written language was invented because signs made of sounds are transitory. As such, signs could be thought of in terms of sounds and characters or in terms of significa-tion. Thus, the *Port-Royal Grammar* was organised into two parts. The first studied the signs that were represented by nature, that is, letters, vowels and consonants, syllables and words considered as sounds, and letters considered as characters. The second part turned its attention to the manner in which man employed them, providing signification to them.

Still according to the *Port-Royal Grammar*, to understand language requires thinking about the operations of the mind: conceiving, judg-ing and reasoning. 'Conceiving' is the simple attention of the mind to objects. It can be purely intellectual, such as when we think of duration or God, or it can be accompanied by an image, such as a dog or a circle. 'Judging' is the affirmation of the existence or otherwise of a thing. For example, having conceived the earth and its roundness separately, we can then state that the world is round. 'Reasoning' is the correct use of two judgements to make a third. It can be considered to be an extension of judging. Judgement is always a proposition, which is composed by a subject, a predicate and a connection, a copula, between them. The subject and predicate are objects of thought and belong to the opera-tion of 'conceiving'; the copula is an action of thought and belongs to 'judging'. Objects of thought are nouns, articles, pronouns, participles, prepositions and adverbs; actions of thought are verbs, conjunctions and interjections. The first can be substances or modifications of them, that is, accidents. Substances can exist by themselves, while accidents depend on substances for their existence. Therefore, there are substantive (such as earth or sun) and adjectival nouns (for example, good, just and round). However, since discourse is not just a mirror of thought, this would require a modification. Regarding signification, people call a 'noun' all words that exist by themselves, even if they are accidents, such as wisdom or whiteness. Likewise, words that signify substances are called adjectives if they need to be joined to other nouns in discourse. Therefore, in the first part, the authors of the *Port-Royal Grammar* continue to explain each one of the objects of thought and their relations.

Therefore, the intention of the *Port-Royal Grammar* was to separate the different parts of language. It demonstrated how language was conceived during the seventeenth century up until the end of the eighteenth century and how it was the language at that time that enabled thought to be represented. Man is conscious of the *modus operandi* of language, as it is a component of thought and that is what permits representation. Language became 'discourse', which was 'merely a representation of itself, represented by verbal signs' (*OT*, p. 81).[6] Discourse was the first representation of thought.[7]

While considering that moment in history, if we understand language, we can then understand the analysis of wealth, natural history and general grammar. Knowledge is 'a well-constructed language'. Language was studied in accordance with its operation. Hence, it was studied in order to analyse thought, as language is an analysis of thought. In this sense, the analysis of wealth, natural history and general grammar became a possibility:

> This is why *general grammar* assumed so much importance for philosophy during the eighteenth century: it was, at one and the same time, the spontaneous form of science – a kind of logic not controlled by the mind – and the first reflective decomposition of thought: one of the most primitive breaks with the immediate. (*OT*, p. 83, original emphasis)

Following the episteme of the classical period, general grammar accomplished a taxonomy of language. It should 'also study the way in which words designate what they say, first of all in their primitive value (theory of origins and of the root), then in their permanent capacity for displacement, extension, and reorganisation (theory of rhetoric and of derivation)' (*OT*, p. 92).

3.3.2.2 *Natural history*

Concerning natural history, the objective was, as in general grammar and the analysis of wealth, to identify and name the visible. 'Natural history is a well-constructed language' (*OT*, p. 138). To know living beings consisted of describing them, ordering them and putting them in a table in accordance with a plan. First, a *structure* of an animal or plant should be investigated. They should be described according to their visible elements. Hence, the *structure* allowed the animal and plant to be placed in discourse. Through the definition of their *structure* it was possible to pass them from representation into language (*OT*, p. 136). A *structure* alone did not enable them to be placed in a table. Beyond naming their elements, it was necessary to differentiate them or establish their *character*. Whereas *structure* was related to *visibility* and a *description* of their individuality, *character* identified their area and adjacencies. *Character* separated them following two techniques: method (classifying natural beings within determined empirical groups, according to their characteristics) or system (classifying them in accordance with determined groups of characteristics: kingdoms, species, families, genera and so on). The classifiers established their character by:

> comparing visible structures, that is, by correlating elements that were homogeneous (since each element, according to the ordering principle selected, could be used to represent all the others): the only difference lay in the fact that for the systematicians the representative elements were fixed from the outset, whereas for the methodists they were the gradual result of a progressive confrontation. (*OT*, p. 226)

Natural history consists of methods of discrimination to identify similarities and differences, and to describe living beings through their visible structure. That is why Foucault called 'natural history' an 'empiricity'. Plants and animals were analysed following four variables: form, quantity, position and relationship, and magnitude. Living beings should be classified into kingdoms, species, families, genera and so on. All that was regarded as knowledge in the Renaissance should be excluded from 'natural history' (ibid., p. 72).

3.3.2.3 *Foucault's General Table*

Foucault provided what he called 'The General Table', intending to illustrate the conditions of possibility of thought in the classical age. His table is reproduced in Diagram 3.1, with additional comments added to his own diagram (*OT*, p. 201), aiming to improve the comprehension of the epistemic context.

In this section, the theory of language, which is represented in the diagram, is explained. Its relationship to the analysis of wealth is explained further in Chapter 5, when the archaeology of political economy is investigated.

This diagram illustrates Foucault's understanding of the three empiricities according to his interpretation of the theory of language during that period. The General Table is a quadrilateral, designating each of its vertices to one of the four theoretical segments borrowed from the general grammar: *Attribution, Articulation, Designation* and *Derivation*.

As Shumway (1989, p. 80) points out, the General Table was not a rhetorical success for Foucault. The diagram was usually ignored and even when it was not, the analyses were either confusing or led to misunderstandings of Foucault's argument.

A description in support of his arguments is at the heart of his epistemological point of view, which is undoubtedly one of his greatest contributions to

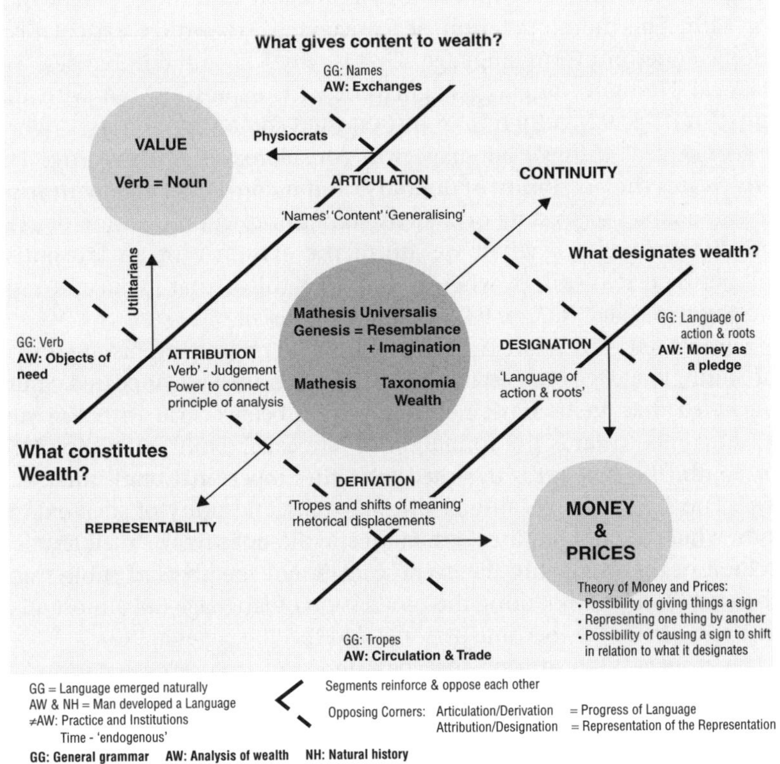

Diagram 3.1   The General Table – the analysis of wealth

an understanding of that era. Foucault believed that to understand the way economic thought analysed wealth depends upon the comprehension of the *modus*, according to which general grammar broke up language. Through the scrutiny of language, Foucault intended to demonstrate that some analogies, amongst different branches of knowledge, allow us to apprehend the underlying configuration of thought. Therefore, it is fundamental to understand how those four vertices are related.

With respect to language, attribution is the theory that corresponds to the function of the verb in a proposition. In relation to the *Port-Royal Grammar*, attribution is what allows the mind to judge. In this sense, the 'verb is the indispensable condition for all discourse' (*OT*, p. 93). Language 'existed only by virtue of the proposition: without at least the implicit presence of the verb to be and of the predicative relation for which it provides authority, it would not be language that we were dealing with at all, but a collection of signs like any others' (*OT*, p. 119).

A proposition consists of a subject, a predicate and the copula, which is a verb. The mere operation of 'conceiving' (to which 'articulation' belongs) does not form language. That is why Foucault emphasises: 'For Classical Thought, language begins not with expression but with discourse' (*OT*, p. 92). When man just emitted some simple noises (when he 'conceived' things), language was considered as not existing. The verb creates the possibility of discourse and it concerns judgement insofar as it enables us to state or to deny something. 'A proposition exists – and discourses too – when we affirm the existence of an attributive link between two things, when we say that this *is* that', Foucault says, quoting Condillac (*OT*, p. 94, original emphasis).

Foucault refers to Adam Smith (1983) while reinforcing his argument. For Smith, language only established itself when the verb appeared. Smith concluded that 'verbs must necessarily have been coeval with the very first attempts towards the formation of language' (Smith, 1983, p. 215). For Smith, the first verbs invented were the impersonal ones, such as *it rains*. This happened because of the simplicity and unity of such expressions, which did not require abstraction and did not involve 'metaphysical division of the event into its several constituent members of subject and attribute' (ibid.). Only during the progression of language did almost all of the impersonal verbs become personal and the adjectives appear.

Therefore, a verb affirms the coexistence of two representations; it designates the representative character of language. '[T]o speak is at the same time to represent by means of signs and to give signs a synthetic form governed by the verb' (*OT*, pp. 95–6). In this sense, 'the proposition is to language what representation is to thought' (*OT*, p. 92).

Articulation is the theory related to the function of naming. In grammar, it is an investigation related to how and why naming is a required part of language, since it makes representation possible, through the creation of names for signs. The elements of articulation name the 'thing to be judged – the *judicandum* – and the thing judged – the *judicatum*', Foucault writes, quoting Domergue (*OT*, p. 96). Therefore, articulation deals with the non-verbal elements of the proposition. It 'gives content to the pure and still empty verbal form of the proposition' (*OT*, p. 115). Articulation 'gives content' because it is only through 'names' that language can be used in order to express or explain thoughts or feelings.

Articulation results from the operation of 'conceiving'. The name is as a result of the necessity of discourse, to express the 'whole content of a representation'. 'Once this [the articulation] has been established, everything can become discourse' (*OT*, p. 99).

Nouns basically perform the function of articulation. A word is 'in its very nature' a noun or name (*OT*, p. 97). However, nouns could proliferate *ad infinitum* in accordance with the number of things that exist. Hence, some kind of generality becomes necessary to designate many representations using just one noun, a common noun.

The common noun can be achieved in two ways: through horizontal and vertical articulation. The horizontal articulation results in substantives (as 'nouns' were called in the grammar), which group individuals according to identities and differences in a language grid. For example, through horizontal articulation we arrive at a *taxonomia*, such as an animal, a quadruped, a dog, and finally a spaniel. The vertical results in adjectives, whose distinction is in the impossibility of existing on their own, given that they refer to modifications, features, accidents or characteristics. Foucault reminds us of Adam Smith, for whom adjectives manifested a metaphysics. Smith (1983, p. 207) stated that '[t]he invention, therefore, even of the simplest nouns adjective, must have required more metaphysics than we are apt to be aware of'.

At the same time, articulation concerns the way words are ordered in discourse. In order for language to become really representative, it is necessary that words also designate other complex relations of succession, subordination and consequence. Therefore, articulation also refers to the ordering of the discourse. These words are prepositions, conjunctions, syntactical signs, marks of plurality and gender, declension endings and articles. They 'have no power of signification except in a relative mode' (*OT*, p. 99).

Designation reinforces derivation and is in opposition to articulation, which is emphasised in the following sequence. 'The function of language is to name, that is, to raise up a representation or point it out, as though with a finger, then it is indication and not judgement' (*OT*, p. 104). While attribution is a judgement, designation is indication. Therefore, attribution and designation are in opposition. Language 'is linked to things by a mark, a notation, an associated figure, a gesture of *designation*; nothing that could be reduced to a relation of predication' (*OT*, p. 104, emphasis added).

The theory of designation in 'the general grammar' searched for what was considered to be the roots of a word, identifying the primitive cries. It was the language of gestures, movements and inarticulate cries. 'All this is not yet either language or even sign but the effect and consequence of our animality' (*OT*, pp. 104–5). It is not sign, but a mimesis that allows men to understand themselves universally. Language just emerged after 'the reversible and analysable relations of signs and representations' (*OT*, p. 105).

In order for language to come into being, it was not sufficient for merely an action to be expressed. A sign had to emerge, which was established by people acting and creating together. Words and things were separated by nature, and conventions established that words would designate things and that words would propagate them through resemblance. Therefore, the theory of roots follows from the language of action. Roots resemble what they name and this resemblance becomes a verbal sign, only through the convention 'that brought men together and regulated their language of action so as to create a language' (*OT*, p. 107).

Derivation is the theory that thinks about the way words can modify and reproduce themselves, changing or moving away from their original meanings, forms, application field, sounds and contents. Derivation and designation reinforce each other, whilst derivation is in opposition to attribution.

The opposition between derivation and attribution can be understood in terms of the stability of representation. Derivation deals with 'the continuous movement of words from their source of origin', which is a 'slipping' in the surface of the representation, which is in opposition 'to the single stable bond that links one root to one representation' (*OT*, p. 115).

Designation deals with the roots and language of action, which is related to the way in which words derive from their source of origin. In this sense, designation and derivation are linked, such that one can use the other in order to provide a comprehension of the language as a representation.

As for the sources of such modifications, they do not obey rules, never cease to occur and are 'more or less endless' (*OT*, p. 110). Words, as language's signs, modify and multiply, not following a rational or meticulous analysis of representations, but as a product of imagination and credulity. 'Language gives the perpetual disruption of time the continuity of space' (*OT*, p. 113).

Foucault mentioned some conditions for those theoretical segments and for them to become language (*OT*, pp. 119–20). Attribution exists insofar as relations of identity and difference are possible. Language only exists if a relation of identity or difference between/among things is possible. With regards to the other three theoretical segments, the condition is 'quite different': there must be 'a murmur of analogies rising from things' and, below the relations of identities and differences, 'a foundation provided by continuities, resemblances, repetitions, and natural criss-crossings' (ibid.). These are the conditions 'to derive words from their first source' (derivation), and for 'an original kinship [...] between a root and its signification' (designation), as well as for 'an articulated patterning of representations' (articulation) to exist (ibid.).

Attribution reinforces and is in opposition to articulation. Articulation alone (expressions, nouns and names) does not constitute a proposition, which is an indispensable condition for language, discourse, and hence for representation in the classical thought. That is, 'the articulation gives content to the pure and still empty verbal form of the proposition' (*OT*, p. 115). At the same time, we can see a relationship of opposition between them since, whilst articulation is basically a nomination that differentiates things, the attribution links them both together.

Designation reveals the link to the world of nominations, which were cut out by articulation. It reinforces articulation, in the sense that it can recapture the attachment of the names to their primitive connections and to things through the investigation of the language of action and roots. But designation and articulation are also in opposition to each other. This is because designation deals with 'the instantaneous, gestural, perpendicular' forms of naming, whilst articulation is patterns that are based on generalisation.

Derivation and designation reinforce each other, since derivation is a continuous movement of words from what was first established by designation and, hence, from their source of origin (language of action or roots). They are also in opposition in the sense that whilst derivation is a 'slipping on the surface of representation', designation reveals the 'stable bond' of words to what is represented.

Derivation reinforces attribution because without it designation would not result in generalities that enable the attributive function of a proposition. Derivation and attribution are also in opposition since derivation has a spatial structure, whereas the 'proposition unfolds in obedience to a sequential and linear order' (*OT*, p. 115).

It must still be emphasised that whilst, in the general grammar, these segments are completely separated, they can be joined in the natural history and the analysis of wealth. Foucault argues that this was the case, since general grammar was dealing with a language that had emerged naturally, whereas in the other two domains analysed, man had to build one. Therefore, attribution and articulation are connected in the figure of 'structure' in natural history and in the conception of 'value' in the analysis of wealth. Due to a similar motive, designation and derivation are linked by the concept of 'character' in natural history and by 'the theory of money and prices' in the analysis of wealth.

As these four segments 'confront each other in pairs and reinforce each other in pairs' (*OT*, p. 115), it is necessary to consider the diagram regarding the lateral and diagonal relations between the theoretical segments. The solid and broken lines denote lateral relations of reinforcement and opposition at the same time. As for the diagonal relations between opposing corners of the rectangle, the line between articulation and derivation denotes the progress of language, symbolising how far the words have moved from their original values (which were determined by an act of designation) under the process of derivation, enabling the state of an articulated language. The diagonal between attribution and designation marks 'the endless interleaving of language and representation' (*OT*, p. 166). This imaginary line configures the relation between a word and what it represents, as it is linking an act of judgement in a thing with what it was originally designated. Foucault argues that this line confirms that language is always representing a representation. Here, the duplicated character of representation becomes noticeable: 'words never speak anything other than the being of representation' and 'they always name something represented' (*OT*, p. 116). Representation is not a mirroring. A representation always represents another representation. As Major-Poetzl (1983, p. 154) noticed, the four theoretical segments could be separated into two groups, each one representing one side of the quadrilateral: 'attribution + articulation' and 'designation + derivation'. The former constitutes a 'representation of thought', while the latter constitutes 'a duplicated representation by projecting thought into the world' (ibid.).

3.3.3   The modern episteme

There was another radical change, according to Foucault, towards the end of the eighteenth century, when a discontinuity in the referential guide of thought marked the emergence of the positivity, called political economy. The essential change was that representation could no longer provide the foundation of knowledge by itself. Signs, the analysis of identities and differences, together with their order were not based upon 'the duplication of representation in relation to itself' (*OT*, p. 237). This does not mean that 'representation' disappeared as a 'function of thought', but representation was no longer an unquestionable foundation of knowledge. In the modern order of thought, representation required justification that was obtained from 'outside' of it. '[I]t is no longer simply accepted as a function identical to thought itself' (Gutting, 1989, p. 182). Furthermore, representation is 'the phenomenon – perhaps even less, the appearance – of an order that now belongs to things themselves and to their interior law' (*OT*, p. 313). Therefore, it is now necessary to look at the depth of the objects.

It was Kant's 'Copernican turn', the inquiry into the conditions of possibility of reason, that questioned representation, particularly when Kant raised those three fundamental questions – What can I know? What must I do? What am I permitted to hope? – adding in his *Logic* one other: *Was ist der Mensch*? ('What is man?' – *OT*, p. 341). This was already defined in *Las Meninas* regarding the impossibility of representing the observer of a representation. That is why Foucault writes:

> In Classical thought, the personage for whom the representation exists, and who represents himself within it, recognizing himself therein as an image or reflection, he who ties together all the interlacing threads of the 'representation in the form of a picture or table' – he is never to be found in that table himself. Before the end of the eighteenth century, man did not exist – any more than the potency of life, the fecundity of labour, or the historical density of language. (*OT*, p. 308)

The shift from the classical to a modern way of thinking was not an abrupt one and can be, as Foucault argues, perfectly discerned in terms of its protagonists and chronological boundaries. It occurred during the period of 1775–1825, which presented doubts in relation to the classical way of thinking. This period was still divided into more or less two stages during 1795–1800. What defined this division was the emergence of an invisible element, 'hidden forces', in the representation of the objects of knowledge in the first stage.

In literature, Foucault associates the end of classical thought with Sade's *Juliette*. Foucault called this work 'the last of the classical narratives' (*OT*, p. 242). As *Don Quixote* was on the bridge between the pre-classical and the classical episteme, Sade was considered to be on the border of the modern episteme, since he had questioned the limits of representation after finding out the limits of language with respect to the expression of desire.

Whilst considering the classical age, to know, was to represent the visible – discriminating its identities and differences, unveiling its order – during the years of 1775 to 1795/1800, one invisible element was added to the analysis in each of the empirical domains. This was due to the fact that their subject matter was being conceived as having an 'internal architecture'. Foucault had already depicted this change in human perception in *The Birth of Clinic*, where he declared that at the end of the eighteenth century (in contrast to what Descartes and Malenbranche considered):

> seeing consists in leaving to experience its greatest corporal opacity; the solidity, the obscurity, the density of things closed upon themselves, have powers of truth that they owe not to light, but to the slowness of the gaze that passes over them, around them, and gradually into them, bringing them nothing more than its own light. (*BC*, p. xiii)

In economics, this element was 'labour', as understood by Adam Smith. In biology, the character of living beings was no longer conceived to be directly linked to its visible structure, but through its 'organic structure', linking it to functions that turned it in opposition between the organic and inorganic fundamentals. Antoine-Laurent de Jussieu (1748–1836) began to promote such a shift in natural history. In philology, 'language' began to be studied as a formal structure:

> [L]anguage no longer consists only of representations and of sounds that in turn represent the representations and are ordered amongst them as the links of thought required; it consists also of formal elements, grouped into a system, which impose upon the sounds, syllables, and roots an organization that is not that of representation. Thus, an element has been introduced into the analysis of language

that is not reducible to it (as labour was introduced into the analysis of exchange, or organic structure into that of characters). (*OT*, p. 235)

Nevertheless, during this first phase, knowing was still considered to be a representation of this invisible element and it was only after about 1795/1800 that representation really collapsed. The definite shift between the two epistemes occurred at some time during the second stage, from 1795/1800 to 1825, and it was promoted by David Ricardo, Georges Cuvier and Franz Bopp. Although they were not the first to mention the concepts of labour, organic structure and word inflection, Foucault argues that they certainly disassociated themselves from the structure of classical thought, transforming discourse and changing the concept of the mode of being within labour, life and language. Whilst within classical thought it was regarded that they were conceived as having an underlying order, in modern thinking they were envisioned as having a 'historical process'.

In the first phase (1775–95/1800), temporal concepts were added to discourse and 'time' came to the foreground, while 'space', which had been at the forefront of the classical tabular form of knowledge, was now transferred to the background. Things 'escaped from the space of the table' (*OT*, p. 239) and could no longer be represented according to a *taxonomia*. Labour, life and language started to be conceived as having a temporal constitution, which was what Foucault meant by a 'historical dimension'. Knowledge was no longer simply a means of establishing the relations between/among visible differences, it meant understanding how and why things had those differences. Unlike natural history, which mapped the external structures of plants and animals, biology turned to anatomical studies, searching for organic functions. Differing from the analysis of wealth, political economy did not search for the source of value in things or in the exchange, instead focusing on the process of production. Philology focused on the changes of grammatical forms instead of the constant structures of the language, as in general grammar.

Foucault announced the modern episteme as 'the age of history', employing the term 'historicity' with two meanings: a temporality and an organic structure of the object of the empiricities. 'History' was related to the idea of 'organic structure', an expression employed by Foucault to characterise not only the focus of biology, but also of political economy and philology in the modern era. These positivities sought an understanding of the internal relation between/among elements of their object in order to apprehend their functions.

Analogy and succession were the new 'organising principles', where neither a *taxonomia* of non-quantitative orders nor a table constitutes knowledge. The space of order was shattered, wrote Foucault, and the panorama of knowledge (*savoir*) consisted of: things having their own organic structures, a space that articulates them and a time that produces them, together with a representation that individuals try to know (*OT*, pp. 239–40).

In biology, the main structure in natural beings is contained within their organs, concealed deep within their bodies. They were no longer classified according to the same organ, which was visibly existent in different beings or named according to their appearance and organised into different groups of similar characteristics. Beings started to be studied according to the functions that their organs performed. It is in this sense that Foucault declared that 'life' emerged for knowledge. Living beings began to be seen as functional systems. As Amariglio (1988, p. 588) pointed out, vitalism could not find a place in the discourse of the sixteenth century, since there was no notion of an essential life force that ordered the body from within. A fundamental characteristic of life in the modern episteme was the emergence of another concept of its temporality. Naturally, in the classical episteme living beings existed temporally, but they were not determined by the course of time, as evolutionary ideas by Darwin and Wallace were to express during modern thought.

When it comes to studying language, word inflections were already analysed before the end of the eighteenth century, although they were studied with the intention of understanding how they were derived from primitive cries and their initial roots. In the modern episteme, a comparison of changes, particularly in the root changes between/among different systems of language, became the central aim of philology. Like the temporality of living beings, languages changed following the laws of temporal succession. Philology was to study the internal temporal mutations of language.

In economic thought, as will be further described in Chapter 5, wealth began to be considered as the result of a process of production that was temporal. Whilst the analysis of wealth consisted of identifying its elements and how they were ordered in a system of exchange, in political economy wealth began to be conceived as an 'organic structure', which was to suggest that it had a historicity.

These changes occurred due to 'history' being replaced by 'order' as the main condition of possibility within knowledge. While it is possible to say that 'reason' (meaning analysing and ordering) had been associated with the classical age, 'history' was related to the modern episteme. History was the new 'mode of being' of things.

History was not in the configuration of the classical episteme, since to know was to begin everything again and to look at the visible structure of the subject matter. Thus, Foucault was using 'history' in the sense of searching for the past of knowledge. In the modern episteme, 'history' became essential in the sense of understanding things as having a temporal constitution. Foucault emphasised that 'history' was conceived not as a 'compilation of factual successions or sequences as they may have occurred; it is *the fundamental mode of being of empiricities*' (*OT*, p. 219, emphasis added).

The succession over the course of time is understood as being something significant. Foucault explained the replacing of analysis and the order for analogy and succession as follows:

> the History is going to unfold the analogies that bring together one to the other different organizations in a temporal series. It is this history that increasingly will impose its laws to the production analysis, to the organising beings, after all to the linguistic groups. The History *gives place* to the analogical organizations as the Order opened its identity way and the *successive* differences. (*OT*, p. 299, original emphasis)

Foucault also emphasised the role of history in relation to its importance in the development of the human sciences. The human sciences treated their object – man – as a historical being, as 'history is needed to describe the historical range in which any given psychological, sociological, or literary analysis is valid' (Gutting, 1989, p. 213).

3.3.3.1   *The other: the unthought*

While 'the other' had not manifested itself during the age of resemblance (being only implicit in the figure of antipathy) and it was explicit in the analysis of differences during the classical episteme, it became something 'produced' by the human sciences in the modern episteme. 'The other' in this new episteme refers to everything that is unconscious and that is responsible for the hidden meaning of the sign. 'The other' is indeed the unthought, which includes the Freudian term 'unconscious', although it is not restricted to it.

In the modern era, the *cogito* of the classical episteme was destabilised. 'I think, therefore I am' was no longer attached to certainty, since the one who knows (thinks) is the same as the one who lives under the 'laws' of life, labour and language, whose elements are not totally conscious. That is why the human sciences emerged: to think about this unthought. They attempt to bring to consciousness that which is unconscious. 'Alienation' in Marxism is an example of this, because it refers to the 'disjuncture of man's existence and essence' resulting from the relations of production, based upon private property (Cousins and Hussain, 1984, p. 56). Man is surrounded by things that he cannot express and by a language that he cannot master. The unthought may never be absorbed in the *cogito*; therefore, 'the other' will have no limit. Foucault even suggests that while this unthought had been searched for within man, it could well be external to him and therefore always be in the 'unconscious', the 'unthought'.

3.3.3.2   *The new historical a priori and the analytic of finitude*

In the new 'ontological fabric' (*OT*, p. 272), the view of 'continuity' between beings, which endorsed representability, changed in the classical episteme. A new ontological concept of beings emerged, relating the idea of 'continuity'. From the end of the eighteenth century onwards, if there was this 'continuity', then it should be investigated from within things, relating things to their history. Knowledge became something 'vertical' in the sense that it had to go beneath the surface of things.

When representation became a problem and an object of knowledge, man began to perform two functions in knowledge that were complementary and constituted what Foucault called the 'historical *a priori*' or the anthropological-humanist structure. In the first instance, man was to be the object of the empirical sciences – life, labour and language. Secondly, man was converted into the philosophical foundation for the possibility of knowledge. It is this historical *a priori* that explains the rise of human sciences. Foucault used the term 'anthropology' not to refer specifically to the science of man, but literally as 'a logic of man': 'anthropologism' became the philosophical foundation of all human sciences. Anthropology or anthropologism is 'an ideology which privileges Man at the centre and source of the philosophical and human sciences' (Lemert and Gillan, 1982, p. 128). Man replaced God (age of resemblance) and Logos (classical age). Foucault called the effect of philosophical anthropology on thought 'anthropological sleep'.

Man is 'a quite recent creature, which the demiurge of knowledge fabricated with its own hands less than two hundred years ago' (*OT*, p. 308). One of Foucault's most striking conclusions was that, until the end of the eighteenth century, man did not exist as an object or subject

of knowledge. For Foucault, there was no epistemological consciousness of man as such. Until then, life, labour and language did not exist
as objects of study. As Amariglio declares, 'Man' and his body became
'aground for the representation of "words and things" (such as value) in
the many organised and dispersed discourses that constitute our formal
and informal knowledge' (Amariglio, 1988, p. 586).

The human sciences did not arise by the effect of a certain rationalism
or due to a practical interest or because a certain scientific problem was
solved. They 'arose on the day man set himself up in western culture, at
the same time as the man found what was necessary to think and what
he had to know' (*OT*, p. 308).

In the age of resemblance and in the classical episteme, man could
have 'a privileged position in the order of the world' (*OT*, p. 318), but
he did not have a proper domain (*OT*, p. 308). Hence, those epistemes
'were not able to conceive of man' (ibid.). In the modern episteme, all
that can be known will be deeply anthropological. Knowledge was to be
actually an 'analytic of finitude'.

Man found his finitude. Naturally, this does not mean that man discovered his mortality only in the modernity. Finitude is related here to
his power of knowing and his practicality and capacity for solving basic
questions concerning life, labour and language. For Foucault, that translated into 'the finitude of Man and the finitude of knowledge involve
each other' (Lemert and Gillan, 1982, p. 127).

For the empirical sciences (biology, political economy and philology),
man was a finite being since he was limited by the environment, by the
forces of production and by the linguistic heritage that had formed him
(Gutting, 1989, p. 199). He is subject to the laws of biology, production
and language. In economics, finitude is the realisation of man's conditions of limitation in nature, to make and produce all that is necessary
for his needs and desires. 'Scarcity' also adopted a different meaning
from that of the classical episteme, where it was considered that 'man
should work' in order to respond to his needs and desires. During the
modern episteme, there would be a fundamental 'scarcity'. Nature was
not fecund, as was once believed. Indeed, it was miserly. This new conception led to the 'pessimistic' theory of Ricardo and the principle of
population of Malthus. Man had to confront the threat of death caused
by the possibility of over-population and Marx 'described value as the
product of labour over and against the alienating forces of capitalism'
(Lemert and Gillan, 1982, p. 127). While representation became a problem, language lost its power to communicate things and its transparency, then becoming an issue.

Modern thought was actually an 'analytic of finitude', which is man's reflection on his own conditions of possibility as a subject of knowledge ('fundamental finitude') and object of the empiricities ('founded finitude'). The 'analytic of finitude' 'shows how man, in his being, can be concerned with the things he knows, and know the things that, in positivity, determine his mode of being' (*OT*, p. 354).

In some respects, it is understood that the limitations are produced by man, so he has to fight to surpass them. There is a paradox here: due to his limitations, man began searching for complete knowledge. For instance, it is man that is responsible for representation and it is also man that must construct the language, a formal language, which will then provide him with the tools to surpass his limitations in order for him to be able to act as the subject of knowledge. Language became an object of knowledge and some domains emerged or developed as a result of it, such as analytic philosophy, formal logic and hermeneutics. Logical positivism could now surface as a possible solution.

3.3.3.3 *The instabilities of the modern episteme*

The analytic of finitude is doomed to failure, says Foucault, on account of the three doublets: empirical-transcendental, *cogito*-unthought and the retreat-return origin. These doublets reflect man's constitution and form his mode of being; as such, they are characteristic of the anthropological discourse that constitutes the analytic of finitude. At the same time, the doublets result from man's search for the foundations of knowledge.

As for the empirical-transcendental doublet, the basis of knowledge can be empirical (*a posteriori*) or transcendental (*a priori*) and they can both be confused within the same figure: man. Kant first presented this distinction. For him, empirical knowledge was founded on the basis of a transcendental form of knowledge. However, Foucault argues that it is not possible to determine the separation between empirical and transcendental. What is empirically known is as a direct result of the transcendental constitution of man. To understand the conditions of possibility of human finitude requires understanding the empirical contents of human beings: man's body, man's social relations and man's language. Knowledge is conditioned by historical, social and economic factors. The criticism arises as a means to establish the differences between science, ideology and common sense. Foucault writes that man became:

> an individual who lives, speaks, and works in accordance with the
> laws of an economics, a philology, and a biology, but who also, by

a sort of internal torsion and overlapping, has acquired the right, through the interplay of those very laws, to know them and to subject them to total clarification. (*OT*, p. 310)

At the same time, how do we define how man, as a subject, determines what is known empirically? Man is in an embarrassing position, epistemologically speaking, for it is not possible to presuppose a transcendental reason which is able to separate truth from error or science from ideology. Of course, in this case the discourse becomes the locus of instability. The truth of the discourse is said to be either in the empirical – positivism – or in the transcendental – eschatology. The 'analytic of finitude' seeks to separate these two methods of establishing knowledge, although according to Foucault this will never succeed. The only exit for man is to question his own existence, which is the awkward situation that cannot be surpassed, unless the anthropological discourse of modernity is discarded.

While in the classic episteme, man was not considered to be a representation of the central subject of knowledge (as in *Las Meninas*), in the modern era, man remains the source of all knowledge and he is finite. Man is the being through which knowledge is possible, so it is necessary to clarify the *a priori* conditions by which the empirical contents of life, labour and language are given to knowledge. But it is here that man is in an embarrassing position. It is in this sense that Foucault asserts that man is limited by the ambiguity of the empirical-transcendental doublet.

With regards to the *cogito*-unthought doublet, also related to the empirical-transcendental doublet, it can be considered that there will always be something that is not, and cannot, be thought. In the modern episteme, first established through Kant, knowledge was regarded in terms of who knows and under what conditions it was possible to know, making it explicit that there will always be the unthought; that is, that beyond the *cogito* and the known, there will be always the unknown. The unthought may never be absorbed in the *cogito*.

As for the retreat-return of the origin doublet, it is related to history and to the search for origins. Life, labour and language are historical and have their own history, which leads us to consider the origin. Nonetheless, man will never find his origin, apart from what has already been initiated. On this point, positivism observed man's origin through his evolution and the origin of things through man's evolution. The consequence is the anthropological marasmus, given that it is impossible that something that is finite can form the basis of knowledge and thus the condition of truth.

3.3.3.4   *The human sciences*

Between words and things, a number of unconscious elements were observed. 'Sciences' now needed to consider this unconsciousness, and hence the 'human sciences' emerged.

Foucault's meaning of the 'human sciences' should be clarified, since there has been some confusion in relation to his designation of the term. For example, Cousins and Hussain (1984) treat the term as being synonymous with 'social sciences'. The question concerns the usual classification of these domains of knowledge. Foucault employs 'human sciences' to designate those domains of knowledge that take man as the focus of their analysis (psychology, sociology and the analysis of literature and myths). However, man is not the central category in terms of his biological functions as a living being, his labour activities or his language. Man in these sciences is considered to be the one who represents those biological functions, the activity of production and the language unto himself.

In the modern episteme, knowledge (*savoir*) is organised in 'a volume of space' in three dimensions (*connaissance*), which Foucault called the 'trihedron' of knowledge (*OT*, pp. 346–7):

a   Mathematical and physical sciences, whose order consists in the links within theories of evident or verified propositions.
b   Other positive sciences, such as biology, economics and philology, whose order is established in the linking of discontinuous, although analogous, elements which establish the propositions that can affirm causal relationships and structural constants between the objects.
c   Philosophical reflection. Foucault characterises this dimension as the 'thought of the Same'. It is the domain of the epistemological and ontological, a radical reflection regarding the being of life, labour and language, as well as the conditions leading to the formalisation of thought.

These three dimensions can be taken as planes that define an epistemological trihedron, from which the human sciences (psychology, sociology and the analysis of literature and myths) can be said to be excluded. The human sciences are excluded in the sense that they are neither along these three dimensions nor on the surface of any of the planes that define the trihedron. However, it could be said that they are in a volume defined by these three dimensions, since they are all related to these other forms of knowledge: they aim to utilise at one level or another a mathematical formalisation; they proceed with models or concepts borrowed from biology, economics and the sciences of language; and they have to deal with the radical finitude in philosophy at the same time as they work on its empirical manifestations. Therefore, the human sciences have a fundamental instability that is not due to the complexity of their object, as is usually assumed. Their uncertainty results from their conditions of possibility, which are defined by their relation to the other forms of knowledge (*OT*, p. 347).

The place of the human sciences in knowledge results from a change in the conception of human nature. Foucault argues that these sciences only emerged in the modern era, because they could not exist in the configuration of the classical episteme. Of course, underlying the view of Foucault was his belief that there was no permanent 'human nature'.

In the classical age, the concept of 'nature' was underlying all empirical knowledge in the sense that it was regarded as being on the same level as that of representation. 'Nature' was actually the object of knowledge and it was common to refer to other domains using the expression 'natural history'.

There was a natural order, in which man was included.[8] However, human sciences are not considered to be studies regarding human 'nature' in this sense. The human sciences do not deal directly with man's life, labour and language, instead addressing themselves with regard to the representations through and by which man lives. Hence, they are not concerned with what man is considered to be in nature. They are interested in the systems of representations since, in the modern experience, the empirical contents of knowledge will always be related to the transcendental questions linked to the conditions of knowledge and there will always be the unthought, 'the Other', which is not in man or is no longer present in things (as in a classical way of thinking). In the modern era, the alterity is 'born, not of man, nor in man, but beside him and at the same time, in an identical newness, in an unavoidable duality' (*OT*, p. 326). The question in the modern age is no longer: 'How can experience of nature give rise to necessary judgements? [which was Hume's proposal, for example] But rather: How can man think what he does not think?' (*OT*, p. 323).

With particular reference to economics, the concept of 'nature' changed. There was now something 'exterior' to man, which was no longer a part of his 'nature' or, even if it was, was always 'unconscious', 'unknown'. Man 'begins to exist at the centre of a labour by whose principles he is governed and whose product eludes him' (*OT*, p. 318). The most fundamental question that surfaced while conducting the investigations became: 'How can he [man] *be* that labour whose laws and demands are imposed upon him like some alien system?' (*OT*, p. 323, original emphasis). Man's 'finitude' was revealed. It has to be remembered that in the modern *cogito*, 'I think' does not lead to the truth of 'I am'. Descartes believed that there was one method that could be established in order to avoid errors. However, in the modern age, there was clearly no way of avoiding the 'unthought'. In philology, for instance, when communication was understood to be an empirical implication of language, the questions relating to what experience was and how it could be explained had to be raised. Cousins and Hussain (1984, p. 61) mentioned another example in economics: when a social class interest was regarded as an implication of income distribution, the question related to what 'interest' was and how it could be known was raised for debate.

Nevertheless, political economy is not a human science:

> even though man is, if not the only species in the world that works, at least the one in whom the production, distribution, and consumption of goods have taken on so great an importance and acquired so many and such differentiated forms, economics is still not a human science. (*OT*, p. 352)

For Foucault, although economics refers to man, this does not mean that it is a human science. Economics has to have a representation, which provides it with the patterns of human behaviour, in order for it to be able to define some of its laws. However, economics was not geared towards establishing such a representation. Only a human science is able to do that, since it is not concerned with the figure of man as a worker, who needs to work in order to survive, but rather with 'man' as representing his needs within society and unto himself and, eventually, representing economics itself (*OT*, p. 352). In this sense, human sciences are not about 'what man is by nature' (*OT*, p. 353). Human sciences need to have recourse to the findings of the empiricities, although they go beyond that and have to connect those findings, which enables man to know or seek to know 'what life is, in what the essence of labour and its laws consist, and in what way he is able to speak' (*OT*, p. 353). Foucault remarks:

> the human sciences do not treat man's life, labour, and language in the most transparent state in which they could be posited, but in that stratum of conduct, behaviour, attitudes, gestures already made,

sentences already pronounced or written, within which they have already been given once to those who act, behave, exchange, work, and speak. (*OT*, p. 354)

It could therefore be argued that Foucault was attributing to the human sciences something that was properly associated with philosophy. What is the difference between the human sciences and philosophy? Gutting (1989, pp. 208–9) clarifies this point. The difference for Foucault was that philosophy turned towards the representations as they manifested themselves in man's consciousness, while the human sciences dealt with them as unconscious processes and structures.

Foucault argued that the human sciences were a case of 'reduplication'. They 'duplicate' biology, economics and philology. This was due in principle to a triple relationship that the human sciences had with these three 'sciences', which Foucault prefers to define as the 'epistemological regions'. The triple relationship forms the constituent models for the human sciences and are arranged by three pairs of concepts: *function* and *norm* (from biology), *conflict* and *rule* (from economics) and *signification* and *system* (from philology). Psychology adopts the model of *functions* regulated by *norms* from biology; sociology adopts the model of *conflict* regulated by *rules* from economics, and the analysis of literature and myths adopts the model of *meaning* regulated by a *system of signs* from philology. These all form the analytical models that marked the history of the human sciences from the nineteenth century onwards. The biological model leads to analyses in terms of *function*. The economic model conducts analyses of activity and relations in terms of *conflict*. The philological and linguistic model leads to the propensity of uncovering hidden meanings, becoming a matter for interpretation and clarification of the *signifying system*.

Psychology deals with man as a living being which 'opens itself to the possibility of representation' (*OT*, p. 355) and reproduces from biology man as someone who has *functions*. These functions all refer to physiological and environmental stimuli and the way man copes, confronts and adapts to them while struggling and changing them through *norms* of adjustment. Sociology refers to the way 'the labouring, producing individual offers himself a representation of the society in which this activity occurs' (*OT*, p. 355). Sociology is therefore a reflection on man as someone who has needs and desires and is always considered to be in conflict while attempting to satisfy them. He confronts his interests and those of other men, groups or classes. In order to do this, he establishes *rules*, which both limit and generate conflict. The study of literature and myths was concerned with 'the analysis of verbal traces that a culture or individual may leave behind them' (Gutting, 1989, p. 209). In this sense, this study projects philology, since it is man that speaks or communicates in some way, for instance through gestures, that has *meanings* and constitutes a *system of signs*. Man's behaviour has significations, which are expressed in words, rituals and myths, while meaning is regulated by a system of signs. All these models also reflect a shift in the process of analysing, as observed by Smart (1985, p. 36): the emphasis on conscious processes (*function, conflict, signification*) has been displaced by analyses of elements that are unconscious and inaccessible or unconscious but able to be brought into consciousness (*norm, rule, system*).

Nevertheless, Foucault emphasises that these pairs of concepts are not restricted to the surface on which they appear. Hence, '*function* and *norm* are not psychological concepts exclusively; *conflict* and *rule* do not have an application limited wholly to the sociological domain; *signification* and *system* are not valid solely for phenomena more or less akin to language' (*OT*, p. 357, emphasis added). It is certain that these pairs of concepts form a 'volume common' to the human sciences and that with this comes a difficulty in defining the limits in terms of object and method within these 'sciences'. The human sciences are interconnected. Psychology, for instance, is essentially a study of man in terms of functions and norms. However, this pair of concepts can be interpreted according to conflicts and rules, significations and systems. This also occurs within sociology and the studies of literature and myths. This has led to attempts to 'psychologise' or 'sociologise' something in knowledge. Cousins and Hussain (1984, p. 64) mention other examples: referring to Luther's Reform in terms of his anal retentiveness, stating that the production of a commodity is insane, and explaining Rimbaud's writings in terms of the contradictions in the *petit-bourgeoisie*.

Since these pairs of concepts 'cover the entire domain of what can be known about man' (*OT*, p. 357), the human sciences are definitely linked to the 'problem of representation'. However, unlike philosophy, the human sciences refer to another stratum of man, in which life, labour and language have effects that are not always conscious. The human sciences are directed towards an understanding where representations escape consciousness. They are an empirical and critical analysis of the human experience, since they 'work within a defined area, which is bound on the one side by what is given to knowledge through empirical investigation and upon the other by what is critically established concerning the conditions of knowledge' (Cousins and

Hussain, 1984, p. 54). This changes the whole meaning of the *'cogito, ergo sum'*. It becomes a problem, not a solution (ibid.). The human sciences turn to the investigation of that which escapes the consciousness of thought, the 'unthought' or, as Foucault otherwise referred to it, as the 'will to know'.

There is still what Foucault called the human 'countersciences': psychoanalysis, ethnology and linguistics. The first two are foundational in relation to the human sciences insofar as they 'excavate the ground on which they [the human sciences] are built' (*OT*, p. 215). However, they will lead to the failing of the human sciences, because they question the concept of man. In this sense, they are 'countersciences'.

If in a future episteme man will not be conceived as the being for whom representation exists, man will cease to exist, and it will be possible to speak, Foucault concludes, about the 'death of man'. This has been a very controversial Foucauldian statement. Certeau describes it as:

> It is not the end of man, that Foucault proclaimed, but of the conception of man that believed it had solved, by means of positivism in the 'human sciences' [...] the ever-lingering problem of death. Because every system's downfall is the allusion of having triumphed over difference, the question today is posed in terms of this alienation in language every bit as much (it is, after all, the same thing) as it is in terms of the 'successive systemic collapses'. (de Certeau, 1986, p. 256)

3.3.3.5 *Language in the modern age*

During the classical episteme, language was representation and a grammar should be elaborated since knowledge was 'a refinement of the knowledge implicit in ordinary language' (Gutting, 1989, p. 195). There could be 'languages that were more important than others, because they were able to analyse representations more precisely or more delicately' (*OT*, p. 285). Latin played this important role. 'Discourse' was what had to be studied, in the sense that it was a way of arranging representations in a sequence of verbal signs. Words existed because they represented things. Words possessed 'some immediate discursivity' on their own, as in 'by right of birth' (*OT*, p. 280). In general grammar, words, independently of particular languages, were conceived as having more or less hidden or derived signification that had been given by a primitive designation (archaic cries). Foucault argued that the study of language was about the representative contents of the words, in relation to something that they originally designated. The idea underlying the study of language was that there was an original language that provided the initial bunch of roots and that some subsequent historical events (such as invasions, migrations, political freedom or slavery, advances in learning and so on) led to the differences between languages.

In the last quarter of the eighteenth century, language began to be considered differently by Laurent Coeurdoux and Sir William Jones. Jones was considered a founder of comparative grammar, having studied the relationship between Indo-European languages and the differences between/among Sanskrit, Greek and Latin. Nevertheless, Foucault argues that it was only after Jacob Grimm, Friedrich von Schlegel, Rasmus Rask and Franz Bopp that language became an object of study and philology emerged. This occurred following the problematisation of representation. Language 'is no longer a system of representations which has the power to pattern and recompose other representations', it designates man's 'actions, states, and wishes' (*OT*, p. 289).

Language 'does not cease to have a meaning and to be able to "represent" something in the mind that employs or understands it' (*OT*, p. 280). However, in the modern age it will not have a representative function 'by right of birth' (ibid.) and words now have to obey some rules that are previously established by grammatical organisation, in order to represent. Whilst considering the classical age, grammar was established as it was words that were represented, while in the modern episteme words only represented, on the basis of grammar (*OT*, p. 237). All languages are to have an equal value (*OT*, p. 285).

The main change was in the conception of language in a historicity, as in life and in labour, and in the sense of a temporal and organic structure. In relation to living beings, which were being studied according to the functions of their internal organic structure, instead of their visible external character (classical age), language had to be studied within the internal organisation (relationship between words, their meanings and their grammatical functions in a sentence, for instance). Philology emerged as a study of language, its literature and its historical and cultural contexts. It studied grammar, rhetoric, history, interpretation of authors and critical traditions associated with a given language. Instead of the vertical investigations, which were used to establish the remaining original sounds or cries of the language (as in the classical age – 'designation' in general grammar), they began studying language as a system that imposed its organisation upon sounds, syllables and roots. Foucault writes: 'now it is not a matter of rediscovering some primary word that has been buried in it, but of disturbing the words we speak, of denouncing the grammatical habits of our thinking, of dissipating the myths that animate our words, of rendering once more noisy and audible the element of silence that all discourse carries with it as it is spoken' (*OT*, p. 298). Hence, language has 'unconscious' – the unthought – elements. Philology emerged in order to analyse 'what is said in the depths of discourse' (ibid.).

Foucault summarises philology's new conception of language according to four 'theoretical segments'. First, how a language is characterised internally and is distinguished from others. In the classical episteme, languages were individualised, according to the formal features of their grammars, such as the proportions of vowels and consonants they employed and/or whether certain categories of words were privileged (either concrete or abstract substantives, for instance). Comparisons were then made between the Northern and Mediterranean languages and the barbarous and civilised languages and so on. Philology was to study the modes of combination between grammatical elements in different languages – types of linguistic organisations. There are two basic modes of combination: the elements of language are like atoms, which combine in different ways to form sentences and propositions; and the inflectional system of a language. The 'inflectional system' consists of phonetic modifications and synthetic subordinations. Foucault defines the 'inflectional system' as being 'a certain manner of modifying the words themselves in accordance with the grammatical position they take up in relation to one another' (*OT*, p. 237). Therefore, 'inflections' are now understood in a completely different manner compared to their use up until the end of the eighteenth century, when inflections were analysed on the basis of a common root. In the modern age, 'it is the root that is modified, and the inflections that are analogous' (*OT*, p. 234). For instance, Chinese is distinct from Sanskrit: while Chinese forms complex expressions using juxtaposing autonomous grammatical elements, Sanskrit forms complex expressions by inflectional modifications to the roots.

The second 'theoretical segment' is that philology takes these internal variations not only to differentiate languages but to study them. For instance, while for the classical age, language arose from noises that became letters, philology considers that languages exist when those noises are articulated and divided into a series of different sounds (*OT*, p. 286). 'The whole being of language is now one of sound' (ibid.). Foucault mentions as an example of this event the Brothers Grimm's interest in folk tales and spoken dialects. Language was sought through the spoken word and differed from the classical concept, which was that it was a sign, that it was indeed a 'map' of primitive cries. It 'has acquired a vibratory nature which has separated it from the visible sign and made it more nearly proximate to the note in music' (ibid.).

The third segment is that philology established a new theory of the root, in which language is 'rooted' not in the things perceived (as a representation of things, emerging from primitive sounds), but in 'the active subject' (*OT*, p. 194). For instance, Foucault explains that for Bopp the roots of a certain language can be studied through its properties, within a formal system, without the need to work back to a primitive language and its initial relationship to objects. The roots do not represent objects, but rather the will of a subject. This has another important consequence, argues Foucault, related to the historicity of language. Language is now human. Its mutations do not result from someone or something above but from below (Foucault mentions the learned elite, the aristocracy, the small group of merchants and travellers, and so on), from the people and it is not a product but 'a ceaseless activity'.

The fourth segment is that a 'new definition of the systems of kinship between languages' emerged within philology. During the classical age, the resemblance between languages was established on the basis of either the primitive language or the fact that one originated from another. Perhaps more importantly, they had reference to a representative character. Philology analyses the internal structures of languages and identifies the temporal relations between them. Languages become historical.

Nevertheless, the philosophical thought regarding a new conception of language was much slower than the thought regarding life and wealth. Although it was 'the most immediate' movement, given its close relationship with representation, the perception and acceptance, so to speak, were very slow (*OT*, p. 232). This was due to the close relationship with the perception of words as being representative of things, the significance of which was derived from an earlier designation (archaic cries, for example). The fragmentation of language was the most difficult to perceive and accept, since it was 'the most secret and the most fundamental' (*OT*, p. 307). While living beings were regrouped around 'life' in biology and the processes were regrouped around 'production' in economics, language is kept 'dispersed' in our own days (*OT*, p. 304).

Foucault explains that this 'dispersion' is based on the fact that languages have a historicity for philologists, which meant that language has to be purified in order to establish a universality. Thus, formalisation and interpretation are pursued.

Although language is no longer the archetype of knowledge, it is still considered the means by which knowledge can be expressed. But as language is now historical and has laws of its own, it contains hidden meanings, it may contain meanings that change historically and it can comprise myths and grammatical habits of our thinking. The modern era tries to control this fragmentation through two basic projects: formalisation and critical interpretation. Through formalisation (which, states Foucault, culminates in Russell), man aims to polish and purify language, releasing it from its 'accidents and alien elements' (*OT*, p. 296). That was the dream of positivists and the proponents of a symbolic logic. A critical interpretation of language aims to understand the hidden meanings through an exegesis. In this case, Foucault even mentions *Das Kapital* as being an exegesis of 'value' (*OT*, p. 298). Perhaps *The Order of Things* could also be included as an exegesis in the history of the conceptions of language.

This radical change of thinking in philosophical thought only occurred towards the end of the nineteenth century, or more precisely in the twentieth century, if it were not for Nietzsche. Foucault writes that Nietzsche, the philosopher and philologist, 'even in that field he was so wise, he knew so much, he wrote such good books – been the first to connect the philosophical task with a radical reflection upon language' (*OT*, p. 305). Of course, Foucault was referencing to what had been referred to as 'the linguistic turn' in philosophy and he continues to point out some of the main questions:

What is language? What is a sign? What is unspoken in the world, in our gestures, in the whole enigmatic heraldry of our behaviour, our dreams, our sickness – does all that speak, and if so in what language and in obedience to what grammar? Is everything significant, and, if not, what is, and for whom, and in accordance with what rules? What relation is there between language and being, and is it really to being that language is always addressed – at least, language that speaks truly? What, then, is this language that says nothing, is never silent, and is called 'literature'. [...] We know now where these questions come from. They were made possible by the fact that [...] the law of discourse having been detached from representation, the being of language itself became, as it were, fragmented; but they became inevitable when, with Nietzsche, and Mallarmé, thought was brought back, and violently so, towards language itself, towards its unique and difficult being. (*OT*, p. 306)

3.3.3.6 *Philosophy in the modern age*

In the classical episteme, there was no 'philosophy', which can be understood in two senses: a) reflection about knowledge, ontology and meaning; b) 'philosophy' was depicted as being at the same level as the analysis of language, of wealth and of living beings (Cousins and Hussain, 1984, p. 48). There was 'no philosophy operating at a superior level and performing a separate function from the knowledge of language, wealth and living beings' (ibid.). In the modern age, 'science' was separated from 'metaphysics', as well as epistemology from philosophy. This broke the homogeneity of the classical *mathesis*, and philosophy was positioned on a different level, in relation to the other domains of knowledge.

From the end of the eighteenth century onwards, philosophy was considered to be the domain for thinking regarding the problem of representation, leading to the emergence of epistemology and the human sciences.

When representation began to be put into question, philosophical thought looked for the conditions of possibility of knowledge in three different forms:

1 Focusing on the subject: the conditions of possibility of knowledge must be within the subject. This was Kant's transcendental philosophy.
2 Focusing on the object: the objects make a representation of things possible – transcendental objectivity (life, labour and language).
3 Phenomenalism: Kant's phenomenal world was a representation of all that exists for knowledge. As we know, phenomenalism was proposed by positivists such as Carnap and Ayer, who advocated the fact that all we can know about the external world is in the form of data transmitted by sensory experience. For Foucault, positivism was in this category, as it was not possible to separate it from its own criticism or from what it rejected. It may be possible to consider positivism as a return to the classical episteme. However, Foucault maintains that positivism was in the modern episteme since the 'turn' had already occurred. Positivism dealt with the problem of representation methodologically by simply excluding it and using the notion of 'meanlessness'.

There are basically two strata representing the figure of man. Economics, biology and philology represent the questions of labour, life and language in the simple form of economic, biological and linguistic mechanisms related to man's existence. The human sciences turned their attention to the implications of these forms, such as action, conduct, behaviour, attitudes, norms, ideologies, ideas, beliefs and so on. They refer to a second stratum as confirming the 'problem of representation'. In this stratum, life, labour and language have effects, which have conscious representations in humans and can only be fully understood through what in the representations escapes consciousness and can only be 'known' by the human sciences.

Cousins and Hussain (1984) argue that, for Foucault, 'man' means neither a given object nor a concept. Instead, 'man' is 'a space of knowledge, a set of relations between knowledges', being in tension since he became both object and condition of his own knowledge. The figure of man has three main instances (ibid., p. 62):

1 The psychological or physical: concerned with the biological functions through which man opens up the question of representation, leading to the question of what thoughts should be considered when referring to the terms of a human animal that is traversed by thought. This domain deals with such categories as cognition, perception, memory and consciousness.
2 The social: concerned with man as the being of needs and production and representing the world of needs and production to himself. It uses categories such as groups, classes, beliefs and ideologies. This domain overlaps with the cultural domain.
3 The cultural: arising from the implications of language, which are treated as strings of representations and systems of communication. It requires the categories of myth, literature and of symbolic or semiotic systems.

3.3.3.7 *The Modern General Table*

Foucault recognised a relationship between the four domains that defined the general theory of language in the classical episteme (attribution, articulation, designation and derivation) and a new quadrilateral, formed by what he called the new theoretical segments of the modern episteme: analysis of finitude, empirico-transcendental repetition, the unthought and origin. The diagram provided by Foucault (*OT*, p. 201) is reproduced here in Diagram 3.2. The contents regarding economic thought are explained in Chapter 5.

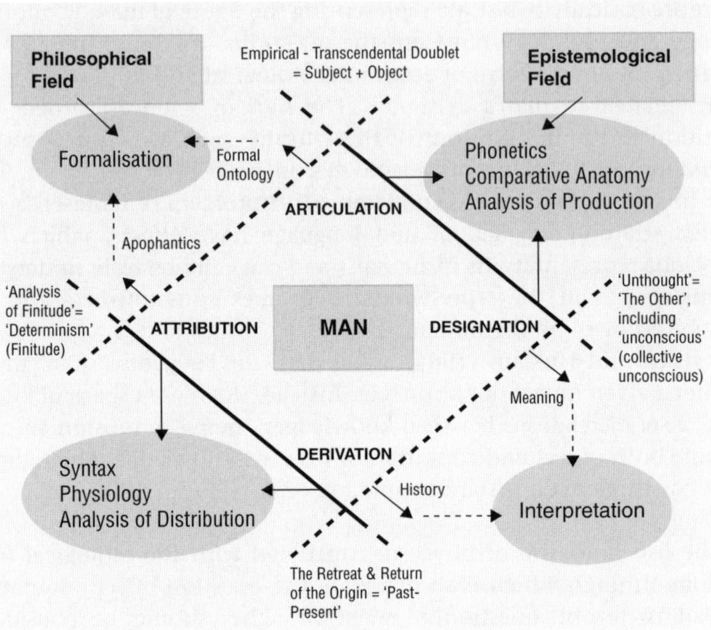

Diagram 3.2   The General Table – the modern episteme

Foucault suggests that we must not consider that this new quadrilateral corresponds to the other one. There is a relationship of resemblance and symmetry, but the underlying configuration of thought is completely different.

The most distinctive characteristic is that the new quadrilateral is no longer a representation of an order that is characteristic of things. This new diagram demonstrates man's representation of things. Therefore, it is no longer considered that the main domains of the three previous empiricities (economics – wealth, biology – living beings, and philology – discourse) are at the centre of the diagram. In the modern episteme, man became the central focus of understanding of all the configurations of thought, and it became possible to imagine him at the centre of Foucault's diagram.

Whilst considering the classical episteme, the *cogito* established man as an individual, a thinking subject. In the modern episteme, man became a 'shifting locus of collective and unconscious determinisms' (Major-Poetzl, 1983, p. 191). The transcendental subject, who is the source of meaning, was separated from transcendental objects such as life, labour and language. This is what Foucault meant by the separation between 'meaning' and 'history' in his diagram, as Major-Poetzl (ibid., p. 184) declared. At the same time, a new metaphysical conception of being emerged.

The 'analytic of finitude' is related to the theoretical segment of 'attribution' in classical grammar. Attribution was the theory of *verb*: how a language could 'overflow its own boundaries' and be able 'to affirm being' (*OT*, p. 336). In the same instance the *verb* was that which allowed language to exist. Foucault states that the analytic of finitude is concerned with asserting man's being, linking the thinking of the positivities (life, labour and language) to his finitude. Man can only be thought through life, labour and language. He is a historical and predetermined being (determinism = finitude).

As with the theory of articulation, which showed how things were named, linking words and things, the empirical-transcendental doublet shows the link between object and subject in the modern episteme. As Foucault states, it 'shows how what is given in experience and what renders experience possible correspond to one another in an endless oscillation' (*OT*, p. 336).

Designation, in classical thought, corresponds to the 'unthought' of the modern era. Designation looked for the ancestors of the words, how initial cries and gestures ('forgotten souls') gave rise to the words (linking representation to things). The modern thought always associates a *cogito* with the unthought that is 'dormant' and 'must be brought to life'.

Finally, in addition to the theory of derivation in the classical episteme, which was looking for the way in which words changed in relation to their primary representation (designation), the retreat and return of the origin doublet is a demonstration of man's eager efforts to find his origins.

3.3.4   The contemporaneous episteme

Although Foucault could not characterise it, he clearly announced a new episteme in *The Order of Things*. The reason he could not describe it in detail was due in part to his own belief that the episteme referred to an unconscious configuration, so it is not understandable by whoever is living within its aegis. However, if he asserts that we are still in the modern episteme ('our thought today still belongs to the same dynasty' – *OT*, p. 243), then his argument appears to be unsubstantiated.

Foucault did not 'evaluate' the pre-classical and classical epistemes, instead criticising the modern episteme and emphasising that the humanism of the modern episteme was the reason for its instability.

He even predicted that the end of the modern era would be marked by the waking up of man from his 'anthropological sleep', and by the return of language to the centre of thought. As for a new configuration of thought, which could be called 'postmodernity', he recognised the instabilities in the modern age that would lead to another order of thought. These instabilities were the three doublets mentioned in the previous section.

This new era is sometimes associated with the twentieth century thought that followed Freud. Freud, Marx and Husserl are regarded as central personages of the modern episteme, since they looked for man's essence in his history (Major-Poetzl, 1983, p. 161). When Foucault announces a moment in history when man no longer has an essence, he also points to a new episteme.

As Gutting (1989, p. 219) remarks, Foucault regarded reflection on language as 'a crucial part of the development of a new episteme, postmodern episteme'. Therefore, structuralism is usually regarded as being part of the new episteme (Shumway, 1989, Caws, 1971 and Major-Poetzl, 1983, for example). Caws defines structuralism as:

> the view that significance arises only out of a matching of the structured complexities of mind on the one hand and the world on the other, is precisely the philosophical outlook best equipped to deal with the post-humanist epoch Foucault anticipates, an epoch in which we will have to come to terms finally with the lack of all transcendence, with the ultimate impossibility of explaining our condition in terms of its origin or history or material basis, and in which the circularity and self-mirroring character of the human will force us, for our own preservation, to an understanding of the structures within which we are confined. (Caws, 1971, p. 34)

Major-Poetzl (1983, p. 153) argues that structuralism reversed the relationship between the same-other, since it 'begins with differences and proceeds to similarities'. The existence of an underlying structure would dissolve the common oppositions within the human sciences, such as the conscious and unconscious in psychology and the normal and abnormal in sociology, and while doing so would form in the content of literature (ibid.). The fact that 'structuralism' had been seen as the threshold of a new episteme may unveil why it was that Foucault changed his mind regarding the subtitle of *The Order of Things* from 'The Archaeology of Structuralism' to 'The Archaeology of Human Sciences'. However, the problem related to the characterisation of the new episteme remains, since Foucault did not mention many of the changes that led to it.

In the new episteme, it is not man who speaks; there is no individual and conscious subject, as stated by Descartes (*cogito*), but the world (Nietzsche: language gives as the illusion of the self; without language, there would not be doers, egos and selves, as written by Davis, 2003, pp. 8–9). The world speaks collectively and unconsciously (as in Mallarmé's works). 'Words only represent other words or, in structuralist terminology, signs signified other signs without external referents' (Major-Poetzl, 1983, p. 156). As Major-Poetzl remarks, time and space emerged together into the foreground of knowledge, leaving no grounding for thought (ibid., p. 153).

3.4   Review

This chapter was essentially based on a conscientious study of *The Archaeology of Knowledge* and *The Order of Things*, attempting to unravel the sometimes difficult relationship between their extremely complex and obscure character. The definitions may vary to some extent and therefore much can be left to the reader's discretion, to conclude and use in future discussion when formalising debate and providing constructive arguments to be deployed in future analysis. Furthermore, Foucault's style appears to alternate between a Nietzschean attitude (where notions such as 'method' and 'theory' would not have a place) and a Cartesian effort to articulate a system.

It is possible to read *The Order of Things* without having read *The Archaeology of Knowledge*, although there is much to learn from both. In the case of *The Archaeology of Knowledge*, it could be considered as a more appropriate read for anyone wanting to apply Foucault's method. He wrote it as a step-by-step description of his inquiry in *The Order of Things* and offered a new method into the history of knowledge, together with a new theory of discourse.

As in all of Foucault's works, the understanding of the series of new notions and concepts that he introduced requires a patient search for the nuances that he introduced as his discourse proceeded. It is clear that he did not solely offer a history as to how epistemology came into being, but that he wanted to develop one as well. As Rorty argues, Foucault 'was not content simply to give a genealogy of epistemology, to show us how this genre came into being' (and Rorty adds 'something he does very well'), but he also wanted 'to *do* something like epistemology' (Rorty, 1986, p. 43). Even if it appears impossible to fully understand his system due to omissions, particularly concerning the articulation of concepts (for example, between the historical *a priori* and the episteme), there is still much that inspires and promotes a rethinking of epistemology in general.

His new theory of discourse comprises notions such as 'discontinuity', 'threshold', 'limit', 'series' and 'transformations' (Carrette, 2000, p. 89). He presented the 'archaeology' as a digging up of historical configurations that established the conditions of possibility of positive knowledge. These conditions were '*a priori*', although they were specific at distinct moments, as they were also historical. That was why Foucault called them 'historical *a priori*'. This seems to be contradictory, although it is justified by the assumption that history was not continuous and events were not linked by causalities. Archaeology intends to unveil the historical *a priori* of knowledge. In particular, Foucault wanted to find out the historical *a priori* of the emergence of the human sciences, which was the same as some empiricities, such as political economy, biology and philology. Whether there exists any distinction between 'historical *a priori*' and 'episteme' is not clarified by Foucault.

Archaeology had to describe and analyse discourses through a new unity, 'the statement', which remains a difficult notion to comprehend, since he defined most of it by what it was not, rather than what it was, while making the particular point of differentiating it from other linguistic terms (sentence, proposition or speech acts). This was because he wanted to make it clear that he was reading the writings of the past not as a grammarian, a logician or even an analytic philosopher, while directing attention towards the understanding of their conditions of possibility. Hence, these conditions of possibility needed to be investigated through the abandonment of the subject that pronounced them and through the connection of utterances in different discourses. Foucault considered these to be the conditions of possibility within a specific 'region of interpositivities', which were the writings in the history of economics, biology and philology, which were investigated as 'statements'.

Discourse was understood by him as a 'group of statements which together have a certain "modality of existence"; they "belong to a single system of formation"' (Carrette, 2000, p. 11). The unity of this 'group' (for example, a discourse called 'political economy') is characterised by 'the type of positivity' of a discourse and should be searched for in a 'system of dispersion', which, although being one of Foucault's ill-defined concepts, refers to his belief that thought was not something controlled by *a priori* axioms and principles, origins and so on, but instead it must be studied by historians as unique to its time. As Foucault declared, the 'archaeology' is also an analysis of 'the type of positivity of a discourse', that is, how 'statements', 'above and beyond books, texts, authors, through time, and independently of the proximity of epistemological validity, scientificity, or truth' (Smart, 1985, p. 40), form their historical 'unity'. Hence, Foucault analysed political economy as a 'group of statements'. He read the works of Smith, Ricardo and others, not taking their utterances as logicians, grammarians or analytic philosophers would otherwise do; instead he sought to investigate 'the statements' shared with other discourses of that time, particularly biology and philology ('interdiscursive domain').

According to his belief in the discontinuity of history, one of his main claims in *The Order of Things* was that reason has a historicity. He stated that rationality was not 'an anthropological invariant' (Foucault, 1987, p. 107) and that we go from one regime of truth to another. Instead of *a* rationality, his archaeology emphasised that the history of knowledge since the sixteenth century had presented very different rationalities, which had led to distinct discourses and practices. He argued that since there had also been four epistemic configurations, characterised by different rationalities (the Renaissance episteme, the age of representation, the age of modernity, and a new configuration – the postmodernity) they cannot be characterised now, since we are in the moment of transition and therefore we can only start to glimpse the instabilities within the modern episteme that may suggest we are actually moving towards a postmodern episteme.

Foucault translated the different rationalities into a set of relations. In his archaeology in *The Order of Things* he selected the following set of relations: the different conceptions of language and representation, perceptions of same/other, the role of such notions as space and time in the constitution of the subject matter, the distinct techniques of isolating it (for example, resemblances or equalities and differences, leading to interpretation, analogy and/or analysis) and the ontological assumption of man's finitude (thought-unthought). These relations characterised the historical epistemologisations of the discourses that he was investigating. They defined different perceptions of the mode of beings and order and then the distinct historical modes of *savoir*.

This suggests that Foucault had a 'structure' underlying his inquiries, which is sometimes regarded as a characteristic that would then place him within a movement referred to as 'structuralism'. However, the fact that this 'structure' was not *a priori*, permanent or transcendental was something that could be taken as a definite distinction from 'structuralism'. In addition to this is the fact that Foucault focused on 'statements' and 'events' rather than 'structures', which presents a contrasting view to that of the structuralist approach.

His epistemological novelty, the *episteme*, is defined by a set of relations, operating as an unconscious referential guide for thought at a given period. It lies beneath distinctive discursive practices ('interdiscursive practice'), establishing epistemological figures, rhetorical schemes, methods of investigation and linguistic devices. For example, Foucault (*OT*, p. xi) declares in relation to the classical episteme that although it was 'unknown to themselves, [...] the naturalists, economists, and grammarians employed the same rules to define the objects proper to their own study, to form their concepts, to build their theories'.

The relations that form the epistemes constitute the necessary and sufficient conditions for a discourse to become possible. Foucault does take them as rules or laws that define knowledge. He quite often used terms like 'rules', 'laws', 'determining' and so on, which might suggest a kind of 'positivism'. For example, he stated that 'we must first discover the law operating behind all these diverse statements' (*AK*, p. 55). He was actually accused of being a positivist (for example, by Le Bon, 1967) and even stated that he could live with the label (sarcastically declaring that he would be a 'happy positivist') if critics could not think of something better. Nevertheless, in respect to the fact that he employs these terms, it should be recognised that he was not merely referring to an epistemological metalevel, but was suggesting that the 'laws' were not transcendental, as positivism would otherwise maintain. *The Order of Things* presents a demonstration of certain regularities in the ways that scientists in the classical age used their imaginations to solve scientific problems distinct from those regularities that modern scientists used to approach similar problems.

Foucault not only constructed an epistemology but he also studied the history of epistemology and ontology. He was relating epistemology to ontology in order to identify the different systems of relations between language (words) and perceptions of reality (things). Hence, he wanted to unveil the unconscious conceptions of being that were underlying epistemological systems. He concluded that the period of the history of knowledge that he was analysing was characterised by three distinct ontological conceptions of being. In sequence, the connection Foucault sees between the ontological assumptions and the epistemological procedures in *The Order of Things* will be stressed.

Up until the end of the sixteenth century (the pre-classical episteme), 'being' was assumed and everything was created by a superior entity that had left 'signs' in the form of resemblances, which were God's signature. Signs were conceived as being in things and man could figure them out through the interpretation of resemblances and analogies between/among things. Language was not considered as a problem, since it was one other thing that was part of the world around them. Words mirrored things and Foucault called the chapter about this episteme 'the prose of the world'. Since God was unique, he and his things cannot be compared. Therefore, knowing was not to compare or to analyse; instead it was to 'interpret' signs already in existence.

From the beginnings of the seventeenth century to the end of the eighteenth century, the *cogito* declared being as a fact, relating it to a subject (I) and to consciousness (I think). Therefore, signs were no longer 'anterior' to knowledge. Man was a subject (*cogito*: I) and the conscious knower (*cogito*: I am) built the signs for knowing, hence a 'well-constructed' language, insofar as its representation was possible through language. During the classical episteme, *mathesis universalis*, a general science of order, played a founding role for knowledge not only for mathematics but also for the empirical domains of analysis of wealth, natural history and grammar. It was not the method (mathematicisation or mechanisation of nature) that these empiricities borrowed from *mathesis*, but the general possibility of establishing an ordered table of identities and differences between representations (*OT*, p. 243).

When representation collapsed towards the end of the eighteenth century, the homogeneous background of *mathesis* was dissolved. Two forms of thought emerged in the modern episteme. The first considered the possibility of representability through the emergence of the transcendental subject. The second questioned the conditions of a relation to actual representations: the force of labour, the energy of life and the possibility of speech. At the ontological level, man as the subject and object was related to the unconscious and collective phenomena, as well as to the changing states (historical experiences). Time, instead of space (which was at the foreground of knowledge in the classical era), became central. Knowledge became an endless task in transgressing finitude. Between words and things, there was man and the unthought. Thought became language. The human sciences emerged to think the unthought, although this would prove to be unsustainable, since there would always be the unthought and they would never find the ultimate origin and oscillate between the transcendental-empirical. Hence, there was no 'progress' in knowledge, but instead a move towards an 'anthropological sleep'.

Foucault's belief in the possibility of discerning the thought of ages through a well-built system has been considered very ambitious and difficult to submit to any kind of criticism. Although it resulted from a very exigent mind, whose continuous reflection protects it from frivolous critiques, some repeated questions have been raised since the publication of *The Order of Things* and some of these will be addressed below.

One of the main criticisms that has usually been directed at his system is related to his notion of discontinuity in history, above all when it is combined with his assumption of incommensurability of epistemes and the fact he did not offer explanations for the shifts between them.

It is possible to see a paradox here, since when Foucault argues that history follows epistemes, perhaps he was seeing some regularity or continuity? Moreover, how is it possible for him to describe the previous epistemes, especially when he states that they are incommensurable? Perhaps there is some kind of continuity between the epistemes perhaps there is another layer that exists and allows us to associate past and present. He claims that he was in a privileged position to see the 'epistemes' and maybe his own, which makes us to wonder about him as an individual and his context. Thus, an investigation into his context certainly adds elements for the understanding of his intellectual project. This was the main objective in Chapter 2.

These assumptions have been particularly difficult to accept and one implication was that they undermine such notions as 'influence' and 'predecessors', although it would appear that Foucault was not opposed to them when they were considered in the same epistemic context. In Foucault's system, consciousness does not play a significant role and it would be possible to write history without considering the people who made it. Ideas emerge derived from that set of unconscious relations. He did not even approach the controversies in relation to individuals' ideas, since he understood them as being a matter of opinion and based on a surface phenomenon. The shifts between epistemes occurred without the interference of anyone, while his archaeology is a history that depicts some impersonal forces that shatter old discourses while establishing new ones. A justification for such a radical position may be found in the unconscious character of those relations, in particular to those related to language. Changes in language and in the conception of it as a means of representation are only perceived *a posteriori*.

Perhaps Foucault's own status as an author-subject is then brought into question, as Major-Poetzl (1983, p. 166) noticed, stating that if language rather than man speaks, who is the author of *The Order of Things*? Is Foucault the 'voice' of our time or is he speaking for himself? If the latter, is he then 'lying' (ibid.)? Nevertheless, something appears to be missing from this argument, given that Foucault made it clear that his discourse was a result of a determined epistemic configuration. Although incoherent on this matter, he declared that we are still in the modern episteme and his discourse would only become possible in a new configuration of thought that followed it.

Following his strategies of thinking, Foucault was indeed 'challenging the boundaries of our thinking' and 'disrupting the binary categories of our thought', as Carrette stated (2000, p. xii). However, it would appear that, in spite of his ardour in keeping this as a central line of his thinking, he could not avoid incurring dualistic perspectives. He was restrictive when he insisted that each age had had one, and only one, episteme. Are shifts between epistemes so pure and definitive, with all those fatal clear-cuts? For example, how can we explain that the *mathesis* of the classical episteme not only continued into physics but went further in influencing the social sciences (White, 1979, p. 102)? How could Foucault explain the existence of two distinct 'modes of thought' (Euclidean-Cartesian and Babylonian) in economics, as argued by Sheila Dow (1985 and 1990) and discussed further in the following chapter? How could one unique episteme define such heterogeneous 'modes of thought' within the same disciplinary discourse at a certain period of time? Foucault sometimes refers to some 'interpenetrability' between and among epistemes, this being the case of 'resemblance' during the Renaissance and in the classical episteme, as well as 'analogy' between the Renaissance and the modern age, which suggests that overlaps must occur between epistemes. For example, he writes: 'resemblance, excluded from knowledge since the early seventeenth century, still constitutes [in the classical episteme] the outer edge of language' (*OT*, p. 120). This raises questions concerning his argument regarding the existence of only *one* episteme in each age. However, it should be noted that he never claimed that epistemes were formed only by original elements, stating that sometimes they change meaning and arrangement. Hence, there is a crucial difference between them, making it unviable to even consider them continuing.

Nonetheless, epistemes may occur according to different strands existing during a given period of time. They may also intersect and/or overlap. Characteristics of one episteme may reappear in another. For example, when referring to the changes in natural history in the classical episteme, Foucault also stated that some of them were a 'return' to Aristotle: 'Thus there is a return in the analysis of living beings to Aristotelian analogies' (*OT*, p. 265). Rationality may be heterogeneous or, as Laudan (1977) argues, there may be 'perennial co-existence of conflicting traditions'. Another fact that was established by Foucault, which supports the view of a non-abrupt shift between epistemes, was that even after having found out his finitude in the modern episteme, man still aimed to surpass it, being the reason for the emergence of the human sciences and movements like logical positivism.

Even if Foucault never openly stated this, his historical studies suggest that he held the view that radical transformations (a term he uses in preference to 'revolution') take place over time. This was the case when he referred to individuals like Cervantes (*Don Quixote*), Sade, Adam Smith in economics, Lamarck in biology, William Jones in philology and Kant, since they were all living during a period of transition. Foucault even uses the expression '*ambiguous* epistemological configuration' to designate the period of transition from 1775 to 1795/1800 (*OT*, p. 140, emphasis added). He identified different 'epistemes' during a certain period of time when he makes the distinction between the classical age and the modern episteme in the works of the contemporaries Destutt de Tracy and Kant respectively. How could Foucault's system start to explain the existence of 'outsiders' such as Nietzsche, the one person that was regarded as his greatest influence? Nietzsche clearly regarded himself as an outsider. All of this presents something of a problem when Foucault insists that the epistemes are incommensurable. We may even consider the fact that discontinuities do not necessarily imply different periods of time and that there can even be discontinuity within a certain era.

Even if Foucault was correct, another problem remains concerning discontinuity, relating to the universality in the concept of episteme, which is that it does not consider the local inherent differences even within the same discipline or within same 'region of interpositivities'. For instance, the Scottish Enlightenment presented substantial differences in relation to the French Enlightenment.

Foucault does not talk about progress since, for him, 'it is more interesting to see, in detail, why philosophers think they have made progress, and what criteria of progress they employ' (Rorty, 1967, p. 2). By comparing the regularities of the concept-formation and the theory-development in his test cases, the classical domains of wealth, nature and language, while comparing those with their respective modern descendants – economics, biology and philology – Foucault established some important aspects that have more in common with one another in a given age than each has with its own inheritor in the next age. There are some who consider, questionably, that Foucault only wanted to demonstrate how things occurred or that they could be different in some way and that he was depicting a retreat in knowledge following the classical age. This argument maintains that there was coherence, order, hierarchy and interdisciplinarity in knowledge, which was then lost in modern thought and, in addition to that, modern thought had no foundation, as with the general science of order of classicism. This argument does not take into consideration the fact that Foucault was not evaluating classical thought but was simply describing it. His intention was to depict how knowledge changed in the modern era, but this turned out to be an evaluation by him. Foucault wanted to describe it in order to show its instabilities and even pointed out an exit route: the waking up from the 'anthropological sleep'. He also stressed that the end of this latest episteme was marked by the re-emergence of language as that which needs to be thought.

Foucault refuses to explain the shifts between epistemes, although perhaps we could even say that those instabilities, in the modern episteme, were actually due to some of the explanations for the shifts from one episteme to another. Furthermore, he does not look for explanations as to why previous epistemes remained intelligible to the subsequent epistemes. The archaeology examines the shifts between epistemes synchronically rather than diachronically. This suggests that he was looking for simultaneous relations in each phase instead of successive transformations. Foucault was clearly aware of such a problem, having already raised the question in *The Order of Things*: 'What event, what law do they obey, these mutations that suddenly decide that things are no longer perceived, described, expressed, characterised, classified, and known in the same way?' (*OT*, p. 217). His only response was that the change 'probably begins with an erosion from outside' (*OT*, p. 50). On another occasion, Foucault provided a reason for not answering this question, stating that trying to find out 'why' the shift to the modern episteme happened would require an 'almost infinite inquiry involving nothing more or less than the very being of our modernity' (*OT*, p. 217), suggesting that there would never be a definite explanation for it. He continued to emphasise that it was impossible to move outside the tacit system of the episteme and it does not take a 'crisis' to explain changes. If we keep in mind the Kuhnian notion of 'normal' science, *The Order of Things* was 'a study of several overlapping and successive "normal" immature sciences' (Hacking, 1979, p. 46). More than in 'revolutions', Foucault was interested in the 'normality' of knowledge in order to understand how systems of possibility define the way in which we think.

The criticism mentioned above in no way detracts from the fact that Foucault's corrosive intelligence and the work he performed was of immense value. His very original and erudite system has offered many elements that have helped to establish change throughout many topical regions. As Toni Negri wrote:

> [W]hat is astonishing – and concerning – is that he never ceases to seek, he makes approximations, he deconstructs, he formulates hypotheses, he imagines, he makes analogies and tells fables, he launches concepts, withdraws them or modifies them. His is a thought of a formidable inventiveness. But this is not its essence: I believe that his method is fundamental. (Negri, 2004)

Even if his assertions are considered to be less interesting than within themselves, he certainly deserves attention for the possibilities and the visions that they have opened up. It would be possible to summarise some of his main proposals as follows: we should be suspicious of meaning and progress in history; history does not follow rationality with ahistorical meaning; and freedom may not be a significant element in history. Foucault may be a choice much more appropriate for philosophical stimulation than for historical accuracy. In this sense, it could be argued that he was above all a philosopher – instead of presenting the history of what is true, he presented a history of what was considered to be true. Instead of founding the history of man as the subject, he could be regarded as demonstrating how the subject was created for knowledge. As he stated himself: 'All my books [...] are little tool boxes [...] if people want to open them, to use this sentence or that idea as a screwdriver or spanner to short-circuit, discredit or smash systems of power, including eventually those from which my books have emerged ... so much the better' (Foucault, quoted in Mills, 1997, p. 17).

The possibilities of fruitful investigations that his new perspective and framework open up are immense. Just as examples, it could be very enlightening to investigate economic thought taking as a reference those different thresholds that he identified in the formation of a discourse in the case of economics. He even gave some hints to analyse the particular case of economics, as well as to accomplish an assessment of his belief that political economy was not a discourse-unit because it referred to either a common object of investigation or a set of concepts and themes.

Following one of the main objectives of this book, which is to provide a conscientious study of the scope of these possibilities to an understanding of economics, the next chapter intends to locate Foucault's perspective amongst others currently explored in economic methodology and the historiography of economics. It is argued that some interests in economic methodology are grouped around the same fundamental question that arises from Foucault's archaeology: is there any underlying configuration that determines knowledge? With respect to historiography, the focus will be on a comparison between Foucault's notion of episteme and the Kuhnian concept of paradigm. Since it is clear that in the Kuhnian concept of paradigm, there has been a fair amount of popularity regarding the rethinking of the history of economic thought, Foucault continues to remain almost unknown in economics. It is believed that only after further investigation can we begin to approach his real archaeology of political economy in depth, which remains the subject of the following chapters.

Part II
The Archaeology and Methodology of Economics

4
The Archaeology, Methodology and Historiography of Economics

4.1 Introduction

The objective of this chapter is to present the perspective offered by Foucault's archaeology through an understanding of economic discourse and by comparing it to other approaches in economic methodology and historiography. As exemplified in the previous chapter, the archaeology provides an important rethinking regarding our past which, Foucault stated, can 'bring some measure of clarity to the consciousness that we have of ourselves and our past' (Foucault, 1984c). It is for the most part an original reflection on how different thoughts and ways of thinking have emerged and existed in economics since the sixteenth century.

It is suggested that Foucault's archaeology shared the same fundamental question raised by other current approaches in economic methodology, which is whether knowledge had an underlying configuration that allowed us to think what we think in a certain spatiotemporal context. In addition to this, his contribution to the historiography of economics is explored, studying in particular the relationships between the Kuhnian concept of 'paradigm' and the notion of 'episteme', since they both have a striking resemblance to each other. It is clear, however, that beyond their similarities, the notion of 'episteme' has been regarded as being at a deeper level in respect to the concept of 'paradigm'.

4.2 Three strands in the history of economic methodology

The thought regarding economic methodology has historically followed at least three major strands, without inferring by that that they are mutually exclusive in any way or that it is an easy task to draw a line between them in time and space.

The first strand was essentially concerned with the question regarding the scientific status of economics as a discipline. Economists interested in economic methodology have thought about '*rules* for what is and is not good science' (Hands, 2001, p. 3, original emphasis). It may be possible to include here the initial concerns raised about methodological questions in economics, which emerged during the same decade as Ricardo's death – the 1820s. These include some classics such as: *Introductory Lecture on Political Economy* by Nassau William Senior (first published in 1827 and later enhanced and published as *Outline of the Science of Political Economy* in 1836); *On the Definition and Method of Political Economy* by John Stuart Mill (first published in 1836 in the *Westminster Review*, the journal of the radical philosophers, and included in *Essays on Some Unsettled Questions of Political Economy* in 1844); *A System of Logic, Ratiocinative and Inductive, being a Connected View of the Principles of Evidence and the Methods of Scientific Investigation* by John Stuart Mill (first published in 1843); *Four Introductory Lectures on Political Economy* by Nassau William Senior (first published in 1852); and *Character and Logical Method of Political Economy* by John Elliot Cairnes (first published in 1857).

The discussions that surrounded these classic writings were primarily focused on the questions related to rationalism versus empiricism (or deduction versus induction), on the demarcation between science and art, whether political economy should be based on some vague assumptions, and the consideration of Ricardo's method (called the 'Ricardian' Vice by Schumpeter, 1954). More recently, and following in this strand, economists have drawn on the philosophy of science. For example, logical positivism has been considered as having had a significant influence on the current method of mainstream economics. The strong increase in importance attached to the mathematical approaches in economics during the post-Second World War period has been associated with a 'formalist revolution' that had its roots in the criteria of scientificity, established by an ideal of science of logical positivism. For example, Ward describes this event as follows:

> The formalist revolution in post-war economics was solidly based on the methodological dream of the latter day positivists. The translation of economic problems into a formal, rather mathematical language was designed to fulfil one of the primary positivist aims: the construction of a well-formed language, of great precision, in which a clear distinction between meaningful and other types of statements could be made. (Ward, 1972, p. 143)

Foucault addressed this issue in *The Order of Things* when he referred to the disputed remarks as to whether the human sciences would achieve a positive character by a formalisation of procedures or by submission to rigorous canons of verification (à la logical positivism). Alternatively, they should otherwise abandon altogether the model of the natural sciences, since their object, man, was a domain of interpretation where hermeneutics would otherwise need to be applied. Foucault stressed that the human sciences could not resist mathematisation, since all empirical investigations involved some relation to mathematics, such as techniques of quantification, of statistical analysis and means of formalisation. However, he argued that these could not become essentially mathematical since they actually emerged from the dissolution of the *mathesis*.

As mentioned in the previous chapter, the human sciences emerged from the collapse of representation and of a project of a general science of order inspired by the mathematical model. This happened when man discovered his radical finitude and the unthought emerged in knowledge. The aim of human sciences was to consider man and the unthought, although they would ultimately fail, according to Foucault, due to the doublets of empirical-transcendental, *cogito*-unthought and the origin retreat-return. For Foucault, this methodological dispute was irrelevant. It was not possible to go back and try to reconstitute an ideal in knowledge of mathematical character.

This case demonstrates that when *mathesis* was dissolved, two fields emerged according to Foucault: analytic and synthetic disciplines. On the one hand, there were the *a priori* sciences, pure formal sciences, deductive sciences based on logic and mathematics and on the other, there were the 'a posteriori sciences, empirical sciences, which employ deductive forms only in fragments and in strictly localised regions' (*OT*, p. 246). It was exactly the dissolution of the *mathesis* that led to the epistemological concern to reconstitute the lost unity through efforts that: classify domains of knowledge according to mathematics; reflect on empirical methods of induction in order to provide them with both a philosophical foundation and a formal justification; try to 'purify, formalise, and possibly mathematicise the domains of economics, biology, and finally linguistics itself' (*OT*, p. 246). Foucault declares:

> It is this event that places formalization, or mathematicization, at the very heart of any modern scientific project; it is this event, too, that explains why all hasty mathematicization or naïve formalization of the empirical seems like 'pre-critical' dogmatism and a return to the platitudes of Ideology. (*OT*, p. 246)

We can even consider the fact that during the aegis of a *mathesis*, there was no attempt to mathematise the empirical domain of economics or that of biology and philology. As demonstrated in the previous chapter, Foucault argued that they were part of the qualitative field of a universal science of order.

The second strand in economic methodology emerged in the last few decades and resulted from a loss of faith in methodological monism, in particular the breakdown of the received view, which was promoted by the work of thinkers such as Paul Feyerabend, Thomas Kuhn and W.V. Quine. This moment coincided with a revival of interest in methodology by economists, which was first associated with a 'crisis' in economics that started at the end of the 1960s and was the result of an end to an economic boom during the post-Second World War period. For example, economic theory did not have an answer to the problem of stagflation. Some economists began to suspect that the previous relative success of the discipline was actually down to the fact that the world economy at that time was in a relatively good position and therefore did not require much. The alleged scientific character of economics became an issue and many works in economic methodology emerged with titles that demonstrated the dissatisfaction with economics, for example, *What's Wrong with Economics* (Ward, 1972), *Dangerous Currents: The State of Economics* (Thurow, 1984), *What's Wrong with Formalization in Economics? An Epistemological Critique* (Woo, 1986), *Truth versus Precision in Economics* (Mayer, 1993), *The Death of Economics* (Ormerod, 1994), *The End of Economics* (Perelman, 1996) and so on.

Hands (2001) has made a substantive contribution to the understanding of a variety of different approaches that have followed this event in economics, including those resulting from what he calls a 'naturalistic turn', as well as those related to the sociology of scientific knowledge. More specifically, Hands emphasised the fact that these approaches have tried to deal with the problems of underdetermination and theory-ladenness. Underdetermination is associated with the so-called *Duhem-Quine Thesis*, which says that no test can be truly definitive, given that a theory comprises a number of auxiliary hypotheses. Theories are never tested in complete isolation, so we will never be sure about the results of a test. Theory-ladenness is associated with Kuhn's *The Structure of Scientific Revolutions* and his view that scientists 'do not just "see"', as Hands (ibid., p. 103) puts it, but 'they "see as"', they follow a 'paradigm'. The 'paradigm', according to Kuhn, determines the way scientists look at and interpret the world, which leads to the 'incommensurability' of different theories. There are striking similarities between Foucault's archaeology and Kuhn's system, the relationship of which will be a focal point of the sequences that follow.

In parallel to the second strand, a third trend followed the studies on language and discourse. Indeed, it may be argued that this was not exactly a new approach in economics, having been present since at least the time of Adam Smith, who, as previously mentioned, investigated the matter, according to Foucault's archaeology, following the epistemic context of the classical age (this is discussed further in Chapter 6). In his studies on human nature, the Scottish thinker accomplished an inquiry into principles that could explain the origin and development of language, together with scientific investigation and how the human mind organised different kinds of discourse to attempt to influence, teach or persuade. Another important moment is found in the writings of the protagonists of 'the marginalist revolution', including Jevons, Pareto and Walras. These writers were committed to clarifying why they thought that mathematical language could and/or should be employed in economic enquiry. For example, in the Introduction to *The Theory of Political Economy*, a book that has been considered pivotal in the formation of neoclassical economics, Jevons wrote:

> It seems perfectly clear that Economy, if it is to be a science at all, must be a mathematical science. There exists much prejudice against the attempts to introduce the methods and language of mathematics into any branch of the moral sciences. Most persons appear to hold that the physical sciences form the proper sphere of mathematical method, and that the moral sciences demand some other method, – I know not what. My theory of Economy, however, is purely mathematical in character. (Jevons, 1871, pp. 3–4)

Although studies on language and rhetoric are not regarded as new approaches among economists, they acquired new perspectives (see, for example, Henderson *et al.*, 1993). New approaches associated with the philosophical linguistic turn have challenged the old view that suggested that economic methodology could prescribe rules for the practice of economists without dealing with problems related to language and discourse. Among them, discourse began to be approached, especially through rhetoric studies which emerged and have been stimulated by the work of McCloskey (1983, 1985) and Klamer (1984).

4.3   Rhetoric versus archaeology

Foucault's perspective may be considered to be very close to that of rhetoric. Indeed, Foucault's archaeology has itself provided elements for the rethinking of rhetoric, such that Corbett and Connors (1999, p. 541) called Foucault a 'rhetorician' and asserted that when the next chapter in the history of rhetoric is written, books like *The Archaeology of Knowledge* will need to be discussed. They placed Foucault alongside the great contemporary rhetoricians, such as I.A. Richards, Richard Weaver, Stephen Toulmin, Chaim Perelman and Kenneth Burke, as a must-read for rhetorical scholars.

In one of the most recent handbooks on contemporary rhetorical studies, Jasinski (2001) often analyses Foucault's contributions to the field, in particular when referring to his archaeological project. He refers to Foucault's work when he writes about episteme, critical rhetoric, the effects of rhetorical practice, rhetoric as epistemic, power and so on. Jasinski describes episteme as being a concept that 'challenges rhetorical scholars to come to grips with the range of forces that enable and constrain situated discursive practice' (ibid., p. 171) and declares that 'Foucault's approach to discourse has had a substantial impact on rhetorical and communications studies' (ibid., p. 218). Examples of Foucault's influence on rhetoric are Blair (1987), Foss and Gill (1987), Gaonkar (1982) and Gemin (1997).

The concepts and notions introduced by Foucault in *The Archaeology of Knowledge* and discussed in Chapter 3, such as 'discursive formation', 'statement', and 'systems of dispersion', have been appropriated by rhetorical scholars. Jasinski continues to point out that it was due in particular to Foucault's influence that:

> Scholars now read and analyze novels, poems, scientific papers, scholarly essays, political speeches, everyday conversations at home and at work, newspaper and magazine articles, interoffice memos, self-help books, and judicial opinions (to name only a few specific examples) as instances of discourse or discursive practice. (Jasinski, 2001, p. 169)

For example, Foss and Gill (1987) explored the Foucauldian notions of discursive practices, rules, roles, power and knowledge for a formulation of a theory that explained the process by which rhetoric was epistemic, and exemplified Foucault's theory through an analysis of Disneyland. McKerrow (1989, p. 101) argued that rhetorical texts must be seen as fragments of much larger discursive formation, instead of units with self-contained meaning and with a beginning, middle and end. Jasinski calls this approach the 'fragmentation thesis'.

Foucault's archaeology, and in particular the concept of episteme, has prompted the growth of a new disciplinary movement in rhetoric that sees discourse practice as epistemic (Jasinski, 2001, p. 218), which started with Robert Scott's essay 'On viewing rhetoric as epistemic', published in the *Central States Speech Journal* in 1967.

Whereas it may be considered a mistake to call Foucault a rhetorician, as clarified later in this chapter, his approach certainly shows close proximity to that of rhetoric. The similarity may be summarised by the fact that both perspectives want to establish how some forms of argumentation were adopted and were more convincing than others. Both of these approaches are, in some way, trying to find buried layers or structures that explain what and how some statements are privileged. For example, McCloskey (1983, p. 482) quotes Wayne Booth's definition of rhetoric: 'the art of probing what men believe they ought to believe, rather than proving what is true according to abstract methods'. Paraphrasing this definition, archaeology probes why and how men believe in what they believe, insofar as it offers a reflection on the conditions of possibility of our beliefs.

Rhetoric and archaeology are both searching for rules of discourse in a critical way. They claim that it is necessary to make conscious some rules that underlie discourse. McCloskey wrote: 'I claim to have noted some of the rules of economic discourse' (McCloskey, 1992, p. 270). Whilst rhetoric aims to make us critical of the presumed rationality of our discourses, Foucault wants us to see that there have been different historical rationalities and even goes to the point of providing us with a characterisation of the different rationalities in the history of economic thought since the sixteenth century. He showed that they comprise a fundamental set of relations that can be investigated by an archaeological approach. It is here that his approach becomes 'critical' in a different, Kantian sense, as mentioned in Chapter 2. Archaeology is 'critical' since it looks for 'the conditions of possibility' of the emergence and existence of discourse. It provides elements that enable us to see that discourse could/can be different from what it was/is. Rhetoric is 'critical' in another sense. McCloskey, for instance, aims to demonstrate that it is possible to improve the rules of discourse and in doing so had certainly identified some common rhetorical devices in economics. McCloskey claims that economists have unduly limited their rhetoric by arguing 'on grounds of certain limited matters of statistical inference, on grounds of positive economics, operationalism, behaviourism, and other positivistic enthusiasms of the 1930s and 1940s' and that there is 'a tension and disjunction between what economists write and how they talk' (ibid.).

There is also another point of contact between archaeology and rhetorical studies. The rhetorical approach, like archaeology, looks for what is unofficial, what is implicit in arguments, considering what have been called 'the precepts of modernism'. McCloskey (1983, p. 484) and Klamer (2001, p. 81) have pointed out some principles of 'modernism' that have guided argumentation and persuasion in economics. Beyond mentioning some 'modern' methodological maxims, such as formalism, objectivism, findings of laws and demarcation between science/non-science and positive/normative, they continue to touch on issues emphasised by Foucault's archaeology that are central to the understanding of modern thought. This is the case when Klamer remarks that the 'problematisation of representation' is the main characteristic of 'modernism'.

Indeed, the archaeology sheds light on the debate regarding the characteristics of what has been called 'modernism' and illustrates the different perspectives of both approaches. Despite their proximity, rhetoric focuses on the 'surface', while archaeology actually investigates how these principles came into being. Therefore, the meaning of 'modernism' differs between archaeology and rhetoric enquiry.

This is the case, for instance, in relation to the view of a Cartesian epistemology informing mainstream economics. Foucault's archaeology shows that the Cartesian representative approach to knowledge collapsed at the end of the eighteenth century and that formalism already emerged as a way to overcome the problem of representation. The problem of language was already present in the emergence of formalism. In this sense, the usual characterisation of 'modernism' in economics is not historically accurate. This may have led to an establishing of the 'wrong' so-called enemy and therefore any proposals to deal with them may have been superficial. The problems with mainstream economics may go well beyond a Cartesian epistemology. Indeed, the hegemonic method of neoclassical economics already represents the problems associated with representation and language. In this new approach, McCloskey suggests that economists should pay particular attention to the way in which their persuasions may become superficial, especially if it is not properly understood that discourse is language in action. Economics today may need more than rhetorical self-awareness. For example, McCloskey has been criticised for not having a theory of discourse. When new conversation on rhetoric in economics says that we have to pay attention to the ways in which arguments are constructed, a very indispensable Foucauldian notion springs to mind, which states that in addition to ideas and explanations that win out over others, there is always a struggle for power and when they win, they become knowledge and truth. In a Nietzschean sense, they become so not because they are the truth, or because they are universal and eternal, but because one group had managed to be more persuasive and imposed their will over others.

Rhetoric and archaeology are opposed to the Cartesian dogma that only the indubitable is true. Actually, as McHoul and Grace note:

> Foucault is dubious about notions of absolute truth [...] but this does not mean that 'there is no truth'. On the contrary, there can sometimes be many truths, each with its own rationality. But the question is: which of these, at any given period, comes to predominate and how? So, instead of mobilising philosophy as the search for truth as such, Foucault tries to take this continual desire for a single truth (particularly on the part of the human sciences). (McHoul and Grace, 1995, p. 19)

Foucault does not imply that there is no truth; rather, that there may exist many historical and cultural truths. He wants 'to determine the ways in which historically specific practices of separating, dividing, distinguishing the true from the false came to be established' (Baynes *et al.*, 1987, p. 97). This reminds us of the distinction McCloskey makes between Truth and truth. For McCloskey, we would not be able to know that we found Truth, even if we had found it, since we do not have 'a path to God's understanding'. Anyway, argues McCloskey, we do not need Truth, we need truth with a small t to solve our practical problems of everyday life. As such, their similarities may well stem from the fact that they are not questioning the true value of what is said, but rather finding out how, against other possibilities of discourse, one possibility succeeds in imposing itself. However, their perspectives diverge in regards to some aspects of importance. It is possible to emphasise their distinctiveness according to the level of investigation, the conception and theory of discourse, and the relation to ontology and epistemology.

As for the 'level' of investigation, 'episteme' refers to something 'anterior' to rhetoric. As McCloskey (1983, p. 483) defines it, 'rhetoric is exploring thought by conversation'. It is concerned with unveiling the argumentative context. Rhetoric studies want to show that there is a language game in discourse. They both proclaim, as did Foucault, that there is something 'not-said', which is itself required, in order to explain what the project was not looking for. As previously mentioned in Chapter 3, archaeology analyses statements (what has been said) without concerns about 'what they are hiding, what they were "really" saying, in spite of themselves, the unspoken element that they contain, the proliferation of thoughts, images, or fantasies that inhabit them' (*AK*, p. 123). Archaeology searches instead for the 'mode of existence' of what has been said. In this sense, it is not about 'the surface of discourse'. Considering rhetoric as a *connaissance*, Foucault even stated that he could have done an archaeology of rhetoric, adding that he would probably have found a system of relations that would at least have overlapped with those he had found in economics, philology and biology (*AK*, p. 176). From an archaeological point of view, the 'episteme' is in a deeper layer, so to speak. It is not concerned with 'internal' forms of argumentation or persuasion. As we have discussed in the previous chapter, it is a search for the configuration of certain notions and relations that make thought and discourse possible in a certain direction and not another. Concerning Foucault's approach to discourse, Habermas wrote:

> The facts of discourse would then have to be treated not as autonomous nuclei of multiple significations, but as events and functional segments gradually coming together to form a system. The meaning of a statement would be defined not by the treasure of intentions that it might contain, revealing and concealing at the same time, but by the difference that articulates it upon other real or possible statements, which are contemporary to it or to which it is opposed in a linear series of time. (Habermas, 1987, p. 241)

As for the term 'discourse' (and as mentioned previously), Foucault's archaeology does not regard it in the same sense as rhetoric analysis does. While rhetoric takes the discourse as an oral or written production in order to understand how it is constructed so as to persuade an audience, the search for the conditions of possibility of thought (archaeology) looks for what, and how, certain ways of thinking allowed such a discourse (and form of argumentation) to be produced.

As for a theory of discourse, the rhetorical approach in economics has not offered a proper 'theory' as to how to analyse discourse in order to unveil what is buried beneath it. Archaeology, as mentioned in the previous chapter, is a new method and Foucault did go as far as to provide a 'theory' to demonstrate how discourse could be historically analysed through a set of relations.

Finally, archaeology differs from rhetoric concerning its explicit relationship to ontology and, as previously mentioned, the archaeology comprises an ontology and epistemology. Archaeology provides a history of the ontological assumptions that underlie the conditions that allow a certain rhetoric scheme to emerge and be favoured by others within a special context of culture and time.

4.4   'Radical' perspectives in economic methodology

Other approaches to discourse in economics are actually much closer than rhetoric is to the radical perspective of Foucault's archaeology, in the sense that they search for the 'roots' of economic discourse. In an attempt to understand the discourse of economics, economists have turned their attention to thinking about the underlying configurations that may define it. Like Foucault, studies regarding Cartesian/Euclidean and Babylonian 'modes of thought' (Dow, 1985 and 1990), about the existence of 'modern' and 'postmodern' configurations of thought and, following Kuhn's approach of paradigms, for instance, maintain that there are some historical conditions that determine rhetorical, linguistic or methodological devices. Their proximity to Foucault's archaeology may be seen in the following quotation, where he describes what he was looking for:

> A modification in the rules of formation of statements which are accepted as scientifically true [...]. It is a question of what governs statements, and the way in which they govern each other so as to constitute a set of propositions which are scientifically acceptable, and hence capable of being verified or falsified by scientific procedures. (Foucault, 1984a, p. 54)

In spite of all the controversies related to these and other approaches, they all have a common important basis, exerting efforts to enhance and better understand the current character of economic discourse through a search for deeper conducive factors that culminate in a certain state of affairs in economics. If we were to regard historiography and methodology in economics in terms of questions, these perspectives would all present the same questions: is there any configuration that determines the way of thinking, theorising, speaking, writing and so on? Although they address different levels, these new approaches raise or touch on the same fundamental question.

Dow (1985) identifies two modes of thought that have guided the history of Western thought: Cartesian/Euclidean and Babylonian. Dow argues that the 1960s marked the divisionary line between the predominance of these two lines of thought: the Cartesian/Euclidean being predominant until the 1960s, after which the Babylonian (although this was not applicable in the case of economics) became predominant. Whilst Cartesian/Euclidean privileged an axiomatic logic, borrowed from the mathematical model, Babylonian (as its own denomination suggests), which was never considered an ideal, takes resources from a diversity of approaches and arguments. Sheila Dow continues to suggest that the Babylonian mode of thought characterises the philosophy of Keynes and stressed that he employed the term when referring to Newton's scientific method as being in contrast to the usual view of it as positivist and mechanicist. Dow's approach also overlaps with an archaeological perspective and does reflect a problematic aspect of Foucault's method. Foucault's contribution to this type of approach was to look for the conditions of possibility that led to the emergence and existence of these different modes of thought. Following his archaeological inquiry, the Cartesian/Euclidean mode was made possible according to a belief in representation and language, which collapsed by the end of the eighteenth century, perhaps marking the emergence of a Babylonian form of thinking. However, as disagreement continues to exist regarding the real period in which a change from one mode to another mode of thought occurred, or even whether we might consider that these different modes of thought still coexist in the current economic thought, Foucault's assumption about discontinuity and incommensurability of epistemes is certainly brought into question. As Dow suggests, previous modes of thought, such as the Cartesian/Euclidean, remain 'instilled in us' (Dow, 1985, p. 10). It would appear that the collapse of representation did not lead to a complete dissolution of an ideal of a mathematical model for knowledge. This is indeed one more argument to support the view that the shifts between epistemes may not be as clear-cut as Foucault implied and, if they are, they may not be immediately obvious and/or absorbed.

4.5   The historiography of economics

As explained by Klaes (2003), the term 'historiography', though etymologically designated as 'the writing of history', has been employed with different meanings: an historical account of the past or the reflection on how historians account for the past. Here it refers to the latter meaning, a methodological reflection on how the history of economic thought has been and/or should be written. Therefore, 'historiography' can be considered as a part of 'methodology'.

Following a general rethinking about historiography in general history, in which Foucault and Kuhn are situated, the 1960s witnessed the emergence in economics of the subfield of 'history of economic thought' (Klaes, 2003, p. 496). In the 1970s, the subdiscipline had a new impulsion motivated by the dissatisfaction of practitioners with the state of affairs of economics (ibid., p. 497), which resulted from a particular increase in the formalist approach. Some economists believe that when economics turned to formalism, it lost its contact with reality and empirical observation. Certainly, the interest in the history of economic thought has developed in the last few decades, as a result of the reflections on the methodology of economics. Some economists believe that economics was well practised in the past and that at some stage this was lost. This is emphasised when, for instance, economists show regret for a turn promoted by the 'Ricardian Vice' in the method of economics, understanding that political economists before Ricardo had presented an empirical and historical approach more adequate to economics today.

One of the main reflections in the historiography of economics has been to consider the context of previous writers. Paraphrasing Weintraub (2002, p. 3) when he describes one possibility of assessing the evolution of the subdiscipline of the history of economics itself, this concern regarding context may be defined as a discussion that should 'engage with the local and contingent circumstances of the evolution of the history of economics by reconstructing its context, or several contexts, in a thick and interesting narrative, perhaps in various voices'.

One major issue regarding this point is how to write the history of the past while under the influence of the present. As Dow (2002b) points out, regarding Hume's case, it is necessary to consider both contexts: the context of the text and that of its interpreters. Introducing Foucault can then substantially add to these reflections, offering his insight regarding 'a history of the present' and providing a framework. It is the role of the intellectual 'to try to isolate within their power of constraint, but also within the contingency of their historical formation, the systems of thought that has become familiar to us, that appear self-evident and are integral with our perceptions, our attitudes, our behaviours' (*OT*, p. 384). Foucault provided a singular and radical perspective, questioning how to investigate the past. As mentioned earlier, he proposed analysing the context of the emergence of any work resulting from a historic configuration that encompassed deep conducive factors, which would then be investigated through the inquiry of a set of relations (the episteme).

The historical awareness that his work offers can be very elucidatory when the return is contemplated as an alternative, for instance. Foucault declared that there is no such thing as a return: 'the history preserves us from that sort of ideology of the return' (Foucault, 1994b, p. 359). It is not possible to go back 'to the old good days', which appears to be the basic view proposed by some currently in economic thought: there was a past that was good and a present that is bad. 'History, and the meticulous interest applied to history, is certainly one of the best defences against this theme of the return' (ibid.). In addition, Foucault argues that it is dangerous to take what just happened as our 'primary enemy' because we tend 'to seek out some cheap form of archaism or some imaginary past forms of happiness that people did not, in fact, have at all' (ibid., p. 357). 'There is in this hatred of the present or the immediate past a dangerous tendency to invoke a completely mythical past' (ibid.). For example, Foucault's history of thought in *The Order of Things* demonstrates that it is not possible to go back in time and think about the present in terms of ontological premises and epistemological devices without considering the problems of language.

Foucault's archaeology has striking similarities to Kuhn's work on the structure of scientific revolutions. The similarities have been noticed within the fields of philosophy and history of ideas since the publication of *The Order of Things* in 1966. The comparison of *The Order of Things* and Thomas Kuhn's *The Structure of Scientific Revolutions* was especially part of what was called by Carrette (2000) the first wave of assessments of Foucault's *The Order of Things* (for example, Caws, 1971, White, 1973 and Leary, 1976) within the philosophy and history of ideas. Nevertheless, although the practitioners of the history of economic thought and methodology promptly absorbed Kuhn's ideas, Foucault's *The Order of Things* has, to some extent, been ignored in economics.

Beyond searching for a basis upon which certain knowledge and theory is made possible, the works of Kuhn and Foucault contain an important common claim, which at the very least has helped to promote a definite change in the relationship between the history and philosophy of science. Their works abandoned the search for an *a priori* fundamental basis and the determinants of science, as had been the case with logical positivism and some of its critics. Both Foucault and Kuhn argued that the way sciences emerge and proceed must be regarded in terms of their own history. Previously, philosophers from Ernst Mach to the logical positivists Popper and Lakatos engaged themselves in explaining the processes of scientific research, aiming to find out the rational development of science in the firm belief that the nature of science could be unveiled through some fundamental criteria and that it was possible to describe and/or find out atemporal procedures followed by scientific inquiry. Foucault and Kuhn, following developments in the field of history, did not accept that type of research agenda. They also opposed the Whig tradition, which represented the history of science as a uniform progression from 'error' to an increasingly refined approximation to the 'truth'. They argued that the history of knowledge had not followed a linear continuity, being paradigms and epistemes, which were in some way exclusive to each moment.

Foucault and Kuhn's conception of history emerged in a period of intense discussion regarding the subject (see Chapter 2 for more information on this). They were convinced that, on a deeper level, knowledge had a certain structure, a regularity, which defines its production. Whilst Foucault in *The Order of Things* called it episteme, Kuhn on the other hand brought about the concept of paradigm in *The Structure of Scientific Revolutions*. Both of these concepts refer to a fundamental arrangement of what is produced in terms of knowledge. Although what exactly these authors meant by these terms has been a question for debate, one is certainly reminiscent of the other.

Foucault and Kuhn worked completely independently of each other, although it is worth adding that Kuhn was certainly aware of the discussions surrounding the thought on history at that time and it is particularly interesting for us to note that he mentioned Alexander Koyré as being one of his influences (Kuhn, 1970, p. 3). Foucault actually made the point that Kuhn was influenced by Canguilhem: 'I did not cite Kuhn, but quoted instead from the historian of science who shaped and inspired his thoughts: G. Canguilhem' (Foucault, 1971c).

However, the similarities that exist between their works are greater than their conception of the history of knowledge. Their systems share important internal similarities and this has led some authors to condemn Foucault for not mentioning Kuhn. In a review of *The Order of Things* for *The New York Times*, George Steiner wrote: 'The notion of *episteme* strikingly recalls Thomas Kuhn's well-known definition of "paradigms". [...] The trouble is that Foucault speaks as if he were a solitary explorer, opening up silent seas' (Steiner, 1971a, original emphasis).

Foucault (1971c) answered Steiner's criticism by declaring that he had only read Kuhn's *The Structure of Scientific Revolutions* in the winter of 1963–4, having already written *The Order of Things*.

It may be possible to see reflexivity here since, following their own beliefs, it could be said that they were sharing the same underlying configuration of thought, which in a sense could be called a new 'paradigm' or, on a deeper level, the same 'episteme'. They were certainly promoting a new 'paradigm' together with others for the historiography of thought. However, they were doing all this according to some conditions of possibility of thought, that is, according to an 'episteme'. Foucault actually wrote about the influence of his own epistemic context on his work (*OT*, p. xiv).

The objective of the following paragraphs is to compare the concepts of 'episteme' and 'paradigm'. Since this has not been explored in great depth, in the fields of philosophy and history of ideas, it is considered that this will form a contribution in the development of such a study through a detailed investigation of some central aspects that contain parallels in Foucault and Kuhn's works. With the probability that they shared both a 'paradigm' and an 'episteme', it is possible to underline some prominent notions that are present in both Foucault and Kuhn's systems: the notion of discontinuity in history, the type of historical approach (internal versus external), the notion of incommensurability, consciousness and intentionality of their main concepts, the scope of analysis, forms of identification and the relationship to other domains of knowledge, together with the importance attached to the role of language. All these notions are fundamental to their systems being able to bring about the concepts of 'episteme' and 'paradigm' and help to provide us with an understanding of their distinctiveness. For this reason, the concepts of 'paradigm' and 'episteme' will be compared in detail as follows.

4.5.1   Etymological meaning

Although neither Foucault nor Kuhn undertook an etymological investigation into the terms 'episteme' and 'paradigm', their great erudition and exigent minds allow us to believe that they were fully aware of their meanings and therefore our study can greatly benefit from such examination.

It is not unusual for the term *episteme* to be associated with knowledge. The ancient Greeks employed it to mean 'knowledge' or 'science'. Aristotle used it in *Metaphysics*, dividing it into *praxis* (knowing how to act), *poiesis* (knowing how to make something) and *theoria* (insight, theoretical knowledge), while Plato meant by it: 'knowledge demonstrable from first principles, in contrast to knowledge of the contingent' (Mautner, 2000). However, Foucault's meaning of the word is clearly distinct and it may be related to a specific meaning originating from the Ionic Greek. In this sense, the word was derived from *epistasthai*, which can be translated as 'over stand', that is, from *epi* – 'over, near' – and *histasthai* – 'to stand' (Etymology Dictionary, 2004). Although the term 'over stand' does not exist as such in the English language, it is possible to explore its meaning, especially by contrasting it with 'understand'. It may be said that 'over stand' refers to something that is over and above all of that which is thought. This would appear to be the meaning that Foucault intended to give to the word, since the 'episteme' in his archaeology was the structure that set the conditions and boundaries for thought within a certain historical and cultural context.

The word *paradigm* is usually perceived as being derived from the Greek *paradeigma*, meaning 'model' or 'pattern'. However, there is a more precise meaning to this Greek word, which is mentioned by Agamben (2002). Literally, 'paradigm' means 'what shows itself beside'. It is therefore significant to say that in its literal meaning 'paradigm' refers to something that is manifest (*para*).

4.5.2   The concepts

The work of Margaret Masterman (1970) is well known for identifying 21 different meanings for the word 'paradigm' given by Kuhn in his *The Structure of Scientific Revolutions*. Kuhn admitted such vagueness and affirmed that most of the differences in meaning were 'due to stylistic inconsistencies (e.g., Newton's Laws are sometimes a paradigm, sometimes parts of a paradigm, and sometimes paradigmatic)' (Kuhn, 1970, pp. 181–2). In the Postscript to the second edition of his book, referring to Masterman's analytic index, Kuhn acknowledged that there was confusion between two distinct notions: 'exemplars' and 'disciplinary matrices'. He redefined 'paradigm' as being a 'disciplinary matrix' and stated that the crucial elements of it were 'exemplars'. He explains that 'paradigm' could refer to the following:

1 'Disciplinary matrix': 'the entire constellation of beliefs, values, techniques, and so on shared by the members of a given community'. This is the 'sociological' meaning of 'paradigm' (Kuhn, 1970, p. 175) – 'disciplinary' because it is followed by the practitioners of a particular discipline (who form a type of 'invisible college') and 'matrix', which is composed of ordered elements.

2 'Exemplar': 'one sort of element in that constellation, the concrete
 puzzle-solutions which employed as models or examples, can replace
 explicit rules as a basis for the solution of the remaining puzzles of
 normal science', which Kuhn calls 'exemplary past achievements'
 (ibid.).

He stressed that this second meaning was the 'deeper' one and that, in
this sense, the 'paradigm' could not be 'subjective' or 'intuitive', instead
being 'systematic', 'time tested' and 'corrigible' (ibid.). In short, for
Kuhn, exemplars are concrete problem solutions, which are accepted
by the scientific community as being 'paradigmatic', and disciplinary
matrices are a mix of accepted abstract generalisations, a shared commitment to beliefs in particular models, shared values and shared examples (for example, Aristotle's physics, Newton's principles and so on).

The episteme, as seen in the previous chapter, is an unconscious
structure that defines the conditions of possibility of knowing within
a certain culture and at a given moment in time, and can be identified
a posteriori by the conception of representation (associated with the
experience of language), the relations between the same and the other,
the role of time (history) and space as a foreground and/or background
for knowing the subject matter, the conception of man (object and/or
subject of knowledge) and his finitude within an age (including the
thought-unthought relationship).

4.5.3   Internal or external history

It is worth considering the possibility of classifying Kuhn and Foucault's
approaches in terms of the 'external' and 'internal' categories of history.
'External history' is usually conceived as the approach in which the
historian is concerned with the social, political, technological, psychological and all the social circumstances that are exterior to knowledge
itself and influence the course of science. The 'internalist' historian
focuses on the internal logic of a science, on the history of conjec-
tures, experiments, theories and individuals that promoted scientific
changes.

Kuhn can be said to be operating in both an 'internalist' and 'externalist' history. It is even worth mentioning his views regarding this
distinction. In his paper 'History of science' (Kuhn, 1979), he addressed
the issue by calling attention to the necessity to work on the relations
between these two approaches. He wrote that for years he had been calling for 'efforts to bring them together' (ibid., p. 123), although without
success and he went on to denounce the lack of models that could

help 'internalist' historians to interact with external approaches. In this reference, he mentions Foucault as a philosopher that could 'provide some help' (ibid., p. 124).

Kuhn was right: if it were possible to sort out Foucault's work in terms of this distinction, then it would certainly be classified within a certain type of category, being as a result of the investigations into the relationship between 'external' and 'internal' history; that is, that Foucault's *The Order of Things* and *The Archaeology of Knowledge* do not fit into any of these particular categories, although his work does provide elements for investigating their relationship. For Foucault, the 'interiority' of thought is a doubling of what is outside of thought (Carrette, 2000, p. 3). Foucault's archaeology is much more interested in what is said and how it is said than who said it or the social environment of who said it. For example, he does not take events like the emergence of capitalism or the French Revolution to explain changes in economic thought. He did not see the 'strategies', that is, 'themes and theories' of an age as a 'hypocritical translation of an interest masquerading under the pretext of a theory' (*AK*, p. 77). Referring specifically to the economic thought of the seventeenth and eighteenth centuries, he declared: 'the Analysis of Wealth is more than the conflict of interest between a bourgeoisie that has become a land-owing class, expressing its economic or political demands through the Physiocrats, and a commercial bourgeoisie that demands protectionist or liberal measures through the Utilitarists' (*AK*, p. 77). He was not concerned with the biographies of authors who wrote profound texts. His archaeology is not based upon the individuals or their particular achievements and puts little emphasis on dating scientific events by means of the calendar (Kusch, 1991, p. 8), at least those that are usually taken for granted by historians.

Foucault was attempting to employ a way of thinking that he had already explored in his work on Blanchot (Foucault, 1987) and which he called 'the thought from outside', which is particularly noticeable in *The Archaeology of Knowledge*. This has been regarded as the search for 'a language without subjectivity, without humanistic constructions' (Carrette, 2000, pp. 88–9). Although Foucault looks at the process of knowing 'from outside', he cannot be called an 'externalist' in relation to the above meaning. He was not applying the techniques of psychology or sociology to a certain branch of knowledge. His 'gaze' was indeed 'historical-philosophical' (see O'Farrell, 1989). In *The Order of Things*, it is worth noting that Foucault was looking for the conditions that made the emergence of economics, biology and linguistics possible, since they formed the basis upon which came the emergence of the human sciences. His goal is to find out the 'discursive mode' that is shared by all the main texts of these disciplines in a specific age. Another way of distinguishing between these two thinkers is to suggest that, whilst Kuhn on the one hand focused his efforts on finding out regularities that formed the basis for a 'corpus of theses', Foucault turned his attention to the 'system of possibility' of some branches of knowledge (Hacking, 1979, p. 40). Foucault was much more ambitious than Kuhn in this respect.

4.5.4   Domains of knowledge

One of the major differences between the systems of Foucault and Kuhn was that, whilst Kuhn spoke exclusively about natural sciences and always stressed that point, Foucault worked on the archaeology of human sciences. In order to do so, Foucault included within his enquiry what he termed as 'empirical domains': one natural science (biology), one social science (economics) and a 'counterscience' in his conception (linguistic). Foucault considered linguistic to be a 'counterscience' because, like psychoanalysis and ethnology, it threatened the endeavour and existence of the human sciences.

The fact that Foucault focused his attention on the human sciences and that he was looking 'from outside' at different fields of knowledge *en bloc* distinguishes his approach from all those that have preceded him. As he remarks: 'In *The Order of Things* I have attempted to mark the play of the correlations, analogies, and differences within several domains of knowledge in a given epoch (theory of language, natural history, political economy, theory of representation)' (Foucault, 1971b, p. 60).

Foucault was interested in philosophical questions related to the way in which a given historical context creates some intellectual interests, making no distinction according to the traditional divisions of science (natural sciences, human sciences and social sciences). He was puzzled by the fact that some domains of knowledge had emerged at almost the same time and this is made clear in *The Order of Things* by his attention to the emergence of the human sciences. However, in order to grasp the epistemic configuration of their emergence, Foucault was also able to identify a common underlying structure defining thought in economics, biology and the study of language.

Kuhn always emphasised that his work focused on the natural sciences, in particular physics, declaring his surprise at the interest aroused towards *The Structure of Scientific Revolutions* from those in the social sciences (Kuhn, 1970). Indeed, he declared that 'paradigm' could not be a concept suitable for social sciences: 'it remains an open question what parts of social science have yet acquired such paradigms at all' (ibid., p. 15). However, this has been disputed and it has been argued that there was a lack of self-understanding on his part. For example, Hacking (1984) suggests that although Kuhn referred to and indeed underlined the fact that he was only approaching the natural sciences, his system was not suitable only for the social sciences but, more importantly, did not apply itself to the natural sciences. This has also been considered as an explanation for the fact that *The Structure of Scientific Revolutions* has drawn little attention from natural scientists, instead being more popular among social scientists.

4.5.5   Discontinuity, incommensurability and the explanation of shifts between 'paradigms' and 'epistemes'

Both Foucault and Kuhn's theories are still connected by the notion of discontinuity and the idea of incommensurability. As previously noted, both Kuhn and Foucault's notions were derived from the influence of historical philosophers such as Bachelard and Canguilhem.

For example, regarding 'revolutions', Fuller (2000) refers to the similarity of interests between Kuhn and some French historical philosophers such as Bachelard, Canguilhem and Foucault, stating that they shared the common view of scientific changes through 'radical disjunction'. However, Fuller also advocates the French historical philosophers as being particularly interested in the 'ruptures in worldview'. Although there can be a disagreement regarding the use of the term 'worldview' when referring to Foucault's system, this statement by Fuller conveys the point. Foucault, following in the footsteps of the aforementioned French thinkers, can be considered as being more ambitious than Kuhn, since he was looking for more radical transitions. Fuller continues to suggest that Kuhn would be in agreement with the idea that Foucault's work captures the most radical transitions. Fuller is therefore suggesting that Kuhn would acknowledge the view that 'episteme' is a broader 'conception' of reality than 'paradigm'.

Hence, the 'discontinuity' has quite a distinctive meaning in both Foucault's and Kuhn's systems. With Foucault, the 'discontinuity' of history is total and means that each moment in time and space is marked by a singular arrangement of the conditions that allowed thought, and therefore the knowledge of different subjects.

It is usually suggested that both Kuhn and Foucault referred to 'revolutions', although Foucault did not employ the word 'revolution' and even preferred to use the word 'transformation' (Foucault, 2000a, p. 222). As White (1973, p. 27) states:

> [E]pistemes [...] do not succeed one another dialectically nor do they aggregate. They simply appear alongside one another – catastrophically, as it were, without rhyme or reason. Thus, the appearance of a new 'human science' does not represent a 'revolution' in thought or consciousness. A new science of life, wealth, or language does not rise up against its predecessors, it simply crystallises alongside of it, filling up the 'space' left by the 'discourse' of earlier sciences.

The notion of 'revolution' is not in Foucault's archaeology of epistemes, since it could be associated with the idea of a change in all the discourses of an age. *The Order of Things* refers to an 'interdiscursive configuration', a 'region of interpositivities', which, as previously mentioned, does not concern a worldview that is valid for all fields of knowledge.

Differing from Kuhn, Foucault, at least in *The Order of Things* and *The Archaeology of Knowledge*, does not try to explain the discontinuity of history and it may be argued that in the genealogy, Foucault was looking for explanations, particularly through the power/knowledge relations. In the archaeology, Foucault does not look for explanations in the shifts between the epistemes and, more intriguingly, why the previous epistemes should remained intelligible to the subsequent epistemes. It is suggested that he examined the shifts between epistemes synchronically rather than diachronically.

Anomalies are hard to recognise in both Kuhn's and Foucault's systems. However, as Kermode (1973, pp. 9–10) argues, 'Kuhn explains such resistance, and the ultimate acceptance of the rejected theory, in psychological and social terms, whereas Foucault has a much more abstract model of the constraints that act within discourse itself'. Foucault limited himself to depicting the two sides of change: before and after. He was well aware of this problem and as mentioned in the previous chapter (recapping on the definitions of the categories of external and internal history) it would be poignant to point out what appears to be the epistemic transformations resulting from something other than exclusively external and internal events. Foucault emphasises that it is impossible to move outside the tacit system of the episteme and it does not take a 'crisis' to explain changes, although he does point out the moments of 'fatigue' of two epistemes: the classical and the modern (Merquior, 1991, p. 37). As mentioned in the previous chapter, if we consider the Kuhnian notion of 'normal' science, then the archaeology was a study about the 'normality' of knowledge and the search for its conditions of possibility.

There is still an important distinction between 'paradigm' and 'episteme' concerning the discontinuity of history. A new 'paradigm' is somehow related to the old one since, for Kuhn, the roots of 'revolution' and the arising of the new paradigm are always in the limitations of the previous paradigm. Foucault remarks that a new episteme is completely distinct from the previous one, although we can argue that he actually recognises some overlaps, a point that will be explored below.

As for incommensurability, there are important distinctions between Foucault and Kuhn. In Foucault's system, 'it is not theories that are incommensurable, but bodies of discourse, systems of possibility' (Hacking, 1979, p. 49). The incommensurability between Aristotelian and Newtonian theories is not due to different systems of conscious belief, but to an underlying deep system of possibility of thinking. Kuhn meant by 'incommensurability' the characteristic of a paradigm in which scientists belonging to different paradigms, and thus advocating different theories, produce totally distinct theoretical terms or different meanings for the same terms. Kuhn first believed that translation could be the solution to this problem. However, as Kuhn concluded in his latest works, there is no metalanguage in terms of which scientists of different paradigms could rationally discuss (Kuhn, 1999, p. 33). He continued to state that his thoughts relating to the problem had evolved through four stages. Firstly, he stated that the incommensurability was always partial, that is, that it was 'restricted to small sets of interrelated terms, ordinarily terms that must be learned together' (ibid., p. 34). Secondly, he concluded that language imposed constraints and so incommensurability involved more than a gestalt-switch. Thirdly, he held the view that language involved two processes, learning and translation, since even if languages can be learnt, the translation can remain impossible. Kuhn realised at this point that the case was not only that a proposition could be true in one language and false in another, but that the problem also extended to that of a true proposition within one paradigm, and how it too could not be expressed within another paradigm. Therefore, incommensurability exceeded the limits of hermeneutics. Finally, he observed that even an enrichment of language itself could not solve the problem, since there was an important relation between language and different ontological perceptions.

It would appear that the problem of incommensurability provides us with an important insight into understanding the distinctions between the systems of Foucault and Kuhn. Kuhn's final conclusion, mentioned above, provides us with a slight suggestion that perhaps Foucault was closer to an answer. Kuhn realised that the problem was not only in the internal usage of language within a paradigm. There can be 'incommensurability' related to the capacity of language to incorporate the knowledge of the world. In this sense, Foucault, while adopting the view that the conception of language is a central defining aspect of the episteme, was giving an indication as to why incommensurability can emerge.

At this stage, the point relating to discontinuity has to be addressed. Foucault argues that each age has one and only one episteme, whilst Kuhn in the later version of his theory concluded that 'any period of scientific development is marked by a large number of overlapping and interpenetrating "paradigms"', and that 'some of these may be incommensurable but certainly not all of them are' (Blaug, 1980, p. 141). Nevertheless, despite Foucault's radical position, epistemes also seem to overlap or to operate like parallel strands. Foucault even states that some elements of one episteme can be found in different moments in time and space, these having been referred to in the final comments of the previous chapter. For example, in economic thought, Foucault argues that Adam Smith was in the transition between classical and modern epistemes.

4.5.6 Consciousness and intentionality

It appears that an essential distinction between the notions of 'paradigm' and 'episteme' lies in their degree of consciousness. For Foucault, 'epistemes' are always unconscious, emerging and operating without human intention. Foucault was looking for the unconsciousness of knowledge. The 'episteme' is not only unconscious but may not even be articulated in thought by the occasion of its dominance. Although 'paradigm' seems to follow manifest or 'unconscious' elements, shifts between paradigms, that is, revolutions, occurred because there was a period of growing consciousness of the problems and limitations related to the paradigm in vogue.

We can continue to comment on Foucault's system and the signs, especially linguistic signs, which exert a fundamental role in knowledge, preceding and conducting the activity of thinking. Nevertheless, man only perceives the changes in signs and language after they happen. Therefore, differing from the concept of paradigm, changes of episteme occur without being perceived and so they are much more complex in terms of establishing their motivations.

Kuhn is not explicit about the (un)consciousness of a paradigm, although it appears that he did include unconscious elements within the wide definition of 'paradigm' as a 'disciplinary matrix'. However, when he mentions these elements, he would seem to be referring to 'intuitive' elements, stating that they can become manifest. Indeed, in the Postscript of his *The Structure of Scientific Revolutions* he stated that he did not mean by 'intuitive' that it was something 'individual' or 'unanalysable' (Kuhn, 1970, p. 191). He explains that he does not mean that it is not 'potentially fully explicable in terms of neural-cerebral mechanism' (ibid., p. 192). Kuhn is saying that individuals have stimuli, which can and will be interpreted according to the group they are part of, producing sensations in accordance with their group's language, experience and culture. In this sense, he declares, the stimuli will become exemplars. Therefore, it may be possible that a 'paradigm' has 'intuitive' elements, which manifest themselves by the occasion of perceptions; there is a process of interpretation, 'a deliberative process by which we choose among alternatives as we do not in perception itself' (ibid., p. 94). In this process, 'we do seek and deploy criteria and rules'. Kuhn is even more emphatic, saying that he was 'opposing [...] the attempt, traditional since Descartes although not before, to analyse perception as an interpretative process and as an unconscious version of what we do after we have perceived' (ibid., p. 195). Therefore, he argues that knowledge results from a 'neural process that transforms stimuli to sensations' according to a process of transference through education and according to a choice of what is 'more effective than its historical competitors in a group's current environment' and which 'is subject to change both through further education and through the discovery of misfits with the environment' (ibid., p. 196).

Hence, if we are to consider either Masterman's study of the concept of 'paradigm' or Kuhn's later reformulation of it, then the following point can be stressed: its 'consciousness'. This is a great difference compared to the episteme, which is unconscious and never becomes manifest in the scientific community at the period of its dominance. Regardless of which concept of paradigm we take (exemplar or disciplinary matrix), it continues to refer to something on 'the surface of knowledge', from a Foucauldian perspective. Paradigms, within the context of normal science, are frameworks that are accepted by the scientific community. If it is not very apparent to the scientists during the period of normal science, then it has to become so by the time of 'revolutions'. New paradigms simply take place after a long process of accumulation of anomalies along with unsolved puzzles. Scientists have to perceive these problems in order to promote the 'revolution'.

This reinforces the idea that 'episteme' is anterior to 'paradigm' and, following Foucault's archaeological approach, the 'episteme' is at a deeper layer of knowledge and gives rise to different paradigms.

4.5.7 Language

Language is a fundamental element in both Kuhn's and Foucault's systems. A linguistic problem inspired Kuhn in the thinking that led to *The Structure of Scientific Revolutions*. As he explained, it emerged while he was still a graduate student and he needed to read Aristotle in order to give a few lectures on Galileo. He stated that he only started to understand why Aristotle appeared so absurd and so incomprehensible to him when he thought in terms of language: 'All at once the text (Aristotle's) made sense to me, but only if I changed my way of reading, altering some of the concepts – the meanings of some of the words – that I, coming from a later age, had brought with me to the text' (Kuhn, 1999, p. 33).

In this we recognise that Kuhn clearly acknowledges the same problem as Foucault when he stresses that the events of history can only be understood in terms of what is contemporaneous with it, which is indeed the 'history of the present' for Foucault.

Furthermore, Kuhn declared that it was also his attempt to understand Aristotle that led him first to the problem of incommensurability (Kuhn, 1999, p. 33). Kuhn not only defined incommensurability as a problem of language but also believed that translation should be the solution. It was only in his latest works that he concluded that incommensurability transcended the problem of language and had to be seen in terms of differing ontological assumptions.

Likewise, language is also the foundational of Foucault's system. As Hacking declares, *The Order of Things* was:

> among other things, a story of abrupt transitions in what is said. One of these breaks, for whose description Foucault is rightly admired, is a matter of language. General Grammar became philology. Language ceased to be the double means of representation: double because words and sentences were considered to represent ideas and mental discourse, while able to represent things and facts. With the advent of philology, language was no longer studied primarily as a system of representation. Individual languages were treated as historical entities, and the focus of attention was grammar and word formation. (Hacking, 1988, p. 266)

Language is therefore a very important element in both Foucault's and Kuhn's systems. However, Foucault takes the conception of language of each age as a means to apprehend the laws that govern the discourse and thus knowledge, and his concern is with language as a semiotic structure. As mentioned in the previous chapter, language is fundamental to Foucault's argument in *The Order of Things*. He argues that during the sixteenth century (pre-classical episteme) language was part of the system of universal resemblance and analogy. Language was one more element created by God and through it man understood the signatures of God (resemblances). Language could even be interpreted as a signature of God. This transparency of language was not lost in the classical period and although sign and signified separated, and words and things were no longer linked by transcendental reason, language maintained its power to say things, although it should be submitted to an ordering, following the establishment of a 'mathesis' as a 'general science of order'. Knowing was to build a well-formulated language and this changed at the end of the eighteenth century, when language lost its transparency and became an object of study, rather than a medium of knowledge.

Perhaps one way of understanding the relationship between 'episteme' and language is through the understanding of the relation between the archaeology and hermeneutics. Hacking (1979) refers to this matter, providing some insight. He argues that Foucault's archaeology is 'the very opposite of hermeneutics'. The argument suggests that, recalling the etymology of the word 'hermeneutics' derived from Hermes, the messenger of the gods, hermeneutics 'is the art of interpreting what Hermes brought'. That is, hermeneutics looks for the meaning that is beneath the sentences that have been written 'if not by God, at least by the past'. Archaeology is the opposite since it does not want to interpret the texts, but to find out and to show the relationships 'between sentences that explain why just these (relationships) were uttered and those were not' (Hacking, 1979, p. 45). In addition to finding the meaning, the archaeologist looks for what it is, from the outside, that is systematised and allowed and that renders some sentences connected in order to say something. Hacking quotes Foucault: 'What counts in the things said by men is not so much what they may have thought or the extent to which these things represent their thoughts, as that which systematizes them from the outset' (Foucault, quoted in Hacking, 1979, p. 45).

4.5.8 Identifying the regularities

In relation to 'paradigm', there are two basic ways of identifying it, depending on the intuitive or manifest nature of its elements. As for the intuitive nature, it could be unveiled through an investigation of the conventions, traditions and ideology that influences the scientific community in relation to the manifest elements, through an inquiry into the classic works, textbooks, tools of research, organising principles, accepted concrete problems and solutions, shared examples and so on.

In contrast to the beliefs of Kuhn, Foucault searched for regularities underlying knowledge, pursuing them through a survey of a vast terrain of discourse. More specifically, Foucault believed that the knowledge in each age could be regarded as a theory of signs and representations and, given that the most important signs are linguistic, he turned his study to the theory of language. Even the ideas of 'author' and oeuvre were scrutinised and denied by Foucault. For example, when he mentioned authors, he employed expressions like 'the figure whom we call Hume' or 'the individuals we term Hobbes, Berkeley, Hume, or Condillac' (*OT*, p. 63). He did this to emphasise how Hobbes, Berkeley, Hume and Condillac as individuals were the result of some conditions of possibility, which could be discerned through the analysis of the discourse of his age.

One other significant difference between the systems of Foucault and Kuhn was that the 'episteme', in contrast to the 'paradigm', could only be unveiled *ex post*. Those under its aegis could not know it.

4.5.9   Epistemology, sociology and psychology

One remarkable distinction that can be made between the systems of Kuhn and Foucault is that Kuhn was essentially committed to the epistemological tradition, in the sense that he aimed to uncover how rationality operated in pursuing knowledge. This does not mean that he believed in finding the truth. In contrast to Foucault's *The Order of Things*, Kuhn is attempting to establish how scientists proceed in their search for knowing. He wants to know how the scientific community applies the cognitive apparatus, launching a sociopsychological gaze, so to speak, at the way in which scientists proceed. For example, Kuhn (1977) takes the case of a child in a zoo learning how to differentiate between swans, geese and ducks for the first time. He explains that the child first discovered that they existed through his father, who was also teaching him the differences. Kuhn used this example to explain the concept of 'exemplars' and how the processing of knowledge formed a part of a socialisation procedure. He explains that at the moment the child was given some 'exemplars' by his father, this could then lead to the establishing of certain rules which, once defined, could lead to knowledge even without the necessity of perceiving similarities.

Foucault's archaeology is concerned with the conditions that make discourse possible, these being prior to the development of theories. For Kuhn, science is a cultural phenomenon in the sense that scientists produce theories according to a paradigm that is followed by the research community where he is present. In his system, scientists follow a conceptual network of their cultural and intellectual environment and a sociopsychological inquiry provides the elements to unveil the paradigm that is conducting the scientific community. Foucault's approach differs in this context, since he looks for the rules that underpin the discourse independently of subjectivities.

We can take the example quoted by Naughton (1982) in order to understand this distinction. He says that in order to understand the concept of 'heat' in Sadi Carnot's theory, we could not try to understand it through the modern concept of entropy. We should relate his concept of 'heat' to the usage conventionally employed in the texts to which we know he had access. This is a Kuhnian approach. The context of a concept has to be thought of in terms of the set of theoretical beliefs, accepted standards, procedures and exemplars (which together form the paradigm) taken by the scientific community of that moment. Foucault would look at the same context, trying to establish why the thinking regarding 'heat' became possible and whose conditions allowed the thought regarding 'heat' and its regarded thought to be interpreted in a very specific way and according to a certain concept of signs. He searched for the 'order' of knowledge and the rules underpinning the formulation of such a concept concerning the concept of language and representation. That is, Foucault's gaze was not sociological or psychological, in the sense that he was looking from 'outside' the event (the development of the concept of heat by Carnot), independently of what was being developed by the subjectivity of that moment.

Another good example that takes into account their distinctive approaches can be typified by reflecting on 'formalisation'. Kuhn declared:

> Any account of the cognitive apparatus of a scientific community may reasonably be asked to tell us something about the way in which the group's members, in advance of *directly* relevant empirical *evidence*, identify the special formalism appropriate to a particular problem, especially to a new problem. (Kuhn, 1977, p. 301, original emphasis)

This statement gives us a clear idea as to how Kuhn approaches the issue of 'formalisation' in his investigation. He regards formalism as a tool to be used in the investigation of a given science. Foucault looked at 'formalisation' as being defined by some historical conditions derived from a new conception of man's finitude. Once again, he is looking 'from outside' at different sciences, trying to find out why and how the formalism operates across different disciplines.

4.6   Final remarks

This chapter emphasised that Foucault's archaeology shares the same fundamental question as other current approaches in economic methodology and argued in favour of a Foucauldian system and perspective to provide important reflections for both the methodology and historiography of economics.

Thinking in terms of three great strands in the history of the methodology of economics (the thought regarding the method and scientific status of economics through the influence and inspiration of the philosophy of science; the currents that emerged as a result of the loss of faith in methodological individualism and the breakdown of the received view; and the studies on language and discourse), Foucault's archaeology was considered as having similar concerns, while offering a distinct and enriched perspective. Although his approach may even be confused with the current rhetorical studies in economics, his archaeology actually investigates how some rhetorical devices are brought into being and can be privileged amongst others. In a manner that was clearly different from the usual rhetorical approach in economics, Foucault offered a distinctive theory of discourse as a framework to accomplish such studies. Moreover, his history of epistemology has enlarged our awareness as to how these studies should be developed. Perhaps this will also help to demonstrate the need for economists to go beyond rhetorical self-awareness and to consider language in the context of the post-linguistic turn. Another intention of this chapter was to draw attention to the important contributions of Foucault's system regarding the consideration of a 'return' to the past, along with his project of enhancing the level of awareness of what we are today through an archaeology of the past, which provides the insight into what has prevented us from contemplating old, alternative approaches.

Concerning the historiography of economics, Foucault had a very important contribution to offer which regarded the thoughts applied to investigating the context of historical writings. In respect of this, his notion of 'episteme' was considered to be very close to the Kuhnian conception of 'paradigm', and therefore the relationship between both Foucault and Kuhn's system was investigated further. Although they were clearly referring to very different levels of investigation, this comparison can provide the elements for a better comprehension of Foucault's proposals.

Utilising the claims of their own systems, the many similarities established between the works of Kuhn and Foucault have resulted from the fact that they might well be sharing the same 'paradigm' in the field of history, while at a deeper level maintaining the same 'epistemic' context. This certainly provides a suggestion of reflexivity in their works. The fundamental question was the same to both of them and they mentioned the same issues relating to knowledge, although they provided different systems of explanation.

The similarities result from the same conception – how we should think about history – which followed the course of thinking about the subject by other historian philosophers, such as Koyré, Bachelard and Canguilhem, who also talked about discontinuity, non-progress and incommensurability. However, Foucault and Kuhn turned to the history of knowledge with very distinct purposes in mind. In terms of the categories of 'external' and 'internal' history, while Kuhn was practising both of these, the same could not be said of Foucault, whose work could not be attributed to either of them. Therefore, this can be summed up as being a major difference between the concepts of 'episteme' and 'paradigm', which is derived from the distinct differences in approach to their formulations.

Kuhn followed the tradition of epistemological research and believed that techniques of psychology and sociology could provide the elements to unveil how the scientific community works in pursuing knowledge. Paradigms always refer to a given scientific community and they can be understood through an investigation of the intuitive and apparent beliefs, conventions and procedures of a certain scientific community. Paradigms and shifts between paradigms can be explained. Even if there are unconscious elements defining their behaviour, they can still be uncovered by an attentive mind, provided they have the correct techniques. This is even possible at the moment when the paradigms are dominant. As for the unconscious elements, they have to become apparent by the occasion of revolutions.

Foucault's approach is more ambitious than that of Kuhn, since he looks at a wider set of practices and discourses, pursuing them to find out the underlying unconscious factors that govern the way in which man thinks. He is not interested in analysing the past product of scientific investigation in order to understand how scientists proceeded in their search for the truth. He is not interested in characterising the internal procedures of a science. In his archaeology, he launched a gaze, which he called 'from outside', at the human sciences *en bloc*. He wanted to find out why they emerged and concluded that he needed to understand how man became an object of knowledge, from which the investigation into the emergence of economics, biology and philology became necessary. He had to look at these branches of knowledge collectively. Foucault also stresses that the 'episteme' is unconscious and that it never becomes conscious for the practitioners of knowledge. It seems that Foucault believed that the episteme could only be unveiled by philosophers looking 'from outside' of the science and he finally states that this is only possible *ex post*. Furthermore, Foucault was cautious in as much as he did not try to explain the shifts between the epistemes. However, he did declare that such an explanation was very complex and that, even if it could be formulated, it would never be definite.

Therefore, while it could be said that Kuhn was dealing with *connaissance*, Foucault wanted to understand *savoir* and, because of that, he turned his attention to *connaissance*.

Language is a very important element for both Foucault and Kuhn. However, they both consider language from a very distinct perspective. For example, Foucault takes the theory of language during the seventeenth and eighteenth centuries as a structure to understand economic thought. What is important for him was how the concept of language, at a certain moment, determines if and how man could represent the world, which he refers to as 'the experience of language'. Certainly, the focus is the power of the language to represent things, the relation between words and things. Kuhn sees language as an important factor to comprehend the difference between paradigms, although it appears that he eventually concluded that language was much more important than that. He stated that the problem of incommensurability transcended a problem of translation and concluded that the relation between the ontological assumptions and language determined different paradigms. At this point Kuhn touched on the same approach to language as Foucault, relating epistemology to ontology in order to identify different systems of ordering language (words) and perceptions of reality (things) – epistemes.

The concepts of 'paradigm' and 'episteme' indeed have something in common. They result from the search to understand the underlying structure that determines the way in which knowledge emerges and proceeds. However, 'paradigm' refers to surface effects compared to the 'episteme'. If the history of knowledge is considered in archaeological terms, the 'episteme' is at a deeper level. The 'episteme' is anterior to the 'paradigm' or 'paradigms'. The paradigm is much more related to practice than to the scientific collective unconscious. While Kuhn's paradigm is shared by a group of researchers, Foucault's episteme is much more widespread and evolves much more slowly. Epistemic shifts are not gestalt-switches in the same way as changes of paradigms are in Kuhn's theory. Thinking in terms of gestalt-switches, the episteme can be regarded as the conditions that lead to different perceptions of the gestalt.

One other comparison that must be emphasised is the aspect of 'epistemes' and 'paradigms' being unique and specific to a given moment in time. As discussed in the previous chapter and in opposition to Foucault's belief, it appears that epistemes intersect and/or overlap. Kuhn contemplated the same characteristic regarding paradigms and, as such, it is certainly worth analysing the following statement by Toulmin:

> If we are to make the theory of paradigms and revolutions fit the historical evidence [...] (w)e must face the fact that paradigm-switches are never as complete as the fully-fledged definition implies: that rival paradigms never really amount to entire alternative world views; and that intellectual discontinuities on the theoretical level of science conceal underlying continuities at a deeper methodological level. This done, we must ask ourselves whether the use of the term 'revolution' for such conceptual changes is not itself a rhetorical exaggeration. (Toulmin, 1972, pp. 105–6)

It could be that the understanding of the 'underlying continuities at a deeper methodological level' that Toulmin is referring to could be considered in an archaeological investigation of 'epistemes'. Although epistemic shifts may not occur according to a definite clear-cut strategy, they certainly comprise conceptions that are more fundamental and last for longer periods than a paradigm does. As will be discussed in the next chapter, 'mercantilism' and 'physiocracy' may be seen as different paradigms, but there was only one epistemic configuration underlying them. However, in the case of the shift of paradigm to the classical thought in economics, an epistemic-switch was also occurring. Adam Smith certainly promoted a paradigmatic shift while also representing a figure in the transition from the classical to modern system of thought. The next chapter will investigate the history of economic thought since the sixteenth century in terms of 'paradigms' and 'epistemes', exploring and assessing Foucault's archaeology of political economy in *The Order of Things*.

5
Political Economy as a Paradigmatic and Epistemic Shift

5.1 Introduction

This chapter explores Foucault's archaeology of knowledge through an investigation of his main claims regarding the rethinking of the history of economic thought. In particular, it analyses how he interpreted the epistemic configuration of economic thought in the classical age (mercantilism in the seventeenth and eighteenth centuries and physiocracy), followed by the transition into the modern episteme with Adam Smith and the emergence of the 'modern' political economy with the theory of David Ricardo.

This presents a follow-up to the comparison made between Kuhn's notion of 'paradigm' and Foucault's concept of 'episteme' presented in the previous chapter. The intention is not only to investigate more accurately the application of their two perspectives to the historiography of economics, but also to stress the importance attached to venturing forward and beyond the point of simply trying to establish how economic ideas evolved through an internal logic of the discipline. Given the familiarity of economists with the notion of 'paradigm', it is suggested that such lines of investigation can only enhance the comprehension of Foucault's proposals.

It is argued that while the mercantilists and physiocrats were producing different theories and following different paradigms, they were also thinking in accordance with the same structure, which provided the same perception of the basic signs (regarding wealth, exchange, money and trade) and followed the same concept of language derived from their 'age of representation'. Adam Smith is the main instigating character in the history of economic thought, since his writings not only represented a change of paradigm but also a shift on the epistemic context. Although his economic system was depicted according to a network of representations, which are identifiable in the classic way of thinking, it contains elements that indicate the emergence of modern economic thought. Foucault's representation of David Ricardo is explored, underlining some of the fundamental changes in Ricardo's theory which placed him in a new form of thought.

Following some final comments, the conclusion of this chapter intends to assess some of the main critiques that are usually raised against Foucault's system in the case of economics, while drawing particular attention to the great potential available in applying Foucault's perspective and accomplishments to a rethinking of the history of economic thought.

5.2 Mercantilism, physiocracy and political economy as paradigms

Although the history of economic thought from the beginning of the seventeenth century to the end of the eighteenth century had followed only one epistemic configuration in Foucault's system, a brief survey relating to some of the most important texts on the subject suggests that in the Kuhnian sense, it comprised different paradigms.

As literature on history of economic thought usually recognises, 'mercantilism' is difficult to classify as a 'school of thought', essentially because of the lack of a 'system' or articulated group of theories. The term first acquired significance with Adam Smith, who identified two systems before him, 'the commercial system' or 'mercantile system' and 'the system of agriculture', summarised as 'mercantilism' and 'physiocracy', respectively. It is usually believed that mercantilism was a group of reflections created by some practical men who had made a common claim and who were either merchants or administrators linked to the state. Their central objective was to find out how to increase the wealth and power of the state and/or of the merchants. Mercantilists emphasised the acquisition of money through a favourable trade balance, which was thoroughly debated and became known as 'positive balance of trade theory'.

These main characteristics of their writings have led the most influential writers in the history of economic thought to conceive that they shared a set of common economic and political viewpoints that allow us to see them as following 'the same paradigm'. Blaug (1997, p. 10), for example, writes that they had 'a certain doctrinal thread', and a 'common theoretical core' and Screpanti and Zamagni (1993, p. 23) declare that the mercantilists shared 'a certain homogeneity to the various national economic policies'. This may also have started with Smith, who already pointed out all these main characteristics of mercantilism. Other great historians of mercantilism, although diverse in opinion concerning some specific conclusions, appear to have corroborated Smith's first characterisation of the main issues discussed by the mercantilists (for instance, Heckscher, 1955 and more recently Magnusson, 1994).

One central and most noted characteristic of 'mercantilism' was that 'money was wealth'. Almost all mercantilists saw money as a *nervus rerum*, 'the life of commerce', 'the vital spirit of trade', 'like muck' (Blaug, 1997, p. 11). This has established a criticism that they confused 'money' with 'wealth'. This was emphasised by Smith, who stated that that was the only form of wealth for these men. However, this hypothesis has been rejected in more recent research as being a view too absurd to be held by anyone. Magnusson (2003) argues that for the mercantilists, from the beginning of seventeenth century onwards, wealth was always the result of production and consumption. Magnusson quotes Davenant, who wrote in 1699: 'Gold and silver are indeed the Measure of Trade, but that the Spring and Original of it, in all nations is the Natural or Artificial Product of the Country; that is to say, what this Land or what this Labour and Industry produces' (Davenant, quoted in Magnusson, 2003, p. 53).

Rotwein (1955, pp. xiii–xiv) argues, for example, that mercantilists wrote as if they were making this identification, although 'among a substantial number of mercantilists money was not desired in itself but due mainly to its beneficial effects on trade', such as for 'driving trade'. Rotwein argues that money was still regarded as the determinant of interest rates and so it was necessary to increase its supply in order to have lower production costs, therefore enabling the producer and merchant to compete on terms that are more favourable compared to foreigners.

Regarding this issue, it has been noticed that it is important to separate the 'mercantilists' of the sixteenth century from those of the seventeenth and eighteenth centuries. According to Screpanti and Zamagni (1993), for instance, during the sixteenth century, mercantilists wrote as if they had made an association between money and wealth. They are called 'bullionists'. This appears to have changed towards the end of the sixteenth century. Smith had even conceded the fact that authors such as Thomas Mun and John Locke referred to wealth as not only being gold and silver, but that it also included land, houses, consumable goods (Blaug, 1997, p. 11). In the more sophisticated form, as Blaug points out (ibid.), 'mercantilism' did not confuse money with capital (as in the meaning of specie with wealth).

This issue is especially important in respect to Foucault's periodisation of economic thought in terms of 'epistemes' and highlights the fact that, following his strategy of reversal, instead of looking for the resemblances between 'bullionists' and 'mercantilists', he was searching for their differences. He considered the sixteenth century to be marked by the 'age of resemblance', whilst the seventeenth century and the first three-quarters of the eighteenth century were dominated by another epistemic configuration, referred to as the 'classical age'. In economic thought, up until the end of the sixteenth century, knowledge was made possible by resemblance and analogy. Hence, the ability of money to measure price and to be the unity of exchanges fell upon its intrinsic value. Money was therefore made from precious metals, which were an indication of wealth. The metals were useful for coinage, since the metal had a price and money had value in its own right due to the metals, making it possible to function as a sign of exchange. Money was therefore a sign, signifying due to its resemblance to that which it signified. This was the perception during the period up until Davanzatti. Foucault quoted Davanzatti:

> From here below, we have difficulty in perceiving the few things that surround us, and we give a price to them according to whether we perceive them to be more or less in demand in each place and at each time. The merchants are promptly and very well advised of these things, and that is why they have an admirable knowledge of the price of things. (Davanzatti, quoted in *OT*, p. 174)

'Mercantilism', from the beginning of the seventeenth century onwards, chronologically delimited by Scipion de Grammont and Nicolas Barbon, was in the context of another episteme, the classical episteme. Indeed, for Foucault, these writers marked the rise in economic thought within the configuration of the 'classical episteme', since they introduced the fundamental system of signs into economic thought during the period of the seventeenth century up until the last quarter of the eighteenth century, therefore including physiocracy.

It is interesting that in this case Foucault identifies Scipion de Grammont as being the first main architect of the mercantile system, while Adam Smith considered Thomas Mun to be the first. Beyond the usual criticism that Foucault privileged French writers, in this case it appears that Foucault had a good reason for that. The main published writings of Thomas Mun (1571–1641) were two short treatises, *A Discourse of Trade from England unto the East Indies* and *England's Treasure by Forraign Trade*, which were first published in 1621 and 1664, respectively. However, Scipion de Grammont's main work was *Le Denier royal, traité curieux de l'or et de l'argent*, first published in 1620.

Whilst mercantilism from the seventeenth century onwards and physiocracy can be regarded as different paradigms, according to Foucault they were in the same epistemic context as that of the classical episteme.

To say that physiocracy constituted a paradigm seems to be uncontroversial. It is perhaps one of the easiest examples of a 'paradigm' in the history of economic thought. Physiocrats formed a community (*'les économistes'*, as they denominated themselves) that shared a common set of theoretical beliefs, together with the same accepted standards and procedures used to conduct scientific investigation. They formed a group of adherents, namely François Quesnay, Mirabeau, Mercier de La Rivière, Le Trosne, Baudeau, Dupont de Nemours and Turgot. As Smith stated, the physiocrats promoted a 'system of agriculture', which in relation to the mercantilists followed a very distinct paradigm and emerged in opposition to them. In the words of Kuhn, they promoted a 'shift in scientific perception that accompanies paradigm change' (Kuhn, 1970, p. 117).

Physiocrats emerged in France, all committed to a class of landlords, with a set objective, which was to prevent a rise in the class of merchants and manufacturers. They argued that only land could generate the *produit net*, a basic concept shared by them all, meaning the difference between the wealth produced and the wealth consumed. Their theoretical structure followed the concept that there was a natural order of existence, *l'ordre naturel*, as had been declared by Dupont de Nemours, and that wealth was determined in the form of material goods, 'as the consumable goods annually reproduced by the labour of society' (Blaug, 1997, p. 24). In this sense, they had a very distinct notion, in relation to the mercantilists, regarding the relationship between money and wealth. Quesnay's *Tableau Economique* was the classical work of the school and was possibly regarded as the 'textbook' for this paradigm. Differing from the 'mercantilists', who advocated protectionist policies (although some authors – for example, Magnusson, 2003 – have argued that it is a mistake to interpret all 'mercantilists' as protectionists), the physiocrats saw economic progress as a result of *laissez-faire, laissez-passer*.

As for political economy, most texts on the history of economic thought depict Adam Smith as the founder of a new paradigm, which would mark the existence of the whole of classical economics. Sheila

Dow (1996, p. 51) writes that Smith established 'a new agenda' for economists, which would form the centre of attention for economists for at least a century. According to Dow, the agenda essentially comprised the question of value as a measure of the product, the growth of the national product and the distribution, both as a social concern and as a determinant of capital accumulation to promote further growth (ibid.). Backhouse (1985, p. 13) writes that 'The *Wealth of Nations* was important for containing many of the components from which classical political economy was made up' and adds that 'Smith provided the vision of the economic system which permeated the whole of classical economics'. This author even defined the chapter on Smith as 'Political Economy as a Smithian Creation'.

Although some differences may exist as to what the main topics of this new paradigm are, writers on the history of economic thought generally agree to the presence of a shift. *The Wealth of Nations* is considered one of the reasons that led to this shift, with Smith's new paradigm being devised because of his opposition to what he called the 'Mercantile System'. Blaug (1997, p. 34), quoting Smith, emphasised that 'the whole book is directed against "the mean rapacity, the monopolising spirit of merchants and manufacturers, who neither are, nor ought to be, the rulers of mankind"'.

Smith, who was a contemporary of the physiocrats, having even met some of them, including Quesnay, also rejected the physiocrats' main theoretical claim, that is, that only agriculture could generate wealth. In Smith's view, wealth was the consumable goods annually reproduced by the labour of society. For the physiocrats, although labour could not create wealth, it could alter it. For Smith, any kind of productive activity would generate value. Labour was at the core of what created economic growth and although Smith held agriculture in high regard, particularly since it was deemed the main economic activity in Great Britain, he did not share the view of the physiocrats, which was that manufacturing was 'sterile' in the sense that it did not generate *produit net*. For him, both agriculture and manufacturing should equally be considered and labour was responsible for the *produit net*.

Schabas (2005, p. 90) had an alternative explanation as to how the notion of 'labour' had changed in Smith's view. Schabas argued that, prior to Smith, labour could only alter goods but not create them. In other words, labour could not embed itself in objects or create value. 'Smith, it appears, was the first to view labor as an alienable stuff that could, in the case of productive labor, be packed into other objects' (ibid.). Schabas even quoted Hume, who wrote in the *Treatise*: 'We cannot be said to join our labour to any thing but in a figurative sense. Properly speaking, we only make an alteration on it by our labour' (Hume, quoted in Schabas, 2005, p. 90). Schabas's insight makes the clear distinction between Hume and Smith, although Foucault's archaeology challenges the idea that, for Smith, 'labour created value'.

Smith was above all concerned with the forces that determined the growth of wealth, which he understood as the total of commodities produced by a community. In respect of this, Foucault emphasises that one of the differences between Smith and the 'economists' of the episteme prior to him was directly related to this concept of wealth. While the 'mercantilists' of the sixteenth century saw wealth as equating to the precious nature of metals from which the money was made, Smith, like the mercantilists of the seventeenth and eighteenth centuries, understood 'wealth' as comprising the amount of objects of need, utility, pleasure and rarity that are produced over a period of time.

Smith raised many criticisms regarding the ideas of the mercantilists and physiocrats, with the intention of solving the many inconsistencies and omissions that existed in their system. Whilst the mercantilists associated the wealth of a nation with the balance of trade and the physiocrats saw it as a result of the product of the land, Smith related it to the division of labour, the accumulation of capital and technical progress. Wealth depended upon the productivity of labour, which was a function of the degree of specialisation or the improvement of dexterity of men, the saving of time and the use of better instruments for working ('labour-abridging machinery'). This formed the emergence of a new paradigm.

In Smith's system, the division of labour was also limited by the extent of the market, which was then related to international trade. Within this, Smith presented one other important distinction from the mercantilists view regarding protectionist policies. Smith's view on international trade was such that the earnings of one nation did not lead necessarily to the loss of another. Therefore, he argued in favour of liberalism, given that an open market could lead to the improvements in the division of labour and that all nations could then take advantage of the increase in productivity. He also argued in favour of free trade within the internal market, stressing the advantages of competition to engender equal rates of return and eliminate excess gains that would lead to the optimum allocation of labour and capital. It is sometimes stated that he was against any form of barrier or regulation, although he did advocate institutional measures to control monopoly power, as argued by Dow (1996, p. 51). Blaug (1997, p. 57) declares that Smith was aware of the utopian character of a complete freedom of trade and that protectionist measures were justified in some cases, such as infant industries and retaliation against foreign tariffs. However, for Smith, it was necessary to enable the 'invisible hand' of the market to operate at a benefit to the society. He believed that self-interested individual behaviour would promote the best situation for society.

As for a theory of value, although the idea of value, determined by the amount of labour necessary to produce things, was already present during the time of Petty and Locke, Smith was more innovative in his perception of labour as being a stable and reliable measuring device for calculating the value of things. This aspect of his system is especially important here insofar as it is one of the main characteristics of his system that Foucault saw as distinctive from Ricardo's theory of value and that places Smith still in the epistemic context of the classical age.

As Foucault insisted in his 'history of the present', the problem with writing history as a continuous process or not considering the specific context of events may be exemplified by the usual interpretation that Smith was 'the prophet of the Industrial Revolution'. Blaug (1997, p. 34), for instance, referring to this statement, argues that this is 'wrong' and that 'indeed, there is nothing in the book [*The Wealth of Nations*] to suggest that Smith was aware that he was living in times of extremely unusual economic change'. Blaug argues that when Smith mentioned the role of the invention of machines, for an increase in productivity of labour, he was not referring to what is today considered to be 'the industrial revolution', in addition to which he was citing examples of innovations from the Middle Ages. Moreover, Smith never referred to any important innovations during his time and it was only after the publication of *The Wealth of Nations* that the British industry really took off.

5.3   The epistemic shift in the emergence of political economy

5.3.1   The epistemic context of mercantilism and physiocracy

Concentrating on the 'mercantilism' from the seventeenth century onwards, together with 'physiocracy', whilst these could both be regarded as different 'paradigms', as far as Foucault was concerned, they were both part of the same epistemic context: the classical episteme.

As mentioned in Chapter 3, Foucault depicted the moment that is usually referred to as 'the age of reason', according to Descartes's dream of a *mathesis universalis*. Knowledge was indicated by comparison and by an analysis of the object of study through the identification of similarities and contrasts – the relations between the same and the other – with the aim of establishing its 'order'. Because 'order' was the 'mode of being' of things (*OT*, p. 219), which was the ontological conception underlying the entire epistemological endeavour, knowledge followed a 'general science of order' that resulted in a project of a *mathesis universalis*. Therefore, space was privileged in the construction of knowledge and to know was to organise things in a certain table of identities and differences as if they were part of a plan. For example, in natural history, knowing consisted of describing living beings according to their structure and character. Living beings should then be classified into kingdoms, species, families and so on and in accordance with their visible characteristics. At that stage, there was no concern with the internal constitution of living beings, their organs and functions (this was to be a characteristic of the modern age). Knowledge was only to analyse, order and 'name' things (taxonomy).

Table 5.1 summarises the main characteristics of the three epistemes within economic thought, together with the shifts that marked them, while intending to assist in their comprehension.

During the classical episteme, economic thought adopted money as a sign of a network of representations. The relationship between wealth and money was based on circulation and exchange. Metals were instrumental in the coinage of money since they were also the best materials for producing it. Economic thought was all to do with wealth and its components. It was about that which was representable by money and was the object of desire, necessity, utility, pleasure and rarity. Wealth was a composition of elements (objects of needs and desires) that could be replaced by one another through an exchange of money. Every item of 'wealth' could be converted into money and by this it means it could circulate (as characterised by every natural being that finds its place in a taxonomia). Everything could be named and find its place within an articulated language. Every representation could signify and find its place in order to be knowable.

Foucault called the economic thought of the classical age 'analysis of wealth' since, following a science of order, it established 'wealth' as what should be analysed and ordered within discourse. Foucault also emphasised that 'wealth' meant in the classical age something different from what it had been in the age of resemblance, as well as from what we understand by it today. It was clear that no longer did the nature of the precious metals matter; instead, it would be based upon everything that was an object of need, utility, pleasure or rarity. It was not

Table 5.1 The three epistemes – main characteristics: *connaissance* of economic phenomena

	Episteme – *Connaissance* – Economic Phenomena		
Main Notions/Concepts	Pre-classical Until Davanzatti (1529–1606)	Classical From Petty to Adam Smith (who was in the transition to the modern episteme)	Modern From Ricardo until present day(?)
General Domain	*Money*	*Wealth*	*Production*
Fundamental Category	*Money (Value & Prices)*	*Exchange*	*Labour*
Mode of Savoir	Analogy: Money is a sign because it is wealth	Analysis & Order: Wealth analysable in exchange	History: Forms of production differ according to the productive power of Labour
Interpretations// *Representational*	Interpretation: Signs created by God	Network of representations, where money is a sign that represents all that is in the network	Interpretation: Signs created by Man
Space/Time		Space: Wealth analysable through exchange & circulation. Circulation is more important than production	Time: Process of production involves a historicity, which is given by forms of production. Production became more important than circulation

Epistemology

(*Continued*)

Table 5.1   Continued

	Money	Money has an intrinsic value: precious metals	Money is a pledge	Money is a pledge
Ontology	**Value**	Value = Money	Value is only created in exchange, as a function of a network of representations	Value results from the productive power of labour
	Finitude		Production of land can provide the means to satisfy Man's desires & needs	'Scarcity'
	Ontology		Needs and desires of the body	Labouring character of the body
Language	**Language**			Formalisation; to surpass the finitude, to deal with the empirical-transcendental doublet

Source: Author's own work based upon Foucault (1970a).

even a 'notion', writes Foucault, in the sense that it was not interpreted because of the interaction between some economic concepts (value, price, trade, circulation, income and interest). In fact, 'wealth' was a 'general domain', 'the ground and object' of the economy.

The analysis of wealth was 'the domain of needs' and Foucault declared that Petty and Ricardo marked its chronological frontiers (*OT*, p. 57). Petty began the classical episteme and Ricardo started the modern age in economic thought. Foucault included in this episteme the 'mercantilism' of the seventeenth century onwards (chronologically delimited by Scipion de Grammont and Nicolas Barbon) and physiocracy. He added to his inquiry the 'utilitarism' as defended by some thinkers during the eighteenth century: Condillac, Galliani, Graslin and Destutt de Tracy.[1]

Given that it was the 'age of representation' and because of its complexity, 'wealth', as with natural history and grammar, could and should be 'named' through a 'taxonomia', although Foucault pointed out that two important differences existed between economic thought and the other empiricities in the classical age.

In the first instance, he emphasised that economic analysis was not formed by the following of the 'same curves' or obeying 'the same rhythm' as was the case with other empiricities, since this involved practices and institutions. Unfortunately, he did not develop on the point and was limited to stressing the distinct, abstract character of economic thought. Foucault's thoughts regarding this matter suggest a continuity of genealogy in relation to archaeology. It must be stressed, however, that although the analysis of wealth differentiated from others in this aspect, all of them were grounded on the basis of the same arrangement of knowledge, namely one episteme.

In addition, between the interplay of signs and representations, the analysis of wealth had a temporal index, which was not found in other areas of the theory of order (*OT*, p. 189). For example, in order to consider the prosperity or poverty within a nation and in relation to the fluctuations of quantity of money and hence prices, economists had to analyse the cycles, the movements of population and so on, when beginning to think in terms of progress. Time had to be considered as a factor when dealing with the relationship between growth and the quantity of money. Foucault argues that time also became a variable in defining money as a pledge when assimilating it into credit. This occurred at the end of the seventeenth century, when it became necessary to consider the duration of credit, the rapidity with which repayment fell due, the velocity of money over a given period and so on. This was a particular characteristic of the analysis of wealth. In natural history, in order to carry out a taxonomia, the structure and character only required a certain continuity of nature; time merely intervened 'from without'. Nonetheless, in the analysis of wealth:

> [T]ime belongs to the inner law of the representations and is part of it; it follows and modifies without interruption the power possessed by wealth to represent itself and so analyse itself by means of a monetary system. Where natural history revealed squares of identities separated by differences, the analysis of wealth reveals 'differentials' – tendencies towards increase and towards diminution. (*OT*, p. 189)

Since it was considered a taxonomia and did not have a method, as algebra was for *mathesis*, the analysis of wealth required a system of signs, which were established by the mercantilism of the seventeenth century. According to Foucault, mercantilism brought about the thinking of price and money at the level of representation and established a system of signs through which wealth could be exchanged or analysed into elements that enabled relations of equality and inequality, which were signified by comparable elements called precious metals (*OT*, p. 179). Mercantilists established the notion that 'all kinds of wealth in the world are related to each another in so far as they are part of a system of exchange. From one representation to another, there is no autonomous act of signification, but a simple and endless possibility of exchange' (*OT*, pp. 179–80). Foucault wanted to emphasise that the sign only constituted itself at the moment of exchange. Money, the sign of wealth, only had value when it was placed in exchange.

The analysis of wealth consisted of the theories of value, money and prices, Foucault writes. It began with the same problem during the Renaissance: how to understand money and its relationship to prices in an exchange. However, during the classical episteme, given that it was an age of representation, money was taken simply as a sign of wealth. Money only has value as a representation of wealth in an exchange and during circulation. Wealth increased because goods could circulate through money and hence multiply. This suggests a system of exchange, employing different kinds of wealth, all related to one another and that all form part of a system of exchange. There was an 'articulation' that took money as the instrument of representation and analysis of wealth, and made wealth into the 'content represented by money' (*OT*, p. 175).

Foucault summarised that the aim of the theory of value was to answer the following questions: 'why are there things that men seek to exchange; why are some of them worth more than others, why do some of them, that have no utility, have a high value, whereas others, that are indispensable, have no value at all?' (*OT*, p. 190). Thus, he argued, the theory of value was not in the asking of:

> what mechanism or kinds of wealth can represent each other (and represent themselves by means of that universally representative wealth constituted by precious metals), but, why objects of desire and need have to be represented and how one posits the value of a thing, together with why one can affirm that it is worth this or that. (*OT*, p. 190)

Hence, Foucault declares, the theory of value 'vertically' (therefore in depth) investigated the 'horizontal' area that was the object of the theory of money and trade.

Value only existed within the process of exchange. In principle, there were two strands of thinking regarding value during the classical episteme: the 'utilitarians' (Condillac, Galiani and Graslin) and the physiocrats. The difference between them was in the way they regarded exchange. The utilitarians *analysed* value as anterior to exchange and as a primary condition without which exchange could not take place, whereas the Physiocrats analysed value in the act of exchange itself. Both the utilitarians and the physiocrats employed a similar mode of analysis, the difference being the point of origin and the direction each one chose 'to traverse a network of necessity that remains identical in both' (*OT*, p. 191).

Condillac, Galiani and Graslin started from the exchange of utilities as the subjective and positive foundations of all values. Anything that satisfied a need would therefore have a value. Any transformation or transference in it, creating the possibility to satisfy a greater number of needs, constituted an increase in value. It is this increase in value that makes it possible to remunerate workers, by giving them an amount which is deducted from this increase and which is equivalent to their subsistence.

For the physiocrats, exchange needed to exist in order for value and wealth to become possible. Quesnay and his followers analysed wealth based on what was given in exchange. They began their analyses with the object itself, which was designated a value and which existed prior to the system of wealth (*OT*, p. 195). Exchange created value. All transformation of the products of the land and all that work on them are remunerated by the worker's subsistence; it must therefore be debited from the totality of goods as a diminution; values arise only where there is consumption. For value to be created, nature must be endowed with an endless fecundity.

Foucault argues that physiocrats and their opponents had a common body of fundamental propositions (*OT*, p. 199): that wealth springs from the land, that the value of things is linked by exchange, that money has value as the representation of wealth in circulation, and that circulation should be as simple and as complete as possible.

The theory of money and trade, writes Foucault, is in response to the following question: 'how, in the movement of exchange, can prices characterise things – how can money establish a system of signs and designation between kinds of wealth?' (*OT*, pp. 189–90). Following his own view of a spatial plan in thought, he characterised the theory of money and trade as being a horizontal investigation of the process of exchange. The theory investigated the relations between/among things or the type of wealth. This was because what articulated wealth was a system of exchange. Types of wealth were related to one another in as much as they were all part of a system of exchange. In this sense, value only existed within the process of exchange.

Money was conceived as a pledge. Since money was a deferred exchange, it had to be a pledge. However, Foucault questioned how this pledge could be sustained. He identified two points of view: those who saw money as a sign and the upholders who saw money as a commodity. There were those who considered that money should be guaranteed by some merchandise exterior to a monetary pledge (for example, land) or by the king (money-as-sign), and those who thought that money should be guaranteed as if it were coined in precious metals (money-as-commodity). Foucault refers to 'Law and Partisans' as being in the former position. He argues that Law and his partisans (Terrasson, Dutot, Montesquieu and Chevalier de Jaucourt, for example) were not 'in opposition to his age as the brilliant – or imprudent – precursor of the fiduciary currency' (ibid.). Law defined money in the same way as his opponents (Paris-Duverney, Chancelier d'Aguesseau, Condillac and Destutt, for example): as a pledge. The difference between them was in what they meant by pledge. Law believed that money should be guaranteed by some merchandise exterior to the monetary pledge, whereas his opponents thought that it would be guaranteed if the money was coined using a precious metallic substance. Law's perception was that money could be printed and destroyed in accordance with the needs of exchange, which would be a problem if it were made from metals.

According to Foucault, although the quantity theory of money had already emerged in the sixteenth century, it had a different meaning from that of the classical episteme. For Davanzatti and Bodin (during the sixteenth century – the age of resemblance), there was an intrinsic devaluation of money due to an inflow of metals from America, causing an abundance in Europe. However, at the end of the seventeenth century, those such as Locke, for example, thought of the quantity of money as a proportion of the whole trade. Money began to be thought of as a sign, which was representative of wealth (*OT*, p. 183).

Foucault argued that the circulation became one of the fundamental categories of analysis and that this was possible due to the space opened up by the relations between money and signs, or in other words wealth and representation, which developed into the metaphor 'the circulation of blood' that had recently been adopted. Foucault was of course referring to Harvey's discovery of the circulation of blood in 1628 and his well-known influence on Quesnay's *Tableau Économique*. In the case of Foucault, it was the epistemic configuration of that age, in particular the change in the conception of signs and representation, that allowed Quesnay, a physician, to think about economic life in terms of the circulation of wealth amongst the social classes. Foucault also mentions Hobbes, for whom the circulation of money happened with duties and taxes; the state could redistribute it among private persons in the form of pensions, salaries or remuneration for provisions that were bought by the state. This would stimulate the exchange of wealth, manufactures and agriculture.

Therefore, Foucault concludes that economic thought occurred within a space of 'circular and surface causality' where 'everything occurred in terms of the reciprocal relations between what it was representing and what was represented' (*OT*, p. 255), that is, that there were explanations as to how money could flow into a country or out of it, how prices could rise or fall, and how production could grow, stagnate or diminish. All these 'movements' obeyed a kind of tabulated process, in which all the values could be representative of one another. More specifically, prices would increase when a representative element, such as money, increased faster than the elements represented (commodities) and production would diminish when the instruments of representation (money) diminished in relation to the things being represented (commodities). Hence, value was clearly understood as a system of exchange. However, this was about to change in the modern age, when value was to be seen as a result of the productive power of labour, Ricardo being the first economist to present this concept. With respect to Ricardo, Foucault writes that labour started to be considered as the only source of value. Therefore, there was no need to relate one value to another in an exchange mechanism. In this sense, value should not to be regarded as a sign in a network of representations, as was the case during the classical age.

5.3.2   The epistemological model for the analysis of wealth

As previously mentioned in Chapter 3, the term 'knowing' in the classical age meant to build a well-constructed language and Foucault went on to develop an epistemological model for economic thought, based upon those four theoretical segments taken from the grammar. He depicted that age through a diagram and explained a part of the representation of the theory of language, arguing that while language emerged naturally in the general grammar sense, man had to build another language to determine the analysis of wealth and natural history.

Thinking in terms of a sentence, such as 'money is wealth', 'money' and 'wealth' are language elements that correspond to a form of 'articulation'. They are nouns that give names to two things. The verb 'to be' allows one to attribute 'being' to the statement. It reflects the operation of the mind in making a judgement, although, more importantly, it is what allowed language to come into being. The entire sentence represents a thought. The duo 'designation + derivation' refers to the projection of the language to the world outside, to the reality: there is something called 'money' and something called 'wealth'. 'Designation' refers to that with which the words designate or signify: there were primitive cries or gestures that gave origin to the words 'money' and 'wealth'. These words designate something outside of a language. Derivation refers to theories that explain the changes in a language: if and how the words like 'money' and 'wealth' changed in relation to images; are these words figurative or metaphorical? Therefore, both 'designation' and 'derivation' are always relating language (a 'representation of thought') to the world around us. Hence, they are indeed a duplication of representation and a projection of thought onto the outside world.

As in relation to language, Foucault wanted to establish the conditions that gave rise to thought within economic phenomena at that moment and to find out its constraints. He argued that the theory of language and economic thought were isomorphic. Economic thought only occurred inside the quadrilateral, which is understood in terms of the four theoretical segments of grammar. In the first instance, economic thought was only considered possible due to the concept of representation that underlined all thought. Similarly, to know the economy was only possible through a formulation of a type of grid showing identities and differences. In its fundamental stage, economic thought first defined 'wealth' as the term to be placed in the grid and it was then necessary to build a language around it in order to discuss it properly. In an analogy to the study of language, Foucault affirmed:

1 What the theory of language stated in relation to 'attribution' and 'articulation' corresponds to the 'theory of value' in economic thought. First, the role played by the verb in language was analogous to the objects of needs and desires with respect to the thinking of 'wealth', while the 'exchange' corresponded to the other elements of a proposition in language. The theory of value explains how certain objects can be introduced into the system of exchange. Attribution (verb) is what allows the existence of language. In the same way, the 'objects of need' are what determine 'wealth'. Articulation provides content to language (since a 'verb' alone would not form a language) through both the function of 'naming' (that which allows the generalisation of a proper noun in order to achieve a common noun) and the 'ordering' of discourse (relations of succession, subordination and consequence). Analogously, for the 'economists' of the seventeenth and eighteenth centuries, 'exchange' provides content to 'wealth', since it was only through 'exchanges' that 'wealth' could occur and increase. Wealth could not take place through bartering and money had to exist. What 'articulates' wealth is the system of 'exchange':

> All the kinds of wealth in the world are related one to another in so far as they are all part of a system of exchange. From one representation to another, there is no autonomous act of signification, just a simple and endless possibility of exchange. (*OT*, pp. 179–80)

Foucault argued that in this analogy, it is only possible to equate it after making some slight changes. It is necessary to understand that while 'attribution' and 'articulation' were separated in the study of language, they were combined in economic thought. Whilst language, analysed by its general grammar, emerged spontaneously, man constructed another language to explain, name and order 'wealth'. Therefore, the functions performed separately by attribution and articulation in language were combined in the analysis of wealth under the concept of 'value'. 'Objects of need, utility, pleasure and rarity' when 'exchanged' comprised the theoretical elements required to explain 'value' in the science of ordering 'wealth'. The 'value' can be 'appreciative' ('objects of need' *per se*) or 'estimative' ('objects of need' compared to each other in an exchange). 'Wealth' is 'objects of need', but it is only the process of exchange that 'permits each portion of wealth to signify the others or to be signified by them' (*OT*, p. 202). Some economists initiated the analysis of 'value' by the 'objects of need', superimposing 'attribution' upon 'articulation'. They were 'utilitarians' in the sense that the 'value' was determined by the 'utility' of the 'objects of need' and 'value' existed before 'exchange'. For utilitarians, people made decisions about what to produce according to an act of judgement (attribution) regarding the utility of the product. In this sense, 'value' was appreciative. They analysed 'value' based on what was received in exchange. Others began with the 'exchange' (articulation upon attribution: physiocrats). The physiocrats inverted the order and understood 'value' as only emerging during the exchange. Therefore, 'value' was estimative. However, all agreed that the 'objects of need' within the process of 'exchange' established 'value'. Therefore, independent of their different paradigms, 'mercantilists of the 17th century onwards' and 'physiocrats' agreed about the theory of value.

2   'Designation' (the analysis of what gives rise to a certain word – language of action and roots) and 'derivation' (tropes and shifts of meanings of the words) were combined in the 'theory of money and trade' in economic thought. 'Designation' was analogous to the conception that 'money was a pledge', while 'derivation' corresponded to the 'circulation and trade' in economic thought. 'Derivation' explained the 'continuous movement of words from their source of origin' (*OT*, p. 115). We can therefore interpret 'circulation and trade' as denoting a movement of 'wealth'. Foucault declared that the variation of prices could be understood as analogous to 'rhetorical displacements of the original values of verbal signs'. He also stated that the theory of prices and money, in respect to 'wealth', was the same as the study of tropes and shifts of meaning were to language. The 'theory of money and trade' explains how a material form can acquire the signifying function, serving as a sign of an object (playing the role of money) and how the same monetary element can signify more or less wealth. The theory of money and trade in economics is actually the union of 'designation' (studying the possibility of giving things a sign or, in other words, representing one thing by another) and 'derivation' (studying the possibility of one sign changing in

relation to what it signifies) in general grammar. As for designation, mercantilists and physiocrats conceived money as a pledge, the point being that money could be made from any material and there was no longer a prerequisite for it to be made from precious metals. If money was to be made from metals, it was now due to important properties, such as durability, divisibility and so on, which made money more appropriate for signifying things. 'Money as a pledge + circulation and trade' ('designation + derivation') represents duplication in representation of thought regarding wealth.

All four theoretical segments in language and in the analysis of wealth were related and not simply in pairs:

1 Attribution and articulation: it is not so difficult to understand why 'objects of need' and 'exchange' reinforced each other in the theory of value and hence in the representation of 'wealth'. Also, since they formed one single segment in the theory of value, there is no opposition in their relationship.
2 Designation and derivation: in the analysis of wealth, they are combined under the theory of money and prices. The relationship of reinforcement is understood in the sense that the underlying principle of the theory is the conception of 'money as a pledge', which corresponds to how 'wealth' is designated and how it moves through 'circulation and trade'. As in relation to attribution and articulation, there is no opposition between designation and derivation because they compose one single segment.
3 Articulation and designation correspond to the function of 'exchange' and 'money as a pledge', respectively, in the representation of wealth. They reinforce each other since the latter is the concept behind, or at the 'root' of, the system of exchanges. It allows for an understanding of value and how these values are then exchanged in order to generate wealth.
4 'Objects of need' (attribution) and 'circulation and trade' (derivation) reinforce each other, since without the latter segment it would be impossible to understand how the former could lead to the emergence and an increase in 'wealth'.

'Money' in the analysis of wealth corresponds to 'common nouns' in general grammar and 'character' in natural history. Just as 'common nouns' can represent several things and 'character' can represent several individuals, species, genera and so on, a single piece of metal can represent 'several equivalent things (an object, work, a measure of wheat, a portion of income)' (*OT*, p. 185). A 'character' can represent more things since it is simpler. The quantity of things that money can represent depends on the velocity of its circulation. In this sense, the speed of monetary circulation corresponds to 'character' in the General Table.

In the eighteenth century, the speed of circulation was studied in relation to the periods of harvests and to the size of population. Foucault writes that this could not be thought of in terms of mechanisms by which money circulates or fails to circulate, or how it was expended or accumulated, as 'such questions are possible only in an economy that poses problems of production or capital' (*OT*, p. 186). This would only be the perspective during the modern episteme and it should continue to be noted that, given that the quantity of money coined was controlled in accordance to those factors, prices were 'not intrinsically "fair", but exactly regulated' (ibid.).

The analysis of money and prices differed if foreign trade was considered. A relationship between money supply and economic growth was developed and a theory regarding the quantity of money in circulation, together with its impact on internal prices and the effects they had on the wealth or poverty of a nation, was formulated. The relationship to the inflow or outflow of money was devised, with the idea that a larger amount of money in a specific country would lead to an increase in prices. This would stimulate buying from abroad and a reduction in the quantity of metals in the country, and therefore a drop in prices and the tendency for the country to become poor again. Cantillon wrote that: 'The excessive abundance of money, which makes the power of states while it lasts, thrusts them imperceptibly and naturally back into indigence' (Cantillon, quoted in *OT*, p. 187). The ideas relating to a population emigrating from a poorer country to a richer one was raised in order to consider the impact on the tendency for a lack of convergence or, on the contrary, divergence. Foucault suggests that such analyses were important because not only did they introduce the notion of progress but, more importantly, they included the notion of time in 'the interplay of signs and representations' and that was an exclusive characteristic of economic thought. Time was not important in natural history (in the sense that time merely intervened from somewhere outside) or, for that matter, in general grammar. However, in the analysis of wealth, time 'belongs to the inner law of representations and is part of it' (*OT*, p. 189).

The function of money became apparent soon after money was defined as a pledge. If in natural history, character is established by situating beings to their surroundings (continuity thus being necessary), then in the analysis of wealth, monetary prices designate wealth following a movement of growth or reduction (time must be included in the analysis).

5.3.3   Foucault's representation of Adam Smith – the boundaries of classical and modern thought

As discussed in Chapter 3, the most obvious change in the modern episteme was related to the view regarding the 'organic structure' of the object, which was derived from the conception of a historicity (temporal series of the object) and the finitude of man. Whilst in the classical episteme, space was a major figure in knowledge, in as much as the table of visible identities and differences favoured the spatial relationships, time became more important than space in the modern episteme, when the historicity of the object was revealed. This reflected on economic thought throughout the emergence of political economy, where the source of value was sought in the process of production. More specifically, labour was introduced as the unit of value. This started to be the case in Smith's system, although it was only evident in Ricardo's theory, argued Foucault.

Smith is again a fascinating character in the history of economic thought, since his writings denote not only a change of 'paradigm', but also an 'epistemic' shift. More specifically, Foucault saw Smith's works as a representation of the transition in the configuration of thought from the classical age to the modern era.

Foucault emphasised that the main aspect of Smith's work that placed him within a classical context in economic thought was the fact that he was still relating the notion of labour predominantly to an exchange of wealth (instead of production, as was to be the case in the modern age) and he saw economic activity as following a system of representations, where exchange played the central role. Smith also included new elements that pointed to a new epistemic context: he did not consider labour as a unit of value in relation to man's needs, as was the case in the classical age. Instead he saw labour as an absolute unit to measure the exchange value.

Foucault emphasised the importance of remembering how in the first instance Smith neither invented the concept of labour nor gave it a new role to play in economic theory. The notion of labour was already established with Cantillon, Quesnay and Condillac. Foucault was absolutely correct, since it is possible to find 'labour' already mentioned in the work of Petty. Schumpeter (1954, p. 217) even wrote that Petty considered capital as accumulated labour and that labour started being considered as a measurement of the value in exchange long before

Smith. Foucault established this to be 'at least from Cantillon onwards'. Furthermore, Petty was also regarded as the first to relate the idea of value to labour (for example, by Heimann, 1945, pp. 37–8). Heimann declared that Petty introduced the idea of value being related to the quantity of labour spent in its production, as well as suggesting that value was a determinant of price (ibid.). Foucault explained that this was because the configuration of the classical episteme led to a thinking of value in terms of a network of representations. This 'system of representation' followed the underlying project of establishing a 'table', 'an order', which also explains Quesnay's *Tableau* or Cantillon's circular flow of income and expenditure. The 'table' metaphor can still be viewed in the precedence of exchange in the analysis of wealth, which is not difficult to find in the works on economy from that era. For instance, it is explicit in Cantillon's *Essai sur la Nature du Commerce en Generale*.

For Smith, as well as for his predecessors, the 'value in use' was given by man's needs and the 'value in exchange' was defined by the quantity of labour applied to the production. Foucault argued that the distinction between Smith and some other thinkers before him, such as Turgot and Cantillon, was not what historians usually supposed it to be. The distinction between value in use and value in exchange was apparent prior to Smith, the point being that Smith changed the relationship between labour and needs. Cantillon saw a man's labour as equal to the value of what he needed to maintain himself and his family – food was the last resort. Therefore, necessity was used to define the value in exchange. Needs defined the value in use and exchange. The relation between wealth and necessity marked all classical thought. Indeed, the analysis of wealth was about 'represented needs' in a system of exchange.

Although Smith had not changed the function of labour and saw it as a measure of exchange value, he understood labour as an absolute, irreducible unit of measurement and promoted a rupture in the relation between wealth and needs. Whilst in the classical episteme, labour was a measure of exchange 'relative' to objects of need, Smith understood labour as an absolute measure of exchange. In this case, it was Smith that 'discovered' labour as the measuring device to calculate the value of things in exchange. This argument by Foucault agrees, for example, with Schumpeter, who, quoting Walras, declared that Smith chose 'the commodity labour instead of the commodity silver or the commodity gold as *numéraire*' (Schumpeter, 1954, p. 188). However, unlike the theory of Ricardo, Smith was not articulating a theory of value in which labour and production produced value.

With respect to Foucault, Smith still analysed 'wealth' according to the conditions of the classic episteme. The Scottish thinker understood 'wealth' as 'objects of need', which represented themselves in the movements and methods of exchange. There was a form of duplication present here: they represented 'wealth' and they were 'represented' in exchange with one another. Trade and exchange were the basis upon which formed the analysis of wealth. According to Foucault, Smith saw even the division of labour as governed by the criteria of barter. Indeed, Smith wrote that:

> This division of labour, from which so many advantages are derived, is not originally the effect of any human wisdom, which foresees and intends that general opulence to which it gives occasion. It is the necessary, though very slow and gradual consequence of *a certain propensity in human nature* which has in view no such extensive utility; *the propensity to truck, barter, and exchange one thing for another.* (Smith, 1986c, p. 168, emphasis added)

In other words, the division of labour in Smith's system was 'attributed to an inborn propensity to truck and its development to the gradual expansion of markets' (Schumpeter, 1954, p. 187). This attests to Foucault's conception of Smith's system as an exchange of representations: 'Every commodity besides, is more frequently exchanged for, and thereby compared with, other commodities than with labour' (Smith, 1986c, p. 176). In this sense, value was not commonly estimated by labour. This point was made by Schumpeter (1954, p. 309), who stated that Smith was interested in exchange rather than value. Smith declared in *The Wealth of Nations* that his inquiry was about the rules, which '"men naturally observe in exchanging" goods "either for money or for one another"' (Smith, quoted in Schumpeter, 1954, p. 309).

However, the idea of a 'division of labour' was also one aspect of Smith's system that showed his place in the dawn of the modern episteme. This notion implied a figure of man, as he was about to emerge as an object of knowledge (which, argues Foucault, would only occur in economics under Ricardo's theory). Smith even referred to this specialisation as something that could lead to workers being deprived of their 'intellectual, social, and martial virtues' (Blaug, 1997, p. 35). This was regarded by Blaug as an anticipation of Marx's doctrine of the alienation of labour and, as Amariglio (1988, pp. 594–5) emphasises, Smith was responsible for a 'clear interjection of the category of labour, of the labouring body, into the discussions of value and wealth that precede him'. Amariglio also stated that:

> Foucault identified the view of the body, in Ricardo and Marx's works, as having originated from a germ in Smith's work. With reference to Smith, we can see the outline of a body in which desire and need were superseded in the order of things by labour – by Man's incessant struggle against death. Following Smith, production and its progress then became the central issue in an emerging political economy. For Foucault, the political, in political economy, correctly suggests that the shift has taken place. Whereas the analysis of wealth superimposes upon itself a relative equality of humans and Nature and of wealth and its representations, political economy looks directly to manmade institutions of social control as signs of and arenas for the unleashing of Man's essential power – labour and its productive organisation. (Amariglio, 1988, p. 596)

However, as Foucault made clear, Smith was still within the limits of the classical episteme, since it was clear that within his theory of value, it was exchange, and not labour, that determined the value of things. Therefore, Smith certainly did not launch a cost-of-production theory of value. This statement seems to be in agreement with the most influential books on the history of economic thought, including Schumpeter's *History of Economic Analysis*. Schumpeter (1954, p. 189) stated that Smith's 'theory of value is no labour theory at all'. Indeed, Schumpeter had an interpretation of Smith's theory of value that agreed with Foucault's point of view. Blaug (1997, p. 38) also emphasises that 'Adam Smith had no theory of value whatever', meaning that he did not have a theory regarding how the prices of productive services were determined. What this demonstrates is that Smith did not formulate a theory of value in which labour 'produces' value. As such, he had no theory of wages and rents and no theory of profit or pure interest; therefore, writes Blaug, 'he had no *labour* theory of value' (ibid., original emphasis). Blaug goes on to be even more emphatic:

> There is no suggestion in the *Wealth of Nations* that the different factors of production can be assimilated in terms of some common denominator other than money and, in particular, there is no suggestion that the value of capital goods can be reduced to labour expended on their production in the past. (Blaug, 1997, p. 38)

Indeed, Smith wrote: 'But though labour be the real measure of the exchangeable value of all commodities, it is not that by which their value is commonly estimated. It is often difficult to ascertain the proportion between two different quantities of labour' (Smith, 1986c, p. 176). Foucault argues that this confusion, which led Smith to the concept that the quantity of labour indispensable for the production of a thing was equal to the quantity of labour that the thing, in return, could buy in the process of exchange, originated exactly from the precedence of that underlying network of representations, in which 'all merchandise represented a certain labour, and all labour could represent a certain quantity of merchandise' (*OT*, p. 253).

It was only in the modern way of thinking, along with Ricardo, that the precedence of 'production' was able to help clarify this issue.

In Smith's economics, a thing was represented by units of work; labour was analysable into days of subsistence; value was still a sign. Value was defined based on a total system of equivalences: commodities representing one another. Labour was a fixed and constant value exchangeable in all places and all times. In short, Smith was still analysing 'wealth' according to the conditions of the classic episteme and employed the concept of labour to analyse exchangeable wealth. In his system, wealth was still a representative element and he understood wealth as 'objects of need', which represent themselves in the movements and methods of exchange.

Although Smith was writing about this system of representations, he was clearly in the path of transition to a new episteme. For him, wealth was no longer represented by objects of need and desire. Indeed, wealth was represented by labour, which replaced the objects of need and desire as the measure in exchange. In the duplicated representation, objects of need and desire represent 'wealth' and are 'represented' in exchange with one another. Within this duplication, Smith creates 'a principle of order that is irreducible to the analysis of representation: he unearths labour, that is, toil and time, the working-day that at once patterns and uses up man's life' (*OT*, p. 225). If one object can be exchanged with another, it is not because men have comparable desires but because they are subject to time and to labour, which is not merely dependent on his ability or self-interest. Man's labour is also subject to industrial progress, division of tasks, accumulation of capital and the division between productive and non-productive labour. Production signified both the subjective activities of the producer and the objects produced. This is different from economic thought in the classical episteme, which was a circulation of objective things within a closed system.

Therefore, Foucault says that Smith began a movement that surpassed the age of representation. Smith's reflection on wealth was no longer within the analysis of representation and pointed towards anthropology, opening up a space for the emergence of a political economy whose object would not be the exchange of wealth, but instead its production: forms of labour and capital. This was anthropology, since Smith's system placed in evidence man's essence (his finitude, his relation with time and the imminence of death) and how man invests his days of time and toil, without relating this to his immediate needs.

However, Foucault raised one question: how can labour, which has a variable price and changes its form depending on its division, be a fixed, absolute measure of prices? As for the variable price of labour, Foucault argues that Smith saw it as related to the market's situation. For example, in a given country or market and within a certain moment of time, workers may be few and wages may be high, while in other places the number of workers may be high and so the wages may be low. What changes from one thing to another in these situations is the quantity of commodities that each worker can buy per day of work. If the prices are high, due to a scarcity of supply, then each worker will only be able to buy a few of the commodities and these are situations that are determined by the market. The labour itself – as hours spent, 'toil' or 'trouble' – is always the same. If more workers are employed in the production of a product, the product will be more expensive. Foucault quotes Smith: 'Equal quantities of labour, at all times and places, may be said to be of equal value to the labourer' (Smith, quoted in *OT*, p. 223). In response to the second objection (that, due to the division of labour, it cannot be an absolute measure of prices), Foucault again argues that, according to Smith's system, the labour did not change. What did change was the relationship of labour to the production that it was able to accomplish. Foucault says: 'Labour, in the sense of a day's work, toil and trouble, is a fixed numerator: only the denominator (the number of objects produced) is capable of variations' (*OT*, p. 224). The division of labour multiplies the 'productive power' of labour, although, in relation to the price of things, it was not labour that diminished in relation to what could be produced. Indeed, it is the things themselves that appear to shrink in relation to the unit of labour. That is how Foucault interpreted Smith's theory of labour value.

Needs and their exchange are still the principle of economy in Smith's system. Labour and the division that organises it are just an effect of this principle. However, for Smith, it is not needs that play the role of measuring between/among things in exchange, as was the case with the predecessors of Smith. What was compared in exchange in order to find equivalences in terms of identities and differences was no longer defined as the needs. For Smith, there was an absolute measure of that which was imposed in exchange from the outside: time and toil. People exchange because they have needs, but what orders the exchange is the labour that man invests in the objects. It is not the objects of need representing one another in an exchange.

Foucault still regards Smith as being the thinker who promoted a change in the notion of time in economics. Foucault declared that in the classical episteme, the economic thought had already had to think about time (which differed from the natural history and general grammar), but it was only in the modern episteme that time became a fundamental variable. In Smith's economic system 'men exchange because they experience needs and desires; but they are *able* to exchange and to order these exchanges because they are subjected to time' (*OT*, p. 225, original emphasis). Prior to Smith, it was regarded as either a cyclical variable of alternating impoverishment and wealth or a linear variable in which the correct policies of increasing the amount of circulation specie can accelerate production at a faster rate than they can raise the prices. For instance, Hume referred to time in the sense that no country could sustain its economic hegemony forever (Schabas, 2005, p. 93). Since the time of Smith, it has been understood as a variable inside an organic structure. Smith conceived economy as a process that 'grows in accordance with its own necessity and develops in accordance with autochthonous laws – the time of capital and production' (*OT*, p. 226).

This change in the concept of time is an interesting point that Foucault's archaeology highlights in economics. Schabas (2005, p. 93), for instance, argues that the thought regarding the economy developing through large periods of time (as for instance did Smith in Chapter 3 of *The Wealth of Nations*) was something relatively novel in the history of economic thought. Schabas also wrote that 'no mercantilist or Physiocratic writer has the same temporal sweep' (ibid., p. 77). In Chapter 3 of *The Wealth of Nations*, Smith analyses economic development through some prolonged stages. Schabas also draws attention to the fact that this influence of time, which was in Smith's thoughts, was also shared by some naturalists who were his contemporaries at the time, such as Georges-Louis Leclerc, the Comte de Buffon and James Hutton. Again, Foucault's idea of a region of interpositivities, sharing the same epistemic notion – in this case time – is highlighted by Schabas's comment. She mentions that Smith, as well as Hume, were aware of Buffon's evolutionary ideas and *Histoire Naturelle*, and that

James Hutton was actually a friend of Smith and Hume (ibid., p. 76). Schabas even suggests that some naturalists, such as Buffon and Hutton, promoted Hume's awakening to the *longue durée* (ibid., p. 77). Hence, we could also question whether this was not also the case regarding Smith's notion of time.

5.3.4　The emergence of the modern economic thought: Ricardo

For Foucault, it was only through Ricardo that economic thought entered the modern episteme, since he was the first to promote the substitution of the 'circular and surface causality' of circulation by the conception of a 'linear, homogeneous series which is that of production' (*OT*, p. 255). Differing in his system from the economics of Smith, production had primacy over circulation and this was analogous to what happened in biology in as much as two new dimensions were added to the analysis: depth and time. In biology, hidden similarities of bodies began to be considered and temporal organic processes replaced the spatial location of organs within the classificatory systems.

For Foucault, Ricardo was the first person to work on the history of labour. This had been seen as a provocative claim, as Major-Poetzl (1983, p. 154) noted, since Marx was often considered to be the first.

The major difference that Foucault identified between Smith and Ricardo was that labour was analysable into days of work that could be used as a common unit of value for all merchandise and the commodities could be represented in terms of the units of work. In Ricardo's system, however, a quantity of labour determined the value of a thing, since not only could it be represented in units of work but, more importantly, labour was a producing activity and the source of all value. Value was no longer a sign; it had become a product. Value had its origin within labour and it changed according to the quantity of labour devoted to producing things; however, it does not change according to an increase or a decrease in wages, as Foucault stressed when mentioning Ricardo. After Ricardo, it was not trade and exchange that were considered as the basis for an analysis of wealth. Labour was the basis, given that the exchange was based upon the labour. Therefore, the theory of production was to precede that of circulation and this had three main consequences: the emergence of a new form of causal series; the concept of 'scarcity' with a fundamental meaning; and a change relating to the evolution of economics.

In the classical episteme, Foucault argued that economic thought had provided the explanations as to how money could flow into a country or out of it, how prices could rise or fall and how production grew, stagnated or diminished. The difference was that all of these 'movements' obeyed a type of table in which all values represented one another: prices increased when the representing elements (money) increased faster than the elements represented (commodities); production diminished when the instruments of representation (money) diminished in relation to the things to be represented (commodities) and so on. As for Foucault, there was 'a circular and surface causality' in which everything happened in terms of the reciprocal relations between what was representing and what was represented. From the time of Ricardo onwards, labour was regarded as the causality without reference to anything else, other than something peculiar to it, for example, the forms of production according to the degree of division of labour, the quantity of capital applied and so on. When Ricardo promoted this disassociation of the creation of value from its representativity, he made it possible to articulate economics based upon history. Wealth became something that resulted from an historical process. Value was as a result of certain conditions of production, which were determined by the quantities of labour applied to produce them; as such, there was a temporal sequence of production. Economic thought was no longer attributed to spatial analysis according to differences and identities. In what appears to be another provocative statement towards Marxists, Foucault declared that: 'Even before economic reflection was linked to the history of events or societies in an explicit discourse, the mode of being of economics had been penetrated, and probably for a long while, by historicity' (*OT*, p. 256).

Another change that occurred in the modern age was related to the concept of scarcity. This was a decisive step for a theory of utility, along the line of that introduced by the first marginalists at the end of the nineteenth century. Foucault's analysis of this change sheds light on the relationship between economics and psychology as it was about to emerge, demonstrating to us another reason why we should be more careful when applying the expression 'psychological principles' when referring to the predecessors of Ricardo in economics.

'Scarcity', in the meaning acquired during the modern age, was not in the epistemic context of classical thought. The notion may be found in economic writings of the classical episteme, such as in Galiani's work (*raritá*). However, 'scarcity' was related to needs. Again, it is important to stress that economic thought was a representation of needs, conceived as being able to increase or take on new forms and, above all, which could be satisfied by the production of land. For Foucault, this was the view of both the mercantilists and physiocrats. Labour was applied to land and made it possible to overcome scarcity. Man himself was represented by the objects that he did not have, although the land produced, in some abundance, objects that were not consumed immediately and represented others in the processes of exchange and the circulation of wealth.

Although Foucault did not refer specifically to Smith, we should reflect on his writings here. Some interpreters of Smith's system have argued that there was in his writings an 'implicit' understanding of the concept (for example, Kaushil, 1973 and Hollander, 1973 and 1987) and, according to Blaug (1997, p. 39), Smith refers to 'scarcity'. What is really at stake here is the meaning of 'scarcity' in terms of modern thought. Foucault describes 'scarcity' as having emerged in political economy (with Ricardo) with a fundamental meaning related to man's finitude. Therefore, even while Smith employed the term in *Lectures on Jurisprudence* and *The Wealth of Nations*, he had a very different concept. As Brown (1994, p. 152) argues, Smith applied the term 'scarcity' to mean in principle 'goods in short supply relative to demand'.

In this respect, it is possible to reconsider what Schumpeter (1954) asserted regarding Galiani's visionary conception of scarcity. Schumpeter wrote that Galiani 'proceeds to develop these concepts (*utilitá* and *rarità*) in much the same way in which I suspect they are explained in many an elementary course today' (ibid., p. 301). In addition, he went on to declare that Galiani had defined scarcity as 'the relation between the existing quantity of a thing and the uses one has for it', meaning he could then explain 'why a golden calf is valued more highly than a natural calf' (ibid.). This highlights the mistake that can be made from reading the works of the past and trying to relate them to the present.

Blaug (1997, p. 39), referring to the issue regarding the notion of utility in Smith's *The Wealth of Nations*, highlights this issue. Blaug points out that Smith indeed focused his investigation on exchange value rather than use value. Smith actually declared that he was focusing on exchange in Book 1, Chapter 7 of *The Wealth of Nations*. Blaug also argues that Smith had a concept of 'utility' 'not as the power to satisfy a particular want', but 'as the power to satisfy a generalised biological or social need' (ibid.), which is in agreement with the findings of Foucault's archaeology. Hence, Blaug concludes that there was nothing related to the marginal or final utility of individuals in Smith's economic system and writes that 'scarcity' for Smith was 'relative scarcity' governed by demand and supply in the short term and by the cost of production in the long term (ibid.).

Foucault writes that the notion of scarcity has changed and it is actually a fundamental notion in understanding the transformation from classical to modern thought. Ricardo promoted such a change. From Ricardo onwards, 'scarcity' became 'a fundamental scarcity'. The imminence of death became more explicit in the definition of economic thought: 'It is no longer in the interplay of representation that economics finds its principle, but near that perilous region where life is in confrontation with death' (*OT*, p. 257). Scarcity was in Ricardo's theory in as much as he explicitly addressed the question of population increase and the necessity of exploring less productive lands. A relationship began to emerge between economics and anthropological implications as suggested in Malthus's proposition of biological properties of human species that should be prevented by some remedy or constraint.

Foucault was even more emphatic, suggesting that economics emerged as a necessity for knowledge because of the fundamental situation of scarcity. Man must employ all possible means in order to make economic activity (Foucault uses 'labour' synonymously with 'economic activity') overcome the fundamental insufficiency of nature. For Foucault, the concept of *homo economicus*, as it emerged, is related to man's finitude as revealed by Kant. Hence, in regards to economics, man was no longer representing his own needs towards himself, which was the case in the classical episteme: 'Eighteenth-century economics stood in relation to a *mathesis* as to a general science of all possible orders; nineteenth-century economics will be referred to an anthropology as to a discourse on man's natural finitude' (*OT*, p. 257).

This reflected the change in the ontological view which was denoted by Kant's critique. Following on from Kant, the question of finitude was more fundamental than the analysis of representations. Scarcity has its origins not in needs and desires but on an anterior level, given by the imminence of death. That is why need and desire became something subjective, as was later to be the case in psychology.

The last main consequence related to the evolution of economics. The 'rent of land' was not due to the fruitfulness of nature, as it was conceived to be in the classical episteme and even under Smith's system. Nature was to be conceived by its avarice. Theories regarding the rise of population and the necessity of using progressively poorer lands emerged. Population was indeed a central notion for the emergence of political economy: 'The new science called "political economy" arises out of the perception of the new networks of continuous and multiple relations between population, territory, and wealth' (Foucault, 1994a, p. 217). Both the theories of Ricardo and Malthus became possible within this system of thought. The 'rent of land' became a consequence of the avarice of nature. Population increases and new lands, of progressively poor quality, have to be cultivated; the costs of production increase, as do the prices of agricultural products, together with the 'land rent'. The nominal wage of labourers has to increase in order to cover the costs of subsistence, although their real wages would need to remain of sufficient value to cover their costs of clothing, shelter and food. The profit of entrepreneurs decreases in exactly the same proportion as the increase in the rent of lands.

When labour in the process of production began to represent wealth, time became important. In this sense, there were shifts from a spatial to a temporal orientation in economic thought, which led to an economics based on production (rather than exchange) and a conception of man (anthropology) in terms of his alienated relation to time.

Therefore, the shift in economic thought occurred when exchange was replaced by labour as the domain to be pursued in knowledge. Before Ricardo, exchange was the unit of the analysis of wealth. In Adam Smith's work, labour started to be the measure of the price of things. It is only in reference to Ricardo that labour, as a *production* activity, started to be considered as a real source of value. Production took the place of exchange. The value originated from labour and became a product. Therefore, the value was not solely an indicative sign of the exchange amongst things, as it was in the classic age. During this period, the analysis of wealth was made at a level of representation, through signs and their ordination. Economics as 'a modern empirical science' was no longer based on representation, as wealth started to be seen as something that had a specific *depth*. Economics now entered vertically into the wealth domain, being identified by *production* and more precisely by *labour* as a value source. According to Foucault's ontological analysis, economic theory changed from the central aspect of desire of the body to the labouring aspect of it. Now man would be seen as a producer and not someone who simply represented his needs. If there was not scarcity, then there would not be the necessity for production and there would not be labour. The human limitation and finitude lead to work and to production.

5.3.5   The Modern General Table

As mentioned in Chapter 3, Foucault also depicted the epistemic context of the modern age through a diagram, which was reproduced in Diagram 3.2. Foucault did not explain this new modern diagram concerning economic thought. He only mentioned two broad areas of economics: theory of production and analysis of distribution.

As was also shown in Chapter 3, philosophy separated itself from the empirical domains of knowledge in the modern episteme. This separation was shown by splitting the diagram into two fields: epistemological and philosophical. It is important to notice that the lines that separate the philosophical and epistemological fields are not dotted.

The philosophical field is still represented by 'formalisation' and 'interpretation'. The former is the connection between 'apophantics' and 'formal ontology', which are closely related to the spaces previously occupied by 'attribution' ('verb') and 'articulation' in the general grammar. Foucault was suggesting that 'formalisation' has been employed as a means to overflow an analytic of finitude, which has to deal with the empirical-transcendental doublet. Foucault sees 'formalisation' as the way in which man in the modern age tries to escape from his radical finitude, including 'structuralism'. He states: 'Structuralism is not a new method; it is the awakened and troubled consciousness of modern thought' (*OT*, p. 208).

In the epistemological field, Foucault included 'analysis of production' alongside 'phonetics' and 'comparative anatomy' as a new form of theorising that corresponds in some ways, although not without fundamental modification, to what 'articulation' and 'designation' used to represent in the classical age. He implies that the theory of production is indeed at the same discursive level of a new theory of discourse, which has abandoned the search for representative roots of language and now pursues an understanding of inflections in words. Analogously, the study of production corresponds to the comparative anatomy in biology. The point that Foucault is emphasising here is that these empiricities include this new approach in their objects due to the new concept of historicity, which is understood as a temporal and organic structure, as has been explained previously. Foucault then placed 'analysis of distribution', 'syntax' and 'physiology' as the new approaches that correspond to 'attribution' and 'derivation' in the previous epistemic context. At this stage, the study of objects had to be considered, along with internal structures and the functions of the organs, such as in biology. In political economy, the knowledge of 'production', which became the new domain to be studied, required an understanding of the elements and mechanism of distribution.

5.4 Labour, time, neoliberalism, human capital and *homo economicus*

In his lectures delivered in 1978–9, Foucault revisited the relationship between production, labour and time in the classical political economy (the term 'classical' is used here as it is known in the conventional history of economic thought, without any relation to the classical episteme in Foucault's archaeology). According to him, classical economics constantly 'neutralized' the notion of labour, because of the relationship between labour and time, as it had been introduced by Smith's system, but particularly as it was present in Ricardo's theory (Foucault, 2004, p. 226).[2] Foucault argues that Ricardo never defined or analysed labour. He only considered it in the quantitative manner and according to time. The increases of labour could not be anything other than a presence in the market of the additional amounts of workers or hours of work. Foucault argued that this Ricardian reduction of the problem of labour to a simple analysis of the quantitative variable of time meant that economic analysis never really analysed the very nature of labour. Foucault writes: 'from this, the classical economics never really comes up' (ibid.). However, it was not only with classical economics that this occurred. Keynes did not introduce any more elaborate a theory of labour than that of Ricardo, and with Keynes, labour was also only another factor in production, which is passive when considered in the sense that it only found its activity in relation to a certain amount of investment. For Foucault, this changed only with the neoliberals, amongst whom he mentions Becker and Schultz. They provided a critique of classical economics, which promoted an essential change in the notion of labour.

From Smith until the beginnings of the twentieth century, the object of economics was to study of the mechanisms of production and exchange and the consumption within a given social structure. The neoliberal critique established that economic analysis needed to consider the nature and consequences of choices, while referring here to the definition of economics by Robbins as a study of the way in which individuals allocate scarce resources according to their alternative ends. Foucault argues that Robbins could be considered as a founder of the neoliberal doctrine. In this sense, economics was no longer an analysis of a relational mechanism of things or processes of capital, investment and production. Robbins understood that the task of economics was to analyse human behaviour and the internal rationality of this behaviour. Thus, 'economics is no longer to be considered an analysis of processes; it is an analysis of an activity. It is not the analysis of the historical logic of processes [here Foucault is referring to the historicity introduced in the modern episteme], it is the analysis of the internal rationality, of the strategic programming of the activity of individuals' (Foucault, 2004, p. 229). And this change does not mean only to reintroduce labour into economic analysis. It is indeed 'to know where labour is placed between capital and production' (ibid.). The question is not how labour is bought or what value labour adds. The fundamental issue became to know how labour uses the resources that it possesses. In this new epistemological approach, the worker was not only an object in the labour market, who sold their labour force for a given price that was deduced by the equilibrium between supply and demand. Workers were not a labour force but an active economic subject. Since it was now considered, under the neoliberal theory, that salary becomes an income and given that 'income' is the product or earning of capital, salary becomes the income of capital. Labour was not a commodity that was reduced, through abstraction, to become a force of work and time. The capital of labour was deduced by skills and competence or, as the neoliberals describe it, it is a 'machine'.

Foucault emphasised the many consequences that this transformation of labour into capital would have. Firstly, capital was understood as something that could not be separated from whoever possesses it. Although a worker's competence and skills could be seen as a 'machine', it could not be dissociated from the worker. This provided an important consequence relating to the notion of alienation, as understood by Marxist theory. For Foucault, the concept of human capital may still be regarded as, in some way, the worker's competence becoming a 'machine', although now it is regarded in a positive sense, given that it produces a flow of revenues. It is not a concept of 'force of labour' but 'capital-competence' that is remunerated by salary – salary-revenue. Naturally, there is a complete distinction here from the Marxist interpretation of labour-force being sold. The workers themselves now appear as a kind of entrepreneur of themselves. Economic analysis would now have to include not only individuals, processes or mechanisms as its object, but especially enterprises. Economics now becomes the study of a society which is made of 'enterprise-units'. In these conditions, Foucault argued, neoliberalism changed the classical conception of *homo economicus*. For the classical economists, *homo economicus* was a partner in a process of exchange. This conception led to the requirement of a theory of utility, which meant that economics had to study man and his behaviour and the analysis of his needs, emphasising the necessity for a theory of utility. It was through a study of man's needs that utility became the basis of the process of exchange. Neoliberalism returned to the notion of *homo economicus*, although, now, rather than as a partner in exchange, he became an entrepreneur, an entrepreneur of himself, with investments and revenues. He was now his own capital: he was a producer and became the source of his own revenue – his earnings. This also changes the concept of consumption. The man who consumes was solely on one side of the exchange. He was a producer of his own satisfaction. This means that consumption should be seen as an activity of enterprise, insofar as the individual who possesses a certain capital produces some things that will be to his own satisfaction. Sociological, psychological and even genetic analysis becomes fundamental. It is now imperative to study the way in which this human capital was formed and how it was accumulated. As Foucault reminds us, this change was a consequence of technological progress, defined as 'innovation' by Schumpeter.

5.5   Review

Whilst the history of economic thought can be told through different paradigmatic revolutions, from the mercantilists to physiocrats and then to Smith's political economy, Foucault provides a new perspective, which is through the conditions of possibility that made them possible. According to this new perspective, these 'paradigms' were indeed made possible by some epistemic contexts. Mercantilists should be understood under two epistemes: the age of resemblance until Davanzati, and the age of representation from Scipion de Grammont to Nicolas Barbon. From the period of Petty to Smith, economic thought was under the aegis of the age of representation and Ricardo was at the start of the modern age. Indeed, Smith already represented the elements of a modern way of thinking and it is particularly interesting in the sense that his approach demonstrates a change of paradigm and epistemic conditions. Smith was promoting a change of paradigm while in transition between two epistemic sets of conditions of possibility of thought.

Foucault's archaeology puts the history of economic thought into a system, providing diagrams for a further understanding of the different historical interdiscursive practices. It is particularly inspiring to think that the context of economic thought in the seventeenth and eighteenth centuries followed a similar system of comprehension to that which took place in the study of language. This epistemological novelty of Foucault is once again difficult to understand. Indeed, most of the commentators and interpreters of *The Order of Things* have paid little attention to it, although Foucault himself gave priority to it by dedicating many pages of his book to its careful explanation. It appears that it was not really a rhetorical success for him. Nonetheless, the careful study has shown the great potential for the comprehension of his proposal and for the possibilities that they open up in future investigations into the history of economic thought. The study was especially important when better apprehending his suggestion of an interdiscursive practice underlying economic thought. Not only is this important for that specific moment in history, but it can also create an impetus for the study of other periods. Indeed, some economists have already followed this perspective, even if subconsciously (for example, Mirowski, 1984 and Schabas, 2005).

Foucault demonstrates once again a great erudition, which enables us to consider that the criticism placed against him, suggesting that he was biased in some way towards French thinkers, does not apply in the case of economics. He studied the main protagonists of this period in history and offered a range of significant elements, both new and rethought, enabling a reconsideration of it. It has to be considered that he was writing towards the end of the 1950s and the beginning of the 1960s. It is certain that there is a wide range of more recent works on the subject of the history of economic thought which could defy his main conclusions regarding the great writers of economic thought. However, any appraisal would need to be based upon the same level of approach as his own.

One of the first major distinctions in Foucault's reading of the history of economic thought was related to his discontinuous approach. For him, economics today is not the result of a progressive development of ideas that began to be articulated during the sixteenth century. Political economy was not a more accurate version regarding the thought on wealth that had occurred during mercantilism and physiocracy. Political economy emerged in a completely separate context, in respect of ontological and epistemological conceptions.

Foucault's archaeology is particularly innovative regarding the relation between epistemological notions and some ontological assumptions that each age held and how these reflected on the way in which concepts emerged and existed. In economics, this can be roughly summarised as follows.

Up until the end of the sixteenth century (the pre-classical episteme), knowledge was to make analogies, since everything had a supernatural origin and possessed signs in the form of resemblance. This was translated into economics, which focused on how to understand money and its relation to prices in exchange, through the concept of an ability of money to measure price and be the unity of exchanges that rested upon its resemblance to wealth. Money was made from precious metals since they were an indication of wealth. In this sense, Foucault claims that money was a sign that signified, because of its resemblance to that which it signified.

From the beginning of the seventeenth century to the end of the eighteenth century, the *cogito* was declared as being a fact. The supernatural character of things was also brought into question and to know now focused on looking for a natural order. Man was a subject (as in the Cartesian *cogito*: I) and conscious knower (as in the Cartesian *cogito*: I am). He built the signs for knowing. *Mathesis universalis*, as a general science of order, was representative of this model for knowledge. Mercantilism was determined by this context of the classical episteme. Space was privileged in a project of a science of order that made it possible to analyse the elements of wealth according to equalities and differences. However, the most fundamental element in that configuration of thought was 'representation'. All the explanations concerning economic activity obeyed a kind of table in which all the 'movements' happened in relation to the role of money as a sign; that is, everything happened in terms of the reciprocal relations between what was representing (money) and what was represented. Money became a pledge.

In addition, when representation collapsed, the homogeneous background of *mathesis* dissolved at the end of the eighteenth century. On an ontological level, man is a subject and object, related to unconscious and collective phenomena, as well as to changing states (historical experiences). Time, instead of space, became crucial. In between words and things, there was man and the unthought. Thought became language. The human sciences emerged to consider this unthought, although this was completely unsustainable, since there would always be the unthought, they would never find the ultimate origin, whilst oscillating between the transcendental-empirical. Hence, there was no 'progress' in knowledge, but an 'anthropological sleep', given that knowledge became an endless effort to transgress finitude.

Smith began the movement that surpasses the age of representation's borders in economics. His reflection on wealth was no longer within the analysis of representation and it was distinct from the forms and laws of the decomposition of ideas, as well as differing from the search for a taxonomy of wealth. It points to an anthropology and opens space for the emergence of political economy, whose object was to be not the exchange of wealth but its production: forms of labour and capital. This was anthropology, because Smith's system had placed in evidence man's essence (his finitude and his relation with time) without relating this to his immediate needs. Smith's economic system is seen as following an analysis and taxonomy of a natural order, which is proper of an inter-discursive practice, which was shared with the fields of natural history and the study of grammar. This emphasised the centrality of 'exchange' in a system of representations.

However, it was only with Ricardo that economic thought entered the modern episteme, because he was the first to work on the history of labour. He promoted the substitution of the 'circular and surface causality' of circulation by the conception of a 'linear, homogeneous series which is that of production' (*OT*, p. 255). Production has primacy over circulation. Whilst labour expressed value in Smith's economics, it was only with Ricardo that labour produced value. That is the difference Foucault identified between Smith and Ricardo. For Ricardo, a quantity of labour determines the value of a thing not only because it can be representable in units of work in exchange, but also and more importantly because labour as a producing activity is the source of all value. Value is no longer a sign; it has become a product. Value has its origin in labour and it changes according to the quantity of labour devoted to produce things; however, Foucault stresses that it does not change according to an increase or decrease in wages. After Ricardo, it is not trade and exchange that form the basis of the study of wealth. Labour is the basis, given that the exchange is based upon labour. Therefore, the theory of production was to precede that of circulation.

In his later genealogical investigations, Foucault also identifies one more significant transformation in the ontological notion of labour in economics. He argues that labour was not radically investigated in economics until the neoliberals. Because labour was only understood as one more factor of production and through the interweaving of time, it was not analysed in itself. The notion of human capital brought a new epistemological view of labour. Labour is investigated in its essence, its origins and existence. This also promoted a new conception of *homo economicus*, who is no longer solely a partner in an exchange process – he is also an entrepreneur.

A very deep assessment of Foucault's 'internal' statements ('factual' statements or his interpretation of 'theoretical' statements made by writers he mentioned) regarding the history of economic thought would require a considerable number of specialists in a variety of issues, such is the scope and force of his proposals. Nevertheless, beyond the discussion concerning the accuracy of some pointed historical statements, it has been demonstrated that Foucault enlarged our perspective, offering a range of significant elements, both new and rethought, for the rethinking of its historiography.

The analysis of mercantilism and physiocracy as different paradigms coexisting in the seventeenth and eighteenth centuries, underlined by the same epistemic context, sheds light on some important epistemological aspects founded on a particular conception of the mode of being of things. The scrutiny of 'paradigms' may tell us much about the way in which the history of the discipline, to put it in relative terms, happens 'in the surface' of knowledge. The 'episteme' may be able to show us the underlying fundamental framework related, in particular, to the notion of representation and a theory of signs. 'Mercantilists' and 'physiocrats' were thinking according to the same structure given by the same perception of basic signs (concerning what comprised wealth, exchange, money and trade) and following the same conception of language derived from their 'age of representation'. Indeed, economic thought was about represented needs in a system of exchange.

In the transition to the modern way of thinking, Smith combined a perception of finitude with a desire to find out the natural order of things. It can be clarifying to think about Smith's system according to that interdiscursive practice, which the economic thought shared with the natural history and the theory of language. This stressed and shed some light on the issues regarding the centrality of 'exchange' in his system and the understanding of his labour theory of value. Foucault's archaeology showed that although labour expressed value in Smith's economics, it was only with Ricardo that labour began theoretically to produce value. As for Smith's writings on language and rhetoric, they already pointed to a 'dispersion' of language, which led to the emergence of philology. However, Smith could not anticipate the philosophical thought on the being of language that emerged at the end of the nineteenth century. The question about the relationship between current concerns with rhetoric in economics and the linguistic turn verified in philosophy remains to be explored. Although we may not have a final answer to the question, given that this would involve a deep investigation as to how conscious economists engage in this new conversation, it is possible to paraphrase Foucault and say that at least we now know what has to be asked and why we should ask it: 'It is true that I do not know what to reply to such questions [...]. Nevertheless, I now know why I am able [...] to ask them – and I am unable not to ask them today' (*OT*, p. 307).

Finally, the archaeology of political economy placed in evidence the emergence of three fundamental epistemological changes, which marked the 'positivity' of economics (as one of the thresholds of knowledge defined in Foucault's theory of discourse – see Chapter 2): the emergence of a new form of causal series; the emergence of the concept of 'scarcity' with a fundamental meaning; and a change related to the evolution of economics. Regarding the first change, when Ricardo dissociated the creation of value from its representativity, the historicity of economy became possible; that is, instead of finding out a representative table of wealth according to the space of equalities and differences, theorising in political economy became a focus on the temporal sequence of production, its historicity. Then, one began to think in terms of labour, production, accumulation, growth of real costs and so on. In an ontological analysis, political economy resulted from a change in economic theory from the central aspect of the needs and desire of the body to its labouring character. Now man will be seen as a producer and not as one that simply represents his needs. As for the notion of scarcity, whilst it was understood according to the changes in human needs during the previous episteme, it increased considerably, meaning a fundamental anthropological finitude in the modern age. *Homo economicus*, as it arose at that moment, is not an agent that represents needs, but one that has to face this radical finitude. The last consequence for economic thought, which Foucault calls 'the evolution of economics', is that the intertwining of man's finitude and history led to the 'pessimism' in theory, such as Ricardo's 'steady state', or even Marx's revolutionary promise. Thus, Foucault argued that there was no discontinuity between Ricardo and Marx. They were in the same epistemic configuration of thought, following the same conditions of possibility. Whilst Ricardo pointed out to 'an indefinite deceleration', Marx saw a 'radical reversal' as 'the fulfilment of an end to history' (*OT*, p. 262).

Here is an assessment of the critiques usually raised against Foucault's system (which were discussed in Chapter 3) becoming fundamental in the case of economics.

As for the criticism related to his notion of discontinuity in history, in general terms it would appear that it does not apply in the case of economics. The discontinuity in economic thought, as pointed out by Foucault, works very well in helping us to understand the historical specificity of concepts. It is particularly interesting to note the centrality of money in a web of representations during the seventeenth and eighteenth centuries, which led to a focus on a theory of circulation. This was followed by the privileged role played by the notion of space in the approach to wealth and according to a search for the natural order; similarly, at the end of the eighteenth century, labour emerged for thought following a concept of historicity as a temporal and organic structure, which went beyond the visibility of the object of study. Time became a fundamental agent in subject formation. This led to a theory of production that replaced the precedence of a theory of circulation.

As for the implication that discontinuity undermined notions such as 'influence' and 'predecessors', Foucault was indeed not opposing such notions insofar as they were treated as events in the same epistemic context. In this way, it is possible to understand, for instance, the

Petty-Cantillon-Quesnay sequence (stressed, for instance, by Schumpeter, 1954, p. 218) or Hume and Smith's intellectual proximity. As another example, Foucault's classification of epistemes does not undermine Schumpeter's statement: 'Cantillon was to Quesnay and Petty was to Cantillon, what Ricardo was to Marx' (ibid.). In Foucault's archaeology, the latter two were in the modern era, while the former four were in the classical episteme. The case is such that Foucault focused on mutations rather than continuity, but it does not mean that there is no continuity. The problem was that historians used to focus on tradition, influence, evolution and so on. Hence, Foucault declared, we should disturb the tranquillity with which these notions are accepted (*AK*, p. 28).

However, as for the question as to whether Foucault had failed to see diversity within the same epistemic context, it may well exist in the current economic discourse. For example, despite his emphasis on the radical shift of an ontological order of body from 'needs' to 'labour' at the beginning of the nineteenth century, Jack Amariglio, inspired by Foucault's genealogy, has argued that one way of distinguishing current approaches in economic theory is through 'an ontology regarding the order of the body' (Amariglio, 1988, p. 586). In addition to this, Amariglio points out that Marxist and neoclassical economic theory can be distinguished by which aspect of the body is taken as the focus for a theory of value. Whilst the former takes the labouring aspect of the body, that is, 'the capacity and primacy of the body to toil *in* the face of death' as its focus, the latter presumes the predominance of the aspect of 'desire', 'estimated and controlled by the psyche' (ibid., p. 585).

There are few references made to Foucault's archaeology within economics and even fewer examples presented in English, although one remarkable paper is Amariglio (1988). It is more difficult to find a critical review of Foucault's ideas in economics, Schabas (2005) being a rare exception. Schabas argues that although Foucault 'displays considerable erudition about the history of economics', he completely misunderstood the history of economic thought. One of her criticisms was that economics did not develop alongside the other human sciences (sociology, linguistics or even psychology) because it 'has a much older lineage' than these sciences (ibid., p. 17). She declared that political economy was already 'a coherent discourse by the late seventeenth century, in particular because of the texts of Pierre Boisguilbert, John Locke, and William Petty' (ibid.). In this case, it would be necessary to understand what she meant by 'a coherent discourse' in order to be able to assess her statement. However, she provided indications of that when she wrote that 'there is a rich body of literature on money and trade in the fourteenth and fifteenth centuries' and 'Aquinas, Jean Buridan, and Nicola Oresme all took stock of new developments in European commerce in conjunction with Aristotle's teaching' (ibid.). Yet, Foucault never denied these writings and he was indeed exploring the relations between 'political economy', such as those that emerged at the end of eighteenth century, and the emergence of these human sciences. He particularly wanted to show how man became a central figure for knowledge, leading to their emergence. He was not arguing that 'economics' emerged 'alongside' the human sciences in the sense that Schabas suggests. Foucault was not implying that there was no thought about economy before that time. Indeed, her criticism may be more appropriate for those with a traditional view of history in economics that perhaps considers economics to have only emerged under Smith, the father of economics, or when economists have problems understanding 'mercantilism' as a 'school of thought', in the sense that they do not have a coherent discourse in mind.

Another important criticism that Schabas makes regarding Foucault's archaeology is that she is in disagreement with his 'claim that the concept of wealth was a representation in the seventeenth and eighteenth centuries'. She adds that wealth was actually 'conceived of in hard physical terms' at that stage and that 'only later, in the mid-to late nineteenth century, did it become a nonmaterial entity'. So, she argues, it was only then that wealth became a 'representation' (Schabas, 2005, p. 18), noting that 'Wealth went, not from being a representation to an object, but the other way round' (ibid.). Thus, it appears that Schabas has actually misunderstood Foucault's notion of 'representation'. She associates 'representation' with the 'materiality' of the object, wealth in this case. Indeed, she applied the terms 'representation' and 'object' with meanings very distinct from those used by Foucault. As emphasised here, 'representation' is an epistemological notion in Foucault's archaeology, meaning that, at that moment, there was still a possibility of 'representing' thought through language. It would appear that, for Schabas, 'representation' had a sense of 'abstraction', even though it was still difficult to understand what she meant by 'wealth becoming representation in political economy'. However, she stated her agreement with Foucault in terms of Ricardo providing a critical watershed (ibid.). What is even more interesting is that Schabas's book can be considered as a substantive contribution that demonstrates the central argument made by Foucault, which is the fact that, at that time, there was an 'interdiscursive practice', whose investigation can provide considerable understanding regarding economic thought.

Nevertheless, it has been considered that Foucault presented a different 'periodisation' of the history of economic thought that may be proved to be problematic. One of the major divergences is related to the fact that Foucault did not see any important epistemic shift in economic thought from that promoted by Marx. As Foucault suggests, 'Marxism exists in nineteenth-century thought like fish in water: that is, it is unable to breathe anywhere else' (*OT*, p. 262).

The reason why Foucault does not see any discontinuity in his archaeology needs to be considered according to the level of criticism. It is worth stressing that Foucault's archaeology criticises the traditional accounts of the history of economic thought at an epistemological level, without connecting its key shifts to economic or political events, or even to the conceptions of the economic system or society as a whole. His view resulted from a different philosophical point of view and an account of the ontological and epistemological assumptions that underlie thought. As seen in Chapter 2, he criticised the dialectical accounts based on a Hegelian immanent conception of history, since he was under the strong influence of structuralism and phenomenalism. This helps us understand why it is that when he does not see an expressive epistemic distinction between Marx and Ricardo, he is not actually adopting the same viewpoint as other historians, who are mainly concerned with ideological, political or even theoretical aspects.

The fact that Foucault did not identify a distinct place for Marx in his archaeology of *The Order of Things* does not mean that he did not consider any expressive change as promoted by Marx. It may even be said that Foucault was somewhat evasive when he wrote in *The Archaeology of Knowledge* that Marx inaugurated 'an entirely new discursive practice on the basis of political economy' (*AK*, p. 207). When he made this assertion, he was dealing with the thresholds of knowledge (as seen in Chapter 2) and intended to imply that the change of a discursive practice would not suggest the following of a different epistemic formation. However, his statement remains problematic since it appears that, according to his system, a different discursive practice would involve a transformation of the underlying conditions of thought.

Indeed, as emphasised throughout this book, the analysis of Foucault's archaeology criticises the usual approach to history on a different level. In this sense, if Foucault does not regard there to be a substantial difference between Ricardo and Marx, then what he understood referred to the conditions of possibility of both of these thinkers. For Foucault, they could both be considered possible, according to a certain constitution of those relations: language-representation, time-space, thought-unthought and so on. The predominant writings of Foucault that have been ana-lysed here (*The Order of Things* and *The Archaeology of Knowledge*), despite containing elements that will be important for Foucault's later analyses of power, do not provide explanations for the different regimes of power.

Foucault's critique of Marx's economic determinism is not manifest in his archaeology of knowledge. It is only later, while working on the genealogy of knowledge/power relations, that he demonstrated his disa-greement with the Marxist conception of power. He challenged the idea that the human subject and forms of knowledge were given beforehand and that the economic and social conditions of existence were imprinted on a given subject. For him, power relations were neither derived only from the role of the state nor from class struggles. Power is asymmetri-cally dispersed throughout the social body (Foucault's microphysics of power) and cannot be analysed only through its negative role.

Foucault claims that although, of course, Marx and Ricardo presented different 'theoretical' alternatives, they both shared and could not modify a certain epistemological configuration of thought. They had to deal with the same epistemic context, which was especially marked by the relations between scarcity and labour. On the one hand, scarcity acquired a meaning of fundamental anthropological finitude and, on the other hand, labour became historical. This led to Ricardo's 'steady-state' and to Marx's revolutionary promise.

Another important distinction relating to Foucault's 'periodisation' is the fact that he did not consider the 'Marginalist Revolution'. This intellectual movement at the end of the nineteenth century has been considered as a moment of rupture and change within the theoretical scheme and of language use, which led to the emergence of 'neoclassi-cal' economics or mathematical economics. There has been some debate as to whether that moment could really be depicted as a 'revolution' in the sense of a discontinuity regarding the main theoretical conceptions. However, more recent studies demonstrated that it did at least represent a 'methodological' revolution, whilst employing a metaphor imported from physics and adopting the mathematical language in the construc-tion of pure theory (see Mirowski, 1984 and 1989). The point here is that while mathematics had previously been employed, it was mainly used as an instrument for the purpose of quantification and became a language in the formulation of theories at the end of the nineteenth century. It would therefore appear that Foucault had neglected the importance of that moment in the history of economic thought, since he located that movement in the same epistemic context as Ricardo, the modern episteme.

Therefore, there are at least two levels of analysis regarding Foucault's disregard of that moment. First, we could consider the 'theoretical' aspects that in some way would not corroborate Foucault's main conclusions concerning the conditions of possibility of Marx. Second, we should evaluate the methodological change promoted by marginalism and how this alludes to Foucault's characterisation of that moment in terms of the epistemic context.

Regarding the first level above, Birken (1990) argued that Foucault failed to see the break promoted by marginalism. He argued that marginalism, and thus the emergence of neoclassical theory, marked a sharp break in relation to classical economics and that it should be considered as part of a new ('postmodern') epistemic configuration of thought. According to him, the emphasis placed by marginalists on utility pointed to a Nietzschean relativisation of the body, which does not have the collective character that it used to have for classical economists. The neoclassical body had already acquired a 'decentred', 'postmodern' character by the end of the nineteenth century, marking a first moment of 'postmodernism' in economics. He argues that there was a shift from production to consumption, in which desire could no longer be depicted by humanist basic principles. For Birken, Foucault failed to see the break, precisely because of his methodology: archaeology. Birken notes that the problem with the archaeology was exactly that it did not offer elements for understanding exactly when and where the epistemic shifts had happened. However, what is more problematic in Birken's argument is his very unusual conception of neoclassical theory. Amariglio (1990a) has again made a substantive contribution to the debate regarding Foucault on economics by responding to Birken's criticism. He argues that Birken's views resulted from an unsustainable concept of neoclassical economics, which was problematic on four basic grounds: the economic man in the neoclassical theory is not a 'decentred' subject, as supposed by Birken; the neoclassical conception keeps the stable rational connection between desire and preference; the neoclassical notion of equilibrium requires the assumption that there is a universal statute of desire; and *homo economicus* has an essential identity in neoclassical theory. Contrary to what Birken believes, Amariglio agrees with Foucault in that neoclassical economics does not differ from classical economics, in the sense that it maintained the same humanist concern, which was to find the essential principles of the economic man.

As for the 'Marginalist Revolution' representing a methodological shift, it does not mean that it could be considered as an epistemic transformation. As argued throughout this book, Foucault's archaeology of epistemes actually offers us some insights to enable us to understand how different methodological conceptions take place and exist in a certain discursive practice. In this way, Foucault considered the 'Marginalist Revolution' as inserted in the same epistemic context of Ricardo. According to Foucault, the marginalist movement was indeed a response to the conditions of the modern episteme, when the end of representation transformed the thought on language. If one of the main changes promoted by marginalism was to incorporate the mathematical language into economic theory, this could be understood as a means of trying to overcome the limitations of knowledge that marked the essence of the modern episteme, which Foucault called 'analytic of finitude'. As Foucault remarked, formalism, whereby the mathematisation promoted by the main protagonists of marginalism was the first step, became a means of trying to surpass the collapse of representation. In this sense, marginalism was indeed a transformation of method, although it occurred due to the same conditions of thought that marked the emergence and existence of the classical economics from Ricardo onwards. Indeed, Ricardo's way of thinking, which has been said to have already changed the method of economics ('Ricardian Vice'), was also only possible due to the same conditions.

Therefore, Foucault's archaeology can be applied to a study of the historical basis of methodological, rhetorical and linguistic devices. In the next chapter, this potential is demonstrated through the understanding of Smith's writings about language and rhetoric, his method and his notion of the 'invisible hand' under the influence of this perspective. In addition, Smith's case sheds light on the issue relating to the clearcut shifts between epistemes, such as those argued by Foucault. This usual criticism of Foucault's project needs to be reassessed, particularly in the light of his treatment of Smith as a transitional figure. Although Foucault insisted on this characteristic of the episteme, it would appear that Smith is a good example of such changes that take time and are not easy to perceive.

6
Some of Foucault's Contributions to Reconsidering the Debate on Smith's Context and Writings

6.1   Introduction

Adam Smith played a central role in Michel Foucault's work, both in his archaeology of knowledge (including political economy) and in his genealogy of biopolitics. He often mentioned and quoted Smith in *The Order of Things* and on a number of other occasions, such as during interviews and lectures. It is important to emphasise the understanding of Foucault's representation of Smith through the publication of his lectures at the Collège de France during 1978–9 (Foucault, 2004). Essentially, the aim of this chapter is to demonstrate the potential of Foucault's contributions to the current scholarship of Smith's works amongst economists. The previous chapter focused on Smith's economics, following Foucault's archaeology of political economy. The attention will now focus on Smith's writings on language and rhetoric, the methodological conceptions underlying his work according to a common discursive practice of his time, and his role in the emergence of biopolitics according to Foucault's genealogy.

6.2   Smith on language and rhetoric

As referred to in Chapter 3, Foucault placed Smith's 'Considerations concerning the first formation of languages' (hereafter 'Considerations') alongside other works on language and rhetoric by Locke, Condillac and Destutt de Tracy as examples of the conception of knowledge as intrinsic to discourse, and general grammar as 'the spontaneous form of science' in the classical age. Although Foucault mentioned and quoted 'Considerations' many times in *The Order of Things*, we cannot be sure if he was aware of the *Lectures on Rhetoric and Belles Letters* (hereafter *Lectures on Rhetoric*). However, even if we did know, it would be impossible to determine if he really meant to consider all of them in the context of the classical age. Hence, we cannot be sure if Foucault really depicted Smith's writings on language and rhetoric as being about 'discourse' – 'the spontaneous analysis of representation' – and not being about 'language' in the 'modern' sense of the term. This may well have clarified how Foucault interpreted Smith's concept on the possibility of representation. Nonetheless, based on some related facts suggested below, it can be argued that Smith's concern with language also followed a moment of transition into modern thought. Indeed, Foucault's argument regarding Smith's economic thought, being in transition between epistemes, provides a strong case to suggest that this could also be true of Smith's writings on language and rhetoric.

To understand this point requires a clear comprehension of the changes in the concept of language that have occurred since the Renaissance. This was detailed in Chapter 3, although the main ideas will be summarised here.

In the 'age of resemblance', a primary text had been left in the world by a creator, man could find out about it through interpretation and so language was one more sign to be interpreted. In the classical age, language was the first representation of thought. What was studied in general grammar was indeed 'discourse' in the sense of 'a way of speaking, arranging and presenting representations of the world in a logical order' (O'Farrell, 2005, p. 41). Since knowledge, or scientific knowledge (at least regarding the interdiscursive domain of natural history, general grammar and the analysis of wealth), was 'a refinement of the knowledge implicit in ordinary language' (Gutting, 1989, p. 195), a form of grammar became necessary. During the modern age, philology emerged taking 'language' and not 'discourse' in the previous sense as an object of study. Language became an object amongst others to be studied. This reflected the emergence of man as the subject of knowledge. Since man found out the limits of representation and was the one who expressed knowledge, which could only be carried out through a language, language therefore had to be studied. Formalisation emerged as a means of trying to escape from the limits of representation. 'Language, reason and knowledge no longer go together' (Cousins and Hussain, 1984, p. 46). Man is finite and he has to deal with an unthought, which can be unconscious. He actually expressed himself through language, giving meaning to words and things, which were then subjective. Language was no longer representational; if it still represented something, then it did so through man. Hence, during the classical age, representations and things were linked by language, although in the modern era, things were separated from representation. On one side, there are things and on the other, there are representations, which are more or less accurate of the reality that will always be unknown. These representations only occurred through man and, more precisely, through language.

It may be possible to see some of Smith's concerns regarding language as fitting into Foucault's description of the classical period, in which to know was to speak and/or write correctly. Smith was certainly aware of the studies on the origin of language and grammar of his time. He cited Rousseau's *Discours sur l'origine et les fondements de l'inégalité parmi les homes* in 'Considerations' (Smith, 1983, p. 205), where Rousseau himself refers to Condillac's writing on the subject. Smith had read the articles on grammar in the French *Encyclopédie* and Abbé Girard's *Les Vrais Principles de La Langue Français*e, and wrote a letter to George Baird in 1763, referring to a project by William Ward which was published in 1765 with the title *Essay on Grammar*:

> I approve greatly of his plan for a Rational Grammar and am convinced that a work of this kind executed with his abilities and industry, may prove not only the best System of Grammar, but the best System of Logic in any Language, as well as the best History of the *natural progress of Human mind in forming the most important abstractions upon which all reasoning depends*. (Smith, quoted in Mossner and Ross, 1977, pp. 87–8, emphasis added)

Smith even associated the system of language with the system of logic, as seen above. In this sense, we could conjecture about the conception of 'knowledge as a well-made discourse', in which style became a crucial goal in a specific sense. This is evident in statements such as that Smith believed that:

> the best method of explaining and illustrating the various powers of the human mind, the most useful part of *metaphysics*, arises from an examination of the several ways of communicating our thoughts by speech, and from an attention to the principles of those literary compositions, which contribute, to persuasion or entertainment. (Howell, 1975, p. 12, original emphasis)

For Smith, simplicity might suffice. In his belief, there was a clear, plain and perspicuous style which would provide an author with the best skills to deliver his ideas. Perhaps that is why Smith seems to privilege communication rather than persuasion. Brown (1994), for instance, declares that he emphasised 'communication as a general aim of all speech and writing as opposed to the classical emphasis on persuasion' (Brown is here using 'classical' to refer to 'classical rhetoric'). Thus, it seems that the conception of language of the classical episteme was underlying his argument in favour of 'a plain style' that the author should apply in order to achieve his or her aim of communicating or transmitting thoughts.

Nevertheless, a more accurate reading of Smith's writings on the subject suggests that his interest in language surpassed the epistemic borders of the classical age, such as those depicted by Foucault. They certainly went beyond a mere pedagogic concern or an interest related to his local environment of debate, which related to the use of Scotticisms and the concern regarding self-improvement and peculiar to the Scottish Enlightenment, which were actually considered to be an explanation for the popularity of Smith's lectures at that time (see Howell, 1975, for instance).

Although it may be said that Smith was writing before the emergence of philology, there was much in Smith's reflections that placed him in a context of transition to a modern concept of language. They point to a 'dispersion', a 'fragmentation' of language, as was depicted by Foucault's archaeology. This is particularly true considering his *Lectures on Rhetoric*, although it is already possible to see examples of this in 'Considerations', when Smith already referred to a temporality of languages, in the modern sense, which were described by Foucault. Smith deals with the historical increase in the complexity of the composition of languages, derived in particular from the mixture of different languages (Smith, 1983, p. 220). Indeed, the full title of 'Considerations' is 'Considerations concerning the first formation of languages and the different genius of original and compounded languages'.

Smith's *Lectures on Rhetoric* indicates some of the most important characteristics of the modern conception of language, raising questions together with a treatment of language that would soon be classified in the concerns of philology. Smith had a constant concern with the internal structure of languages and conceived that language had to follow some grammatical rules in order to be able to communicate and persuade. As Foucault declared, for Smith, words did not have 'a representative function by right of birth' (*OT*, p. 280).

Smith's conception can be distinguished from Condillac's, for instance. As Berry (1974, p. 138) declared, Condillac, following the *Port-Royal Grammar* tradition, 'believed that in primitive languages every word stood for an idea and that there was accordingly perfect communication between individuals'. For Condillac, the primitive language allowed perfect communication. Smith certainly had a different approach. He privileged the historical changes in grammatical forms instead of the constant structures of the language, which were the case in general grammar and followed the *Port-Royal Grammar*. Smith also sought an understanding of the internal relation between/amongst elements of language, in order to apprehend their functions, as part of their temporality. Hence, he clearly saw language as historical in both senses, which was pointed out by Foucault: temporality and organic structure. Smith compared different systems of language and considered communication as an empirical implication of language. As was the case in relation to his economic thought, Smith's thought on language was permeated by the figure of man as the knower whose life was limited by his body, by the forces of production, by social relations and by his linguistic heritage. When Foucault described the presence of man in knowledge, it was in Smith's writings that man is 'an individual who lives, speaks, and works in accordance with the laws of an economics, a philology, and a biology' (*OT*, p. 310). This is very clear when Smith writes that it is language and our propensity to barter that makes us different from all other species. During the classical age, Smith pointed out that knowing was an 'analysis of representation', a 'decomposition of ideas', 'an anthropology dealing with a man rendered alien to himself and an economics dealing with mechanisms exterior to human consciousness', as Foucault depicted that moment (*OT*, p. 226). Smith's economics already pointed to 'the direction of an anthropology that will call into question man's very essence (his finitude, his relation with time, the imminence of death)' (*OT*, p. 225) and he took the same approach when thinking about language. As Bryce stated in the introduction to *Lectures on Rhetoric* (Smith, 1983, p. 17), language for Smith 'is organically related not merely to thought in the abstract [...]; it bears the "the same stamp" as the speaker's nature' and 'stile [...] not only expresses the thought but also the spirit and mind of the author' (ibid., p. 19).

Smith regarded language as 'developing in step with man's (and society's) development' (Berry, 1974, p. 138). Man, his sentiments and cultural context, for example, were determining meanings. Smith mentioned in *Lectures on Rhetoric*:

> The perfection of stile consists in Expressing in the most concise, proper and precise manner the thought of the author, and that in the manner which best conveys the *sentiment*, passion or affection

with which it affects or he pretends it does affect him and which he designs to communicate to his reader. (Smith, 1983, p. 55)

Statements of this kind occur frequently in Smith's writings and relate to his notion of sympathy. For Smith, the writer should place himself in the reader's position:

When the sentiment of the speaker is expressed in a neat, clear, plain and clever manner, and the passion or affection he is possessed of and intends, *by sympathy*, to communicate to his hearer, is plainly and cleverly hit off, then and then only the expression has all the force and beauty that language can give it. (Smith, 1983, p. 25, original emphasis)

Foucault contrasted the change in the study of language from the written language in classical thought (by the *Port-Royal Grammar*, for example) to a focus on the spoken language in the modern age, which was similar to 'notes of music'. Smith had a constant concern with spoken language and indeed analysed the English language in terms of sounds, employing, coincidentally or not, the same metaphor of notes in music as were employed by Foucault (Smith, 1983, p. 14).

Another important fact that corroborates our conjecture is that the speculations on language in that period did not follow a 'homogeneous' conception, as Berry (1974) argues, which may be an indicator that Foucault's framework of sequential epistemes requires additional considerations. Berry describes four schools of thought within the history of philology in that period. First, there was the 'theological' view, taken by Nicolas Beauzée (1717–89) in France, Johann Peter Süssmilchin (1707–67) in Germany and James Beattie (1735–1803) in Scotland, that language was a divine gift. A second school of thought could be termed as 'rationalist', for whom language 'was an instrument of logical analysis by which a correlation was, or ought to be, established between thought and speech' and therefore language 'was a human invention' (Berry, 1974, p. 132). Protagonists of this school of thought were James Harris (1709–80) in England and Lord Monboddo (1714–99) in Scotland. The third school of thought was 'the organic', which can be said to have had a similar view to Foucault's description of the classical age. In agreement with Foucault's description, Berry claims that Condillac and Rousseau were amongst its members, although Berry also includes Priestley and Mandeville in England and James Dunbar in Scotland. The final school of thought was called 'the emotionalists', who agreed on the origin of language, along with the organic school which included Blackwell and Blair in Scotland. However, Berry stated that the organicists placed more emphasis on the development of language. Berry then affirmed that Smith should be placed 'squarely' in the organic school.

Moreover, Smith was a contemporary of Sir William Jones, who, according to Foucault's archaeology, was a figure of transition to the modern philology. They even had a common friend, Benjamin Franklin. Jones was also a close friend of Lord Monboddo, who shared with him his intellectual views on language and man. Jones's *The Sankrit Language* was first published in 1786, marking the beginning of comparative grammar and Indo-European studies. It can only be assumed that Smith was aware of their ideas.

Another aspect of Smith's writings on language that should be discussed is his study on rhetoric, with emphasis on persuasion. As Dascal (2006, p. 105) remarks, Smith saw rhetoric slightly differently from his contemporaries. He did not understand it as being associated with the 'ornamental' role of language. Smith criticised his contemporaries and argued in favour of a 'plain' style, which 'permitted him to recover the forgotten Aristotelian rhetorical tradition that emphasises persuasion as a main discursive function' (ibid.). According to Dascal, Smith went beyond an interest in language structure and semantics, moving towards an awareness of the language use or pragmatics, which could be attested to by Smith's concern with 'the speaker's "cast of mind", his current interest and communicative intentions, the hearer's capacity of understanding, and – in general the context of use' (ibid., pp. 105–6). This view brings us to the question of how Smith could be considered within the context of current interest in the rhetoric of economics. In the light of Foucault's history, this question would require an understanding of the development of the concept of language, while establishing how this reflects on current conversation regarding the rhetoric of economics, initiated by McCloskey (1983) and Klamer (1984).

As previously mentioned, Smith's writings on language and rhetoric contain elements that point to an awareness in the language break with representation, a 'fragmentation' of language as Foucault put it. But did Smith anticipate the thought regarding 'the being of language' as promoted by those thinkers of the linguistic turn in philosophy? He was certainly not considering the questions Foucault pointed out as marking our age's conception of language. For Smith, there could be imperfections in language, but they were not due to the modern conception of language. For instance, the modern view of language conceives that meanings may not be in the text, but they develop during the process of reading, which might therefore include hidden meanings or intentions. This is indeed apparent when Smith states that the reader did not play a crucial role: 'our words must also be put in such order that the meaning of the sentence shall be quite plain and not depend on the accuracy of the printer in placing the points, or of the readers in laying the emphasis on any certain word' (Smith, 1983, p. 5).

As for rhetoric, Howell (1975) argued that Smith's lectures on the subject followed a new tradition initiated in the middle of the sixteenth century by Ramus that allied rhetoric and logic and became an important characteristic of science in Britain during the eighteenth century.

As for the new wave of interest generated in the rhetoric of economics, although it emerged after the linguistic turn in philosophy and was certainly stimulated by the necessity for thinking about language that this movement expressed, it is not clear that its protagonists were fully taking it into account. Studies on the rhetoric of economics appeared to be aiming more towards a return to the Aristotelian conception of rhetoric rather than to an understanding of a theory of discourse, as developed by thinkers of the twentieth century (in particular some French philosophers, including Foucault). McCloskey had argued that economists should be aware of their strategies of persuasion, since the only way to proceed in science was through conversation. Despite saying that economists should be rhetorically self-conscious, the rhetoric movement had failed to stimulate deeper discussions regarding economic discourse, involving a better comprehension as to how it was constituted historically and how it had existed in relation to the events, epistemological and ontological assumptions, institutions, governmental programmes and technologies, political reason and so on. This would imply a better understanding regarding its own emergence, as well as its connections to crucial philosophical movements, such as much of the continental philosophy of the twentieth century. McCloskey has been criticised for not having a theory of discourse. There could be a change here from a rhetorical self-consciousness to a linguistic self-awareness, which would include a concern about rhetoric devices. The linguistic turn in philosophy led to the idea that meanings depended upon the use of language (more details of this can be found in Chapter 2). Furthermore, in relation to Foucault, the analysing of discourse meant to think about the relationship between language, knowledge and power. However, this has not been the case in economics.

Tribe (1999, p. 618) writes that 'Smith's own approach to the teaching of rhetoric was rather different from this [for instance, McCloskey]: he treated the domain of rhetoric as equivalent to human communication, and therefore a pathway to an understanding of human motivation'. Tribe still points out that Smith was indeed looking for a set of rules towards the style of communicative discourse (ibid., p. 618). The statement by Tribe contains elements that suggest he would be in agreement with Foucault regarding the context of Smith's concern for language during the classical epistemic. Tribe also declares that it was 'much later' that 'this led to the insight that our understanding of *what* was being said or written depended on *how* or *where* it was being said' (ibid., original emphasis). One major difference that the current conception of language presents is indeed related to the Nietzschean question of 'who is speaking?' However, Foucault emphasised, when attributing this change to Nietzsche, that this new thought regarding language encompasses a more radical reflection on the being of language (*OT*, p. 305), exemplified by questions such as 'what is language?' and 'what is a sign?'. However, if the current movement on the rhetoric of economics as a concern relating to the communicative and persuasive character of discourse was understood to be the case, then it could be suggested that there was no real difference between the approaches of Smith and McCloskey.

6.3 Smith's method

Smith's essay 'The Principles which lead and direct Philosophical Enquiries: illustrated by the History of Astronomy' (hereafter 'History of Astronomy'), which was written in about 1750 and first published in 1799, is frequently discussed as an investigation into Newton's influence on Smith. Smith describes the Newtonian method 'as the greatest discovery that ever was made by man, the discovery of an immense chain of the most important and sublime truths, all closely connected together, by one capital fact, of the reality of which we have daily experience' (Smith, 1986c, p. 36). He also presented his views on method in some of the works that were published under the title *Essays on Philosophical Subjects* in 1795, where he argued that scientific enquiry should follow Newton's method. These statements, together with his conception of theories as 'imaginary machines', have been taken as proof of the influence of Newton's method on his inquiries, including economics. The similarity between Foucault's 'genesis', as mentioned in Chapter 3, together with Smith's explorations of the principles that led human nature to knowledge are really striking, although we are unable to deduce for sure if Foucault ever read Smith's works, other than 'An inquiry into the nature and causes of the wealth of nations' and 'Considerations', which were often mentioned in *The Order of Things.*

Although not denying Newton's influence on the method of Smith, it is poignant to consider this event in accordance with Foucault's perspective. In other words, instead of taking the traditional view of 'influence', it is possible to approach the event through the investigation of the discursive practice underlying knowledge. Indeed, if we were to allow such a perspective, we could read 'History of Astronomy' in a totally different light, which might even suggest that Smith was investigating the discursive practice of his time, 'exemplified' by the history of astronomy, as he declared. We may also realise how similar Foucault and Smith's considerations were. It is even possible to read in Smith the description of what Foucault called 'a general science of order', with examples from the classifications of a process in natural history, for instance. Although marginally similar to Foucault's approach, Smith's consideration of the history of astronomy is more like a description of paradigms. As Dow (2010) and Heilbroner (1986) mentioned, there is a similarity between Smith's approach and Kuhn's notion of paradigm. Dow (2010, p. 7) stated that in 'History of Astronomy', 'Smith discusses what we would now refer to as "paradigms shifts" in the understanding of the physical workings of the universe'. Heilbroner (1986, p. 15) points out that Smith's essay is 'an excellent review of the historical development of a science, reminiscent, in its emphasis on the succession of one temporarily successful account by another, of Thomas Kuhn's well-known modern treatment of a science as a succession of vulnerable "paradigms" or conceptual frameworks'.

Hence, instead of concentrating the analysis on the inductivist or deductivist methodological character of Newton's method and how that may have influenced Smith's investigations in economics, we can focus on the investigation of *their* combined contexts. Other important aspects of Smith's writings emerge for consideration, such as his frequent use of examples taken from other fields of investigation. It is of particular interest to note that he used to take examples from natural history, which may corroborate Foucault's view of an 'interdiscursive' practice. Schabas (2005), as mentioned previously, is an example of this type of approach.

Smith described the process of knowledge through an ordering of things. He described and provided examples of what was being done in natural history at that time, according to a process of knowledge and through the analysis and ordering of things, mentioning the examination of plants by naturalists in order to classify them according to species, genera and so on. Smith even presented it as the procedure that followed on from knowledge in general, through an observation of resemblances between objects and the arrangement of them into 'proper classes and assortments' (*HA*, p. 24). Above all, the aspect of analysis and classification, according to equalities and differences, which are the essential characteristic of the classical representation through a general science of order, became explicit in Smith's way of thinking. Referring to the classification (which he called 'assortments') into genera and species in practice in natural history, he stated:

> The further we advance in knowledge and experience, the greater number of divisions and subdivisions of those Genera and Species we are both inclined and obliged to make. [...] Whatever, in short, occurs to us we are fond of referring to some species or class of things, with all of which it has a nearly exact resemblance. (*HA*, p. 25)

Smith also refers to the sentiments that guide human knowledge – 'surprise', 'admiration' and 'wonder' – the latter emerging when man has to order completely new things, that is, things he cannot associate through resemblance with anything he has seen before. He declares that when resemblance is not enough to make such classifications, specifically when something new is presented to us, when our imagination and memory are not helpful, we experience the sentiment of 'wonder', a sentiment of 'uncertain' and 'undetermined thought' (*HA*, p. 26). This description by Smith, referencing the procedure of knowledge in his own time, has a striking similarity to Foucault's characterisation of his epistemic context, where resemblance and imagination played central roles in the process of knowledge.

Therefore, instead of drawing our attention clearly to the question of how and to what extent economics mirrored physics, perhaps this new perspective could provide not only an understanding as to why this happened (since there was a common discursive practice), but also a realisation as to the importance attached to the other aspects of an author's system. For example, the comprehension of Smith's epistemic context highlights the centrality of 'exchange' in his system, which sheds light on the readings of his economics and the many controversies to date. One example is related to Smith's theory of value, which relates the notion of labour to wealth in a network of representations, where the focus was still on exchange (era of representation), while adding elements that suggested a new epistemic context (age of history), this being especially applicable since he did not consider labour as a unity of value in relation to man's needs, which was the case during the classical age; instead he regarded labour as an absolute unit for the measurement of exchange value.

In *The Theory of Moral Sentiments*, first published in 1759, Smith had already argued that there was no antagonism but a harmony of individual interests that could promote the benefits for society, as Mandeville's *Fable of the Bees* (first published in 1723) had suggested. This 'economic harmony' reflected Smith's epistemic context, in the sense that there was the conception of a natural order, which was also present in the beliefs of the physiocrats. Therefore, it has been considered most likely that when Smith turned his attention to the inquiry into economic phenomena, he applied the same methodological system that he identified in Newton's work. For instance, Deane (1978) and Redman (1991) supported this view and argued that *The Theory of Moral Sentiments* contained the central principles that explained human behaviour in his system in 'An inquiry into the nature and causes of the wealth of nations'. The role played by sympathy in the former led to Smith's conclusions regarding the harmony of *self-interested behaviour* in the latter (Redman, 1991, p. 98). Deane argues:

> *The Wealth of Nations* was the result of subjecting to empirical test in one sphere of human activity the theory of society that had been in *The Theory of Moral Sentiments*. [...] By postulating a logical system of economic relationships based upon an underlying law of human nature (analogous to Newton's law of gravity), he set the course of theoretical political economy towards a system-building discipline. (Deane, 1978, pp. 10–11)

Another aspect related to the recent debate amongst Smith's interpreters and from which this new kind of approach could also benefit is a reference to the relation between his system and the later emergence of a general equilibrium theory in economics. This may not only be confusing the idea of 'principles' derived from analytical history (present in Smith's argument) with 'axioms' (present in classical logic), as argued by Dow (2010), but it may also be ignoring the fact that 'formalism', which made the general equilibrium theory possible in economics, only emerged during a modern way of thinking. It was the 'fragmentation' of language, derived from a more fundamental finitude of man and his ambition to control language, which led to the emergence of formalism at the end of the nineteenth century.

As Montes (2004) had argued, Smith could not be considered as a predecessor to the general equilibrium theory, based on Newton's influence of his method. This is because Smith, following the Scottish Enlightenment, interpreted Newton's method correctly under his 'experimental philosophy'. Newton's method combined inductivism and deductivism. As Burtt (2003) claimed, there were no *a priori* certainties for Newton, as there could be for Kepler, Galileo or Descartes. The secrets of nature could not be uncovered solely by an axiomatic-deductive approach. Burtt declares that Newton even declared that some problems could not be properly translated into mathematical language and that mathematics was a useful tool to solve problems presented by experience. Just as Newton derived laws departing from singular facts, Smith was a shrewd observer of history and different societies, and his deductions were empirically based.

Foucault's archaeology also provides a number of important elements for exploring the epistemological conception that underlies the work of Smith. In particular, the change in the conception of human nature and the emergence of an unthought element for knowledge can all shed light on our debate. The fact that Foucault included Hume and partially Smith in the context of 'the age of representation' raises the point regarding his ability to see the real possibility of knowledge within these other thinkers.

In this case, what is understood by 'representation' and mentioned in Chapter 3 is, in its most usual meaning, derived from Leibniz's use of the term that is taken as 'correspondence' to something 'exterior' to man, where man 'represents' things in the world in which he exists. If this was the sense that was used by Foucault, then Hume and Smith could not be considered to be in the same epistemic context, since they did not understand knowledge as an accumulation of 'truths'.

As mentioned previously, Foucault employed the term 'representation' in the sense of man 'representing' thought through language, which was a 'duplicated representation'. It was representation in the sense that thought became clear by means of the transparency of language. Therefore, it would appear that Foucault leaves the question open regarding the relationship between 'representation' and the 'real world'. There could be those who believed that 'thought' reproduced 'reality' and those like Hume who did not.

One of the most important claims of Hume was that knowledge could be considered to be more to do with belief. Deleuze (1991, Preface to the English edition) is even more vigorous in affirming that Hume 'established the concept of belief and put it in the place of knowledge. He 'laicized belief', says Deleuze, 'turning knowledge into a legitimate belief'. For Hume, we believe in a continuing and independently existing world, in our own continuing selves and in causal relations. But from where do our beliefs come? As Norton (1993, p. 11) replies, Hume argued that they are indeed beliefs in 'fictions' because in his system 'neither reason nor the senses, working with impressions and ideas, provide anything like compelling proof of the existence of continuing, external objects, or of a continuing, unified self'. If we had only reason and senses, we would be 'in a debilitating and destructive uncertainty' (ibid.). What permits our beliefs is 'imagination'. Thus, Hume gave 'imagination' a special function in knowledge, rescuing it from the usual prejudice against such a faculty and, as mentioned previously, Foucault actually seemed to have taken Hume's reflections on the role of 'imagination' as an axis upon which to determine an understanding of classical thought.

Although some of Hume's interpreters suggest that his conclusion is that reality did not exist, he actually affirmed that there was no possibility to prove it by experience or observation. For instance, Norton (1993) argues that in Hume's system, neither impressions nor ideas resembled objects. Hume did not take perceptions 'as *representations* of external existences' (Norton, 1993, p. 8, original emphasis). Indeed, in the case of Hume, we cannot determine whether such an order exists or not. It appears that for him, we also believe in 'representations', since we repeat some impressions that are derived from our experience, which provides us with the ideas that serve to 'represent' them. As Dow (2002b, p. 404) argues, they have been attributing to Hume an ontological conclusion which he had never reached. Indeed, Dow states that Hume's conclusion was epistemological, in the strict sense that reality could never be proved; as Norton (1993, pp. 7–9) argues, Hume affirmed that the immediate objects of the mind are perceptions, although he never stated that the perceptions were 'representative of objects'.

Given Smith's non-Cartesian epistemological view, Foucault's characterisation of his thought as being a 'representation' of things, such as in relation to his economic thought, could prove problematic. Since Smith is depicted as being on the bridge of modern thought, his case became slightly different from that of Hume. With Smith, the presence or otherwise of an 'unthought' becomes fundamental in establishing how he is placed in one of these epistemic contexts, even though 'unconscious' has a meaning that goes beyond the usual psychological or sociological meaning attached to it and which is something that may be unveiled by some future therapies or sociological investigations. It is perhaps the 'unconscious' that may encompass the 'unthought', which is something that is not and cannot be thought. Representations in the modern age, which occurred through man and language, are generally seen as being due to the 'unthought', otherwise considered as 'the other'. Modern knowledge always relates to the question of conditions of possibility.[1]

Foucault did not deal with Smith's role in the emergence of psychology and sociology. However, he did consider Hume's influence on the subject. According to Foucault's archaeology, Hume was not establishing or suggesting an investigation of a psychological basis for knowledge. It was only in the modern episteme that the human sciences emerged and it was then that they emerged, due to the change in concept of human nature. Regarding the classical thought, there was a representation of a natural order where man was a part of it. In this sense, Hume was looking for the principles of human nature. The human sciences, including psychology and sociology, emerged as a method of rethinking the relationship between those things that were not a part of nature (even if they were, they would then be part of the unthought). The human sciences do not study what man is in nature. In modern thought, 'I think' is not followed by 'I am'. There may be something 'exterior' to man, something that is not 'part of his nature' or, as mentioned previously, even if it was a part of it, it may also be 'unconscious', 'unknown'. For Foucault, this new conception was translated into economics by the centrality of 'labour'. There is in the modern age something that is not part of his nature and governs his behaviour, even if he is not completely aware of its principles or how to deal with it (*OT*, p. 318).

Following Foucault's explanation of the emergence of the human sciences, we need to ask ourselves the following question: was Smith focusing on a search for the psychological principles of human nature? The common understanding is that psychology is the scientific study of the human mind and its functions, especially those affecting behaviour. In this case, we would not have a problem depicting some of the concerns of Smith and Hume relating to the search for 'psychological' principles of human nature. Otherwise, as Colman (2001) explains, psychology is 'the study of the nature, functions, and phenomena of behaviour and mental experience'. However, while considering Foucault's conditions of possibility within the emergence of psychology, it may be necessary to investigate the presence of the 'unthought' in respect of Hume and Smith.

6.4   Smith, the birth of biopolitics and the invisible hand

While this book primarily focuses on Foucault's archaeology and writings during the 1960s, it has also been necessary to explore his later works and lectures at the Collège de France in 1978–9 when referring to the works of Smith, when referring to Smith's role in the birth of biopolitics and while reflecting on Foucault's earlier studies. This reinforces the argument that there is a direct connection between the two phases of Foucault's work: archaeology and genealogy. Archaeology and genealogy are only stages of his intellectual project and Smith played a central role in both.

The biopolitical analysis proposed by Foucault was developed within the context of his courses at the Collège de France. It is particularly interesting to enhance the understanding of Foucault's representation of Smith through the publication of his lectures in 1978–9 (Foucault, 2004). Foucault focused on the discussion of a genealogy of the knowledge/power relationships, with the intention of demonstrating, that knowledge is built as a result of the relations of power that are established in societies.

The exercise of power is analysed from two fundamental elements: the law, whose judicial rules formally define power, and the truth, which legitimises and renews a power of its own. Power is only exercised through the production of truth, in as much as its implementation presupposes an economy of statements of truth. Such discourses are an expression and are expressed through power devices. These devices include institutions, architectonic organisations, regulating decisions, laws, administrative measures, scientific discoveries and philosophical, moral and philanthropic propositions. In other words, knowledge and truth are produced through power struggles between different fields, disciplines and institutions which are used to authorise and legitimate power. For example, a person can be considered abnormal since the human sciences define him/her as such. 'Biopower' certainly consists of these technologies, which analyse, regulate and define the human body and its behaviour. Thus, power must be analysed as something that circulates, works and can be used in a network. 'Not only do individuals circulate but they are always in a position of using their power or having it used on them; they are never the passive or consenting targets of power, they are always transmission centres' (Foucault, 2003, p. 183). With these devices, power ends up having a more positive than negative character. It produces more than it represses. If there is a need for punishment, there is a greater need for production, creation of knowledge and declarations of truth that will make the exercise of power viable. Hence, each society ends up constituting its own regimes of truth, each one welcoming determined discourses and making them work in practice, and developing its own techniques and procedures in the building of truth.

Foucault identified that one way of analysing the development of biopower was through the history of the state. Before the seventeenth century, the state was seen as a means to an end, which was in the glory of the sovereign and the welfare of the people. From the seventeenth century onwards, the state became an end in itself. The important factor was to be the strength, wealth and power of the state. People were not thought of as ends unto themselves with rights and duties but as resources that had to be taken care of and used to ensure the development of a state. In order to ensure that the population was productive, it was necessary to keep it healthy, strong and safe. The state had to regulate and control its population. This was only possible in two ways: a body of knowledge and an administrative apparatus. The body of knowledge was built upon the emergence of a group of disciplines within the human and social sciences, among which was political economy. The administrative apparatus consisted of 'policing' institutions. 'Police' were not only determined under the sense of controlling criminal activity but also in providing health and welfare, dealt with by the human sciences which provided the knowledge.

Societies thereby constitute an 'economic policy of truth' through which they may generate investments and profits (political and economic). This economy is characterised by the following points (Foucault, 2003, p. 13):

- Truth is built around the form of scientific declarations and the institutions which produce them.
- The truth is submitted to a constant economic and political incitement (a need for truth for both economic production and political power).
- The truth is the object, in many ways, for an immense diffusion of an immense consumption (circulating in the form of an education or information apparatus, whose extension into society is relatively large, although with strict limitations).
- The truth is produced and broadcast under strict control (not exclusive but dominant) of some big political or economic institutions (university, army, media).
- It is the object of political debate and social confrontation.

Foucault's objective in studying power was to unmask it through the discourses of truth, which was supported by the conception of neutrality of the rule and the scientific discourses. He proposed genealogy as a tactic to unveil the discourses of truth. However, he also proposed a genealogy of power that sought to capture the relationships of forces at the micro rather than macro level. Hence, it sought to uncover in history the events that intertwine in the production of relationships of force, enabling genealogy to uncover the making of *the history of the politicisation of problems*. As with archaeology, genealogy aims to expose these relationships not by applying the usual history of science approach, which discusses the process of formation of knowledge, but instead by making explicit, the illusion of truth.

In *Discipline and Punish* (Foucault, 1975), Foucault argues that in the seventeenth and eighteenth centuries, new techniques of power emerged. This is of course connected to his archaeology of epistemes. It suggests that the notion of 'episteme' did not disappear in his late genealogical investigations. The difference was that genealogy was about to encompass the historicity of institutions, disciplines and other activities that were consistent with the fundamental set of relations that used to fall under the heading of archaeology. Hence, genealogy investigated the knowledge-power-truth relationship in order to demonstrate that knowledge and truth were produced by struggles between institutions, fields of knowledge and disciplines. They became truth when they were introduced as eternal and universal.

In the episteme of the Renaissance, the world was God's book and the church had the power to monopolise and authorise discourses. When the church finally lost this power, a number of fields of knowledge, disciplines and institutions emerged to produce and authorise truth and knowledge. Since there was now no God to authorise them, their claims were always a matter of dispute and they had to compete with one another to negotiate support. In the classical and modern epistemes, power was dispersed and it belonged to nobody. Even the power of reigning monarchs was not attributed to them as individuals and people had little belief in their divine rights, as was evident from the executions of Charles I in 1649 in England and Louis XVI in 1793 in France. Power started to function through relations. During the modern age, the idea was that power came from the people, who were the essence of democracy, although it can be argued that the history of the twentieth century showed that individuals and groups would invent and use the notion of 'people' to obtain support for their ideas, agendas and policies. Power was something dispersed, ubiquitous and a complex flow that worked through a set of relations between different groups, and which nobody owned.

Beginning in the seventeenth century, bodies were submitted to a system of confinement, vigilance and examination to acquire certain docility, a sense of discipline, which had a double character: political obedience, which diminished the body's strength; and productivity, in terms of economic utility, which maximised the body's strength. The disciplinary society that emerged was characterised by the diffusion of characteristic architectonic organisations such as schools, hospitals, factories and prisons. The diffusion of disciplinary techniques in society tended to homogenise social space, creating a type of common language amongst the different institutions and organisations. According to Foucault (2003), power in modern societies was exercised much more by the discourses of truth, which was elaborated from the building of knowledge, than by public law.

The technology of power exercised on the individual body and typical of the classical episteme was replaced by a power that was extended to the whole of the population during the end of the eighteenth century. This was connected to the emergence of the notion of 'population', as previously seen in the emergence of political economy. Modern states had to face up to the problems by adopting governmental practices linked to the biological control of populations, such as health, hygiene, birth and life expectancy. Foucault calls this management of population 'biopolitics'. It is in this analysis of the emergence of biopolitics that Smith plays a central role in Foucault's thesis. In the middle of the eighteenth century, a new 'art of government' emerged, which had new mechanisms, effects and principles. Foucault defined 'art of government' as the 'introduction of economy into political practice' (Foucault, 1994a, p. 207). He states that:

> To govern a state will mean, therefore, to apply economy, to set up an economy at the level of the entire state, which means exercising toward its inhabitants, and the wealth and behaviour of each and all, a form of surveillance and control as attentive as that of the head of a family over his household and his goods. (Ibid., p. 207)

As Foucault emphasised, the expression already used by Quesnay captures this very well: 'economic government' (ibid.). This expression became tautological, meaning that 'the art of government is just the art of exercising power in the form, and according to the model, of the economy' (ibid.). It could be argued that the word 'economy' already signified a form of government in the sixteenth century. However, Foucault argued that it was about to acquire a totally new meaning by the end of the eighteenth century.

This 'governmentality' followed the emergence of a rationality, 'the reason of the state', which was not concerned with how power could be obtained and maintained. Foucault defines 'the reason of state' as: 'the state is governed according to rational principles that are intrinsic to it and cannot be derived solely from natural or divine laws or the principles of wisdom and prudence' (Foucault, 1994a, p. 213). States would be focused on finding the answers to questions relating to government, such as the well-being and prosperity of the state. In other words, this rationality was based on how power could be exercised most efficiently. The expression 'reason of state' led to the emergence of three types of knowledge: a diplomatic/military set, concerned with external political security; 'policy', a set of technologies and institutions for the promotion of internal security, stability and prosperity; and political economy.

Foucault writes that it was in the late sixteenth and early seventeenth centuries that the art of government was first formed around the concept of reason of state. Mercantilism was actually 'the first sanctioned effort to apply this art of government at the level of political practices and knowledges of the state' (Foucault, 1994a, p. 214). However, mercantilism did not succeed, since it was immobilised by its own objective, essentially the might of the sovereign using the typical weapons of sovereignty as instruments, such as laws, decrees and regulations. It was only when the theme of economy centred on the problem of population that this reason of state could be properly established – more specifically, it was when the theme of family was replaced by the phenomena of population. New techniques of government emerged, turning to the theme of population alongside the birth of political economy. 'Economy' used to be understood as the management of family property, although it became 'the management of population in its depths and its details' (ibid., p. 219). Population 'emerged as a datum, as a field of intervention, and as an objective of governmental techniques', leading to the isolation of 'the economy as a specific sector of reality; and political economy as the science and the technique of intervention of the government in that field of reality' (ibid.). Political economy is formed within the framework of the objectives that the reason of state established for the art of government (Foucault, 2004, p. 16). *Homo economicus* appears as the basis of a new reason of state in the eighteenth century.

For Foucault, Smith's idea of invisible hand meant a disqualification of the political sovereignty:

> The political economy does not constitute simply a refutation of the mercantilist doctrines and practices. Adam Smith's political economy does not show only how mercantilism made a mistaking technique or theory. Adam Smith's political economy, the economic liberalism, constitutes a disqualification of the project of an economic sovereignty. (Foucault, 2004, p. 288)

Adam Smith's notion of an invisible hand was also opposed to physiocracy. Although physiocracy criticised the administrative regulation through which the sovereign exerted its power over the economy, it did not question the fact that the sovereign was, in principle and by right, responsible for all production and all activity within a country. The sovereign was, after all, the co-proprietor of the lands and co-producer of the product. The existence of a *Tableau Economique* allows the sovereign to know exactly what is happening within his country and allows him to control the economic processes. If the sovereign does not interfere over the action of economic agents, it is because of the *Tableau*. A good government knows exactly what is happening through the *Tableau*, explaining to economic agents what is occurring and what they have to do to maximise their profit. Then there was the *laissez faire* in physiocracy, which coincided with the existence of a sovereign, leading to absolute despotism. Hence, there was clearly a paradox within the physiocratic theory, which changed with the aid of Smith's invisible hand.

Foucault argues that *homo economicus*, while emerging as the object of political economy, differed essentially from *homo juridicus*, having important consequences for the role of political economy as a field of knowledge to conduct the art of government. Foucault takes *homo economicus* as being the 'correlated' of the invisible hand (Foucault, 2004, p. 282), the idea being that it was the 'invisible hand' that allowed him to be the subject of interest. Smith's notion of an invisible hand refers to individuals that, without intending or knowing why, following their own interest, promote the collective benefit. Foucault draws special attention to the idea of 'invisibility': 'it is an invisibility that makes that no economic agent must not and cannot seek the collective benefit' (ibid., p. 283). In contrast to the belief of physiocrats, the invisible hand shows that economic rationality is founded on an 'unknowledgebility' of the totality of the processes (ibid., p. 285). This showed the impossibility for a sovereign to know the totality of the processes. Liberalism emerged, demonstrating this essential incompatibility between the multiplicity, the non-aggregatability of the subjects of interest, referred to as the *homo economicus*, and the aggregatable unity of the juridical sovereign, known as the *homo juridicus*. The political economy then presented itself as a 'critique' of governmental rationality in the proper and philosophical sense of 'critique'. In other words, Foucault employed the term in the Kantian sense, which emerged later, saying that man cannot know the totality of the world. For Foucault, well before Kant, political economy stated that the sovereign could not understand the totality of economic processes. For Foucault, this meant that political economy, although emerging as the field of knowledge in the new reason of state, already showed signs of becoming impossible in this role, while relating to the context of finitude. This reflection provides more elements for the comprehension of Smith's epistemology that deserves further investigation.

6.5   Final remarks

Essentially, this chapter was focused on the potentiality of Foucault's archaeological inquiry into the study of important issues relating to the history of economic thought, whilst applying it to the writings of Smith.

Concerning Smith's writings on language and rhetoric, this study has demonstrated that an awareness of the history of different conceptions of language and how man has dealt with it historically is fundamental to understanding the current interest in the subject of economics.

Although Foucault included 'Considerations' among the typical forms of thought of the classical episteme, a more accurate analysis of Smith's writings indicated that he already introduced elements that pointed to a 'fragmentation' of language, in the sense of a break in the conception of representation. Smith showed an awareness of the historical character of languages as temporal and distinct 'organic' structures, which corroborates this view. As with the notion of labour in his economic thought, Smith also puts man's essence into focus concerning his studies of language. This demonstrates the precedence of his psychological and sociological analysis within his economic thought. As for a 'contemporality' between Smith's concerns with language and the current studies of rhetoric in economics, the Foucauldian analysis provides us with elements to suggest that although there was a philosophical movement that made explicit a new conception of language occurring between them, they remain similar in the emphasis on communication and persuasion.

As for the debate regarding Smith's method, beyond a Newtonian influence on his work, Foucault's archaeology brings about a new perspective that emphasises the discursive practice of his time. Not only does it avoid the mistaken analysis regarding his influence on the method of current mainstream economics, but it also demonstrates the potentiality for future studies on the history of economics.

In Foucault's investigation of the birth of biopolitics, he dedicated a special role to Smith's notion of the invisible hand. Emphasising the idea of 'invisibility', this difference for Foucault was a fundamental element in the emergence of liberalism, since the notion made it abundantly clear that it was impossible for central government to have a complete and knowledgeable role within the economic process.

7
Conclusion

The primary objective of this book was to establish that the ideas of Foucault deserve renewed attention from economists. His efforts to improve our level of consciousness regarding what we are today, together with an understanding of our past, serves as a contribution to us all, providing remarkable benefits to economics. Beyond the instigation of some revolutionary ideas on the interpretation of the history of economic thought, he also offered a novel perspective, together with a range of inspiring notions and a consideration of the ontological and epistemological conceptions underlying knowledge since the sixteenth century, which cannot be ignored by anyone intending to study the methodology and historiography of economics.

Ironically, he employed the expression 'order of things' to refer to the different forms that some relations had combined historically since the sixteenth century (language-representation, time-space, same-other, interpretation-analogy-analysis, thought-unthought, perceptions of mode of beings and order-modes of *savoir*, though not exclusively) to establish the way man ordered things in discourse. He built his own method and terminology to investigate these processes, which he articulated in *The Archaeology of Knowledge*. Beyond an internal and/or external history, he believed in the possibility of discerning the thought of different ages through the set of relations just described, as well as proposing new and fascinating questions and suggestions as a means of answering them.

Some mention should be made of the usual criticism which has been associated with his archaeological project (detailed in the review at the end of Chapter 2), in particular to two of the biggest objections, which are what could be termed as the 'exclusivity' and 'universality' of the epistemes in a certain spatiotemporal context.

'Exclusivity' in this case is derived from his assumption that each age had one and only one episteme, or that there were clear-cut shifts and incommensurability between epistemes, which is of course related to his assumption of discontinuity in history. The 'universal' character of the epistemes prevented Foucault from seeing diversity within that context. These objections even put into question one of his main strategies of thinking, as he himself declared in *The Order of Discourse* (as seen in Chapter 2); that is, the challenging of dualistic forms of thoughts. It appears that Foucault could not avoid them.

Regarding the 'exclusivity' of the epistemes, the study here allows us to conclude that when referring to 'only one episteme', Foucault wanted to stress the epistemic distinctiveness when long periods were considered. He allowed some 'interpretability' between and among epistemes, treating some periods as having different overlapping epistemic contexts. Some prevalent figures in the history of thought illustrated this point, Adam Smith being an example of one who he openly considered as a figure of transition. This was also the case when he referred to others such as Cervantes, Sade, Lamarck and William Jones, and used the expression '*ambiguous* epistemological configuration' for the period 1775/1800 (*OT*, p. 140, emphasis added), stressing that the epistemic shifts may not be promptly perceived, for example, in the case of the concept of language in the modern age.

However, the issue of the universality of the concept of episteme remains problematic. Even if Foucault was referring to a specific 'region of interpositivities', it would appear that he failed to consider the local differences, for example, in relation to the concept of language towards the end of the eighteenth century.

Nonetheless, following on from the main objectives of this book, we should emphasise some important conclusions regarding three fundamental aspects of Foucault's archaeological project. First, this conclusion highlights some elements regarding the understanding of the conditions of possibility in the emergence and existence of economic thought. Second, it stresses some of his main contributions towards a rethinking of the methodology and historiography of economics. Third, it summarises the insights and elements required for a reconsideration of Smith's writings in their temporal context. In addition, it opens up the possibilities for further inquiries in the future.

Foucault's distinct approaches towards 'the history of the present' and 'a historical ontology of ourselves' *per se* are important contributions which open up a new perspective into the studying of our past, which would still appear to be lacking from the methodology of economists.

The usual perception within the history of economic thought has stemmed from an understanding of the past for the sake of itself, for instance, by attempting to determine a better comprehension of an author's work. Additionally, Foucault has taught us that history can be discontinuous and non-teleological, which is again a point missing from economics. Methods, rhetorical devices, linguistic conceptions, concepts and theoretical frameworks – all have their own history. Hence, the main issue in economics changes during a historical period. In other words, the object of economics has a history, which is what Foucault meant when he recommended that we investigate 'the discursive formation' through 'a system of dispersion'. What makes economics 'a unit of discourse' whilst its object and concepts change over historical time? Foucault not only raised these types of instigating questions, he also looked for the answers. For example, even though the main domain of economics was 'wealth' for mercantilists, physiocrats and Smith, they all understood it differently. Concepts like those of 'value', 'money', 'exchange' and so on have to be understood in accordance with the context in which the economic thought was constructed.

As for the consideration of our history as paradigmatic and epistemic shifts, the level of investigation is so diametrically different between the systems of Kuhn and Foucault that it makes us wonder if such a comparison is even possible. However, making clear such differences between the two concepts has enabled us to better comprehend Smith's writings in terms of not only a paradigmatic shift, but also the epistemic transformation and, similarly, has enabled us to clarify some distinct approaches. This was the case in relation to the concept of language during Smith's era, which was emphasised in Chapter 6. Different concepts of language were used to underlie studies on the subject towards the end of the eighteenth century and the diversity went beyond the different paradigms. Whilst Smith was among those who studied language according to the idea of a natural order, some still considered it in terms of a supernatural, almost a divine character. Therefore, it is emphasised that the case for paradigms versus epistemes could be extremely enlightening.

Another major contribution from Foucault was towards a rethinking on the historiography of economics, the idea of an 'interdiscursive practice' underlying thoughts. As already mentioned (in particular regarding the debate on Smith's method), such an approach could shed light on the understanding of important historical contexts in relation to economics and could offer a perspective that leads to rewarding future studies.

Foucault explored in his archaeology the relationship between ontological assumptions and epistemological beliefs (considered to be something he did very well, as observed by Rorty, 1986, p. 43), which determined the ways of thinking in the history of economic thought since the Renaissance. This provides us with the elements to determine how, and perhaps why, some methodological, rhetorical and linguistic devices have been preferred over the others.

Up until the end of the sixteenth century, a supernatural order established the thought of money and prices. According to this order, knowledge was to make analogies according to resemblances, and the ability of money to measure price and to be the unit of exchange fell upon its resemblance to wealth. At that stage, money was made of precious metals, which represented wealth and were an indication of it; as such, it became a sign that signified wealth due to its resemblance to that which it signified.

From the beginning of the seventeenth century to the end of the eighteenth century, the *cogito* questioned the supernatural character of things and the act of knowing became to search for a natural order. Man, as a subject (*cogito* – I) and conscious knower (*cogito* – I am), built the signs for knowing. The mercantilism of this period and physiocracy took over space, rather than over time, as the privileged agent for knowledge, in a project of a science of order that allowed analysis of the elements of wealth according to equalities and differences. However, the most fundamental element in that configuration of thought was 'representation'. All the explanations concerning economic activity obeyed a type of table (of order) in which all the 'movements' happened in relation to the role of money as a sign. In other words, everything happened in terms of the reciprocal relations between what it was representing (money) and what was being represented. Money became a pledge.

At the end of the eighteenth century, representation became an issue. Language no longer allowed for the representation of thoughts. Man became an object for knowledge, included in economics, with the advent of 'labour' as the agent of production and wealth. When man became an object and subject of knowledge, the unthought emerged. From now on, man was always to be considered as related to an unconscious and collective phenomenon, which was to include the historical character in the sense of 'an organic structure' and a temporal constitution. Thoughts and languages were now considered as one. The human sciences emerged as a means to consider this unthought, although this would prove defective, since there would always be this unthought and they would never find the ultimate origin, oscillating between the transcendental-empirical. Smith was on the border of such change from the age of representation to the age of history. His writings depicted the shifts in the conditions of thought that led to the emergence of political economy. The object of knowledge in economic thought transformed from exchange to the production of wealth. Man was now apparent in Smith's economic thought through the notion of labour. Although 'labour' was considered by Smith as a measure of value, it was only with Ricardo that labour began to be conceived as creating value, which is why, in Foucault's view, Ricardo was the first to show a modern way of thinking on economics. With Ricardo, production became more important than circulation, so it was in his work that the network of representations from the previous epistemic context was conclusively broken. In this sense, the discontinuity in economic thought, as referred to by Foucault, appears to work very well in economics. As has been emphasised, even the common criticism that his claim undermines the idea of influence and predecessors does not apply to economics, since economic thinkers are considered to be within determined epistemic contexts.

Thus, Foucault's archaeology offers many important reflections for those economists interested in understanding the fundamental conditions of thought and language/rhetoric in economics. In particular, his history of epistemology has shown that economists must surpass the stage of concern with forms of argumentation and persuasion in order to investigate which rhetorical procedures have been brought into being and acquired privileged position over others and how this has been done. The language issue is in correlation to the problem of representation, therefore the underlying conditions of discourse have to be considered. As Foucault highlighted – when he launched the notion of 'statement', for example – the case is not solely to think about discourse in terms of what it is hiding, or what is 'really' being said, but is instead to understand 'the mode of emergence and existence' of discourse. Such an awareness of how we are built through the past would prevent us, for instance, from dreaming of a 'return' to the past. To think about the current state of affairs in economics implies thinking about language. The language itself has to be considered as 'language in action'.

Related to the previous remarks is yet another important conclusion, based upon a better understanding into the nature of the problems that exist in contemporary economic methodology and which need to be further addressed. This would help prevent us from spending time wondering about alternatives, when the 'enemy' is not the one we have in mind. For instance, contrary to what some economists may still believe, the problem in economics is not a Cartesian view of knowledge. The Cartesian view of knowledge collapsed towards the end of the eighteenth century and political economy emerged following an effort to overcome that situation. Hence, the methodology of political economy emerged in the context of a collapse in the *mathesis universalis*. This line of thought can help to stimulate an important reflection regarding the alternative possibilities to the contemporary tendency towards mathematisation in economics. Moreover, yet another interesting factor to consider in this context is how the formalism of neoclassical economics has emerged and how it exists to deal with the problem of representation and language.

Another example of how a Foucauldian-inspired epistemology could have important influences on economic methodology is provided by the notion of the 'unthought' that emerged in the modern episteme. This appears to be a frequently forgotten factor by new approaches in the contemporary methodology of economics. The presence of an 'unthought' in the modern episteme led to a new conception of human nature and to the emergence of the human sciences. As seen previously, Foucault argued that Smith's system, including his economic system, followed an analysis and taxonomia of a natural order. Hence, it was not only a conception of order that was underlying Smith's thought, but also the belief that this was according to nature's principle. The conception of a natural order led to the search for the principles of human nature by those such as Hobbes, Hume and Smith. In this context, Smith rejected Hobbes's selfish system (to Hobbes, selfishness was the 'state of nature', 'the condition of mankind': *bellum omnium contra omnes*). Smith brought this discussion to the attention of economic concerns and concluded that self-interest could result in the best of natural order. In terms of a paradigmatic environment, while physiocrats analysed the economy according to a circular flow, as illustrated by Quesnay's *Tableau Economique*, Smith analysed it in terms of a natural process in which interests promoted harmony in economic relationships.

Nevertheless, there was a change during the modern episteme in the concept of human nature due to the emergence of the notion of 'unthought', which needs to be explored when referring to Smith since it clarifies his epistemology very well. Smith's system already had an element of this 'unthought', which is corroborated by his studies on language and by the notion of the invisible hand. As for language, Smith already pointed out a split between language and representation. Regarding the invisible hand, if the notion of 'invisibility' were placed in focus, then this would allow us to see the unknowledgeability of the economic process. Although Foucault relates this to the emergence of a new reason of state and liberalism, his reflections can change the history of the notion of *homo economicus* substantially.

As for a reconsideration of Smith's writings on language and rhetoric, Foucault's archaeology enables us to conclude that they had already indicated a 'fragmentation' of language regarding representation. This is emphasised by Smith's awareness of the historical character of language, in the sense of 'organic structure' and temporality, and by the anthropological character of his thought. This leads us to consider Smith's proximity towards the contemporary interest in the rhetoric of economics. The question then becomes whether this transition in contemporary interest has followed the change in the conception of language, promoted by what has been termed 'the linguistic turn' in philosophy, which essentially reflects about the being of language. Smith could not have anticipated such a shift. Judging by the current movement on the rhetoric of economics concerning the communicative and persuasive character of discourse, it would appear that the new approach towards the rhetoric of economics is still not fully aware of it either. Thus, Smith's approach to rhetoric does not really differ much from what is already the case in the contemporary interest of economics.

This book has provided a deep and detailed understanding into Foucault's writings on the archaeology of knowledge and has indicated some ways of exploring them. The examples mentioned above show the potentiality for further scrutiny. To mention just a few other possibilities, *The Archaeology of Knowledge* has a number of other singular notions that could inspire other fruitful avenues of investigation. For instance, a study on economics in terms of those thresholds of knowledge (positivity, epistemologisation, scientificity and formalisation) could certainly shed light on the scholarship of the philosophy of economics. His lectures at the Collège de France in 1978–9 (Foucault, 2004) offered a range of new ideas that through, for example, the notion of *homo economicus* deserve further attention and will certainly be an object for renewed investigation in the future. Therefore, the discourse must end: 'Faced with so many instances of ignorance, so many questions remaining in suspense, no doubt some decision must be made. One must say: there is where discourse ends, and perhaps labour begins again' (*OT*, p. 307).

Notes

2 Foucault's Context

1. Rorty (1986, p. 131) argues that the modern philosophy, which is usually referred to as beginning with Descartes and Hobbes, was not distinguished from science until after Kant, when the theory of knowledge emerged.
2. This influence of a theory of language on social sciences in the eighteenth century is part of the configuration of the classical episteme, as will be seen in the next chapter.

3 The Archaeology of Knowledge

1. A.M. Sheridan Smith, the translator of *The Archaeology of Knowledge*, clarifies that the English word 'language' has two meanings in French: '*langue*', meaning the 'natural' languages, such as French and English, and '*langage*', meaning 'language in general' or kinds of language, such as the philosophical or medical language (*AK*, p. 26).
2. As will be seen in the next section, discursive practices may be called 'positivities' when they surpass the threshold of individuality and autonomy.
3. This view of Foucault will be explained in detail in the section on the classical episteme.
4. This relation is a spatiotemporal axis and can also be identified in *The Order of Things* by Foucault's frequent use of geometric images: circularity of knowledge in the Renaissance; a quadrilateral in the classical and modern ages; and in contemporary times, a triangle formed by mathematics and physical sciences, the empirical sciences of biology, economics and philology, and by philosophy.
5. As will be seen below, it was only in the next episteme, the modern age, that knowledge began to look inside things, 'vertically', writes Foucault, searching for their internal 'organic structures'.
6. In this sense, Gutting (1989, p. 157) used 'discourse' and 'thought' synonymously.
7. There is a distinction between 'language' and 'discourse' here. However, as should be noticed, Foucault was not employing the latter according to his own conception of it (it was only in the modern age that the emergence of man as a subject of knowledge led to 'discourse' in such meanings), but in the sense he believed it had in the classical age. Discourse was 'the spontaneous analysis of representation' (*OT*, p. 232) and so was the object of knowledge. Discourse is studied as a verbal performance of language, as the first representation of thought.
8. It was in this sense that Hume, for instance, proposed the investigation of principles of human nature. As Broadie (1997, p. 31) declared, when Hume spoke of a science of man, he was thinking of human beings as part of nature, which would therefore most appropriately be investigated by means proper to

the study of nature. The case here is that in Hume's episteme there was still a regularity that allowed the association of impressions (resemblance) through imagination, which derived from that conception of human nature. The human sciences link the knowledge of the empirical (living, labouring and speaking) to what man is and what he can know. They analyse what enables man to recognise himself as a living being, as a worker and as a speaking subject.

5   Political Economy as a Paradigmatic and Epistemic Shift

1. One important aspect to be noticed regarding economic thought is that Foucault analysed its main protagonists. It is sometimes suggested that he restricted his sources to a few thinkers, especially French ones. This kind of critique sometimes takes another shape, arguing that the problem is also the fact that he took from a limited group of thinkers, drawing 'conclusions of great proportions' (Leary 1976, p. 291). This critique does not apply to economics. As will be demonstrated, Foucault did take into account the great thinkers usually referred to in the main works of history of economic thought.
2. The edition of *Naissance de la Biopolitique* used as a reference in the book was the original French version, published for the first time in 2004. Only following the writing of this book has it since been translated into English by Palgrave Macmillan (Foucault, 2008).

6   Some of Foucault's Contributions to Reconsidering the Debate on Smith's Context and Writings

1. In this sense, Foucault is located at the centre of modern episteme and is another case that allows us to say that Foucault was actually a Kantian.

Bibliography

Agamben, Giorgio (2002) *What is a Paradigm?* Available from http://www.egs. edu/faculty/agamben/agamben-what-is-a-paradigm-2002.html, date accessed 18 March 2004.

Amariglio, Jack (1988) 'The body, economic discourse, and power: an economist's introduction to Foucault', *History of Political Economy*, 20, 4, 583–613.

——— (1990a) 'Reply to Lawrence Birken', *History of Political Economy*, 22, 3, 562–9.

——— (1990b) 'Economics as a postmodern discourse', in Warren J. Samuels (ed.) *Economics as Discourse. An Analysis of the Language of Economists*. Boston, Dordrecht, London: Kluwer Academic Publishers.

Amariglio, Jack, Cullenberg, Stephen and Ruccio, David (eds) (2001) *Postmodernism, Economics and Knowledge. Economics as a Social Theory*. London: Routledge.

Amariglio, Jack and Ruccio, David F. (1995) 'Keynes, postmodernism, uncertainty', in Sheila Dow and John Hillard (eds) *Keynes, Knowledge and Uncertainty*. Aldershot: Edward Elgar, pp. 334–56.

Arnauld, Antoine and Lancelot, Claude (1975) [1660] *General and Rational Grammar: The Port-Royal Grammar*, Jacques Rieux and Bernard E. Rollin (eds and trans.). The Hague and Paris: Mouton.

Austin, John L. (1975) *How to Do Things with Words*, J.O. Urmson and Marina Sbisa (eds), 2nd edn. Oxford: Clarendon Press.

Backhouse, Roger (1985) *A History of Modern Economic Analysis*. Oxford and New York: Basil Blackwell.

Baert, Patrick (2005) 'Towards a pragmatist-inspired philosophy of social science', *Acta Sociologica*, 48, 3, 191–203.

Barthes, Roland (1972) [1964] *Critical Essays*, Richard Howard (trans.). Evanston: Northwestern University Press.

Baynes, Kenneth, Bohman, James and McCarthy, Thomas (ed.) (1987) *After Philosophy. End or Transformation*. Cambridge, MA and London: MIT Press.

Bellour, R. (1971) 'Deuxième entretien avec Michel Foucault: sur les façons d'écrire l'histoire', *Le livre des autres*. Paris: L'Herne, pp. 189–207.

Bernauer, James W. (1990) *Michel Foucault's Force of Flight. Toward an Ethics for Thought*. New Jersey and London: Humanities Press.

Berry, Christopher (1974) 'Adam Smith's *Considerations* on Language', *Journal of the History of Ideas*, 35, 1, 130–8.

Best, Steven (1995) *The Politics of Historical Vision. Marx, Foucault, Habermas*. New York: The Guilford Press.

Billouet, Pierre (2003) *Foucault*, Beatriz Sidou (trans.). Sao Paulo: Estacao Liberdade.

Birken, Lawrence (1990) 'Foucault, marginalism, and the history of economic thought: a rejoinder to Amariglio', *History of Political Economy*, 22, 3, 557–69.

Blair, Carole (1987) 'The statement: foundation of Foucault's historical criticism', *The Western Journal of Speech Communication*, 51, 364–83.

Blaug, Mark (1980) 'Kuhn versus Lakatos, or paradigms versus research programmes in the history of economics', in Gary Gutting (ed.) *Paradigms & Revolutions. Applications and Appraisals of Thomas Kuhn's Philosophy of Science.* Notre Dame: University of Notre Dame Press.

——— (1997) [1962] *Economic Theory in Retrospect,* 5th edn. Cambridge University Press.

Broadie, Alexander (ed.) (1997) *The Scottish Enlightenment. An Anthology.* Edinburgh: Canongate Classic.

Brown, Vivienne (1994) *Adam Smith's Discourse. Canonicity, Commerce and Conscience.* London: Routledge.

——— (2003) 'Textuality and the history of economics: intention and meaning', in Warren J. Samuel, Jeff E. Biddle and John B. Davis (eds) *A Companion to the History of Economic Thought.* Malden, Oxford, Melbourne and Berlin: Blackwell Publishing.

Burtt, Edwin A. (2003) *The Metaphysical Foundations of Modern Science.* New York: Dover Publications.

Caldwell, Bruce J. (1994) *Beyond Positivism. Economic Methodology in the Twentieth Century,* rev. edn. London, Routledge.

Capaldi, Nicholas (1993) 'Analytic philosophy and language', in Rom Harré and Roy Harris (eds) *Linguistics and Philosophy. The Controversial Interface.* Oxford, New York, Seoul and Tokyo: Pergamon Press.

Carrette, Jeremy R. (ed.) (2000) *Foucault and Religion. Spiritual Corporality and Political Spirituality.* London and New York: Routledge.

Caws, Peter (1971) 'Language and human reality', *New Republic,* March, pp. 28–34.

Certeau, Michel de (1986) 'The black sun of language: Foucault', in Barry Smart (ed.) (1994) *Michel Foucault: Critical Assessments,* vol. II. London: Routledge.

Colman, Andrew M. (2001) *A Dictionary of Psychology.* Oxford University Press. Available at http://www.oxfordreference.com/views/ENTRY.html, date accessed 24 March 2006.

Corbett, Edward P J. and Connors, Robert J. (1999) *Classical Rhetoric for the Modern Students,* 4th edn. New York and Oxford: Oxford University Press.

Cottingham, J, Stoothoff, R. and Murdoch, D. (trans.) (1985) *The Philosophical Writings of Descartes,* vols. I and II. Cambridge University Press.

Cousins, Mark and Hussain, Athar (1984) *Michel Foucault.* London: Macmillan Education Ltd.

Culler, Jonathan (1985) *Saussure,* 2nd edn. London: Fontana Press.

Dascal, Marcelo (2006) 'Adam Smith's theory of language', in Knud Haakonssen (ed.) *The Cambridge Companion to Adam Smith.* Cambridge University Press.

Davidson, Arnold I. (ed.) (1997) *Foucault and His Interlocutors.* Chicago and London: University of Chicago Press.

Davis, John B. (2003) *The Theory of the Individual in Economics. Identity and Value.* London: Routledge.

Deane, Phyllis (1978) *The Evolution of Economic Ideas.* Cambridge University Press.

Deleuze, Gilles (1988) [1986] *Foucault,* Seán Hand (ed. and trans.). London: The Athlone Press.

——— (1991) [1953] *Empiricism and Subjectivity. An Essay in Hume's Theory of Human Nature,* Constantin V. Boundas (trans.). New York: Columbia University Press.

Descartes, René (1985a) [1628] 'Rules for the direction of the mind', in J. Cottingham, R. Stoothoff and D. Murdoch (trans.) *The Philosophical Writings of Descartes*, vols. I and II. Cambridge University Press.

———— (1985b) [1637] 'Discourse on method', in J. Cottingham, R. Stoothoff and D. Murdoch (trans.) *The Philosophical Writings of Descartes*, vols. I and II. Cambridge University Press.

———— (1985c) [1644] 'Principles of philosophy', in J. Cottingham, R. Stoothoff and D. Murdoch (trans.) *The Philosophical Writings of Descartes*, vols. I and II. Cambridge University Press.

Descombes, V. (1980) *Modern French Philosophy*. Cambridge University Press.

Dillon, George L. (1997) 'Discourse theory', in Michael Groden and Martin Kreiwirth (eds) *The Johns Hopkins Guide to Literary Theory & Criticism*. Baltimore: Johns Hopkins University Press.

Dow, Sheila C. (1985) *Macroeconomic Thought. A Methodological Approach*. Oxford and Cambridge, MA: Basil Blackwell.

———— (1990) 'Beyond dualism', *Cambridge Journal of Economics*, 14, 2, 143–57.

———— (1991) 'Are there any signs of postmodernism with economics?', *Methodus*, 3, 1, 81–5.

———— (1996) *The Methodology of Macroeconomic Thought: A Conceptual Analysis of Schools of Thought in Economics*, 2nd edn. Gloucester and Vermont: Edward Elgar.

———— (1999) 'Rationality and rhetoric in Smith and Keynes', in Rema R. Favretti, Giorgio Sandri and Roberto Scazzieri (ed.) *Incomensurability and Translation. Kuhnian Perspectives on Scientific Communication and Theory Change*. Cheltenham and Northampton, MA: Edward Elgar.

———— (2001) 'Modernism and postmodernism: a dialectical analysis', in Jack Amariglio *et al.* (eds) *Postmodernism, Economics and Knowledge. Economics as a Social Theory*. London: Routledge.

———— (2002a) *Economic Methodology: An Inquiry*. New York: Oxford University Press.

———— (2002b) 'Interpretation: the case of David Hume'. *History of Political Economy*, 34, 2, 399–420.

———— (2002c) 'Historical reference: Hume and critical realism', *Cambridge Journal of Economics*, 26, 683–95.

———— (2010) 'Smith's philosophy and economic methodology', in J. Young (ed.) *Elgar Companion to Adam Smith*. Cheltenham: Edward Elgar.

Dreyfus, Hubert L. and Rabinow, Paul (1982) *Michel Foucault: Beyond Structuralism and Hermeneutics*. Brighton: Harvester.

Elden, Stuart (2001) *Mapping the Present. Heidegger, Foucault and the Project of a Spatial History*. London and New York: Continuum.

Etymology Dictionary (2004) Available at www.etymonline.com, date accessed 24 May 2004.

Foss, Sonja K. and Gill, Ann (1987) 'Michel Foucault's theory of rhetoric as epistemic', *The Western Journal of Speech Communication*, 51, 384–401.

Foucault, Michel (1966) *Les mots et les choses. Une archéologie des sciences humaines*. Paris: Éditions Gallimard.

———— (1967) [1961] *Madness and Civilization: A History of Insanity in the Age of Reason*, Richard Howard (trans.). London: Tavistock Publications.

—— (1970a) [1966] *The Order of Things. An Archaeology of the Human Sciences*. London: Tavistock Publications.

—— (1970b) 'The order of discourse', in Robert Young (ed.) (1981) *Untying the Text: A Post-Structuralist Reader*. Boston, London and Henley: Routledge & Kegan Paul.

—— (1971a) 'Nietzsche, genealogy, history', in Paul Rabinow (ed.) (1984) *The Foucault Reader*. London: Penguin.

—— (1971b) 'Monstrosities in criticism', *Diacritics*, Fall, 1, 1, 57–60.

—— (1971c) 'Foucault responds/2', *Diacritics*, 1, 2, 59.

—— (1973) [1963] *The Birth of the Clinic. An Archaeology of Medical Perception*, A.M. Sheridan Smith (trans.). London: Tavistock Publications.

—— (1975) *Surveiller et punir*. Paris: Gallimard.

—— (1980) [1977] 'The confession of the flesh', in Colin Gordon (ed.) *Power/Knowledge. Selected Interviews and Other Writings 1972–1977*. Brighton: Harvester Press.

—— (1983) 'Structuralism and post-structuralism: an interview with Michel Foucault' (interview with Gérard Raulet), *Telos*, 55, Spring, reprinted in Lawrence D. Kritzman (ed.) (1988) *Foucault. Politics, Philosophy, Culture. Interviews and Other Writings 1977–1984*, Alan Sheridan *et al.* (trans.). New York and London: Routledge.

—— (1984a) 'Truth and power', in Paul Rabinow (ed.) *The Foucault Reader*. New York: Pantheon Books.

—— (1984b) *Histoire de la sexualité: l'usage des plaisirs*. Paris: Gallimard.

—— (1984c) 'What is Enlightenment?', in Paul Rabinow (ed.) *The Foucault Reader*. New York: Pantheon Books.

—— (1984d) 'Polemics, politics, and problematizations', in Paul Rabinow (ed.) *The Foucault Reader*. New York: Pantheon Books.

—— (1984e) [1969] 'What is an author?, in Paul Rabinow (ed.) *The Foucault Reader*. New York: Pantheon Books.

—— (1987) 'Questions of method: an interview with Michel Foucault', in Kenneth Baynes *et al.* (eds) *After Philosophy. End or Transformation*. Cambridge, MA and London: MIT Press.

—— (1988a) 'Critical theory/intellectual history', in Lawrence D. Kritzman (ed.) *Michel Foucault. Politics, Philosophy, Culture. Interviews and Other Writings 1977–1984*, Alan Sheridan *et al.* (trans.). New York and London: Routledge.

—— (1988b) 'Politics and reason', in Lawrence D. Kritzman (ed.) *Michel Foucault. Politics, Philosophy, Culture. Interviews and Other Writings 1977–1984*, Alan Sheridan *et al.* (trans.). New York and London: Routledge.

—— (1994a) 'Governmentality', in James D. Faubion (ed.) *Michel Foucault. Essential Works of Foucault 1954–1984. Power*, vol. 3, Robert Hurley *et al.* (trans.). London: Penguin.

—— (1994b) 'Space, knowledge and power', in James D. Faubion (ed.) *Michel Foucault. Essential Works of Foucault 1954–1984. Power*, vol. 3, Robert Hurley *et al.* (trans.). London: Penguin.

—— (2000a) 'The will to knowledge', in Paul Rabinow (ed.) *Ethics. Subjectivity and Truth. Essential Works of Foucault 1954–1984*, vol. 1, Robert Hurley *et al.* (trans.). London: Penguin.

———— (2000b) 'The birth of biopolitics', in Paul Rabinow (ed.) (2000) *Ethics. Subjectivity and Truth. Essential Works of Foucault 1954–1984*, vol. 1, Robert Hurley *et al.* (trans.). London: Penguin.

———— (2001) [1994] *Dits et Ecrits: 1954–1975*, 4th edn, vol. I, D. Defert, F. Ewald and J. Lagrange (eds). Paris: Gallimard.

———— (2002) [1969] *The Archaeology of Knowledge*. London: Routledge.

———— (2003) [1975–6] *Society Must Be Defended. Lectures at the Collège de France 1975–1976*, David Macey (trans.). New York: Picador.

———— (2004) [1978–9] *Naissance de la Politique. Cours au Collège de France. 1978–1979*. Paris: Gallimard Seuil.

———— (2008) *The Birth of Biopolitics. Lectures at the Collège de France, 1978–79*, Michel Senellart (ed.), Arnold I. Davidson (English Series Editor), Graham Burchell (trans.). Basingstoke: Palgrave Macmillan.

Fuller, S. (2000) *Thomas Kuhn: A Philosophical History for Our Time.* University of Chicago Press.

Gaonkar, D.P. (1982) 'Foucault on discourse: methods and tempations', *Journal of the American Forensic Association*, 18, 246–57.

Gay, Peter (1966) *The Enlightenment: An Interpretation. The Rise of Modern Paganism.* London: Weidenfeld & Nicholson.

———— (1969) *The Enlightenment: An Interpretation. The Science of Freedom.* London: Weidenfeld & Nicholson.

Gemin, J. (1997) 'Manufacturing codependency: self-help as discursive formation', *Critical Studies in Mass Communication*, 14, 249–66.

Gutting, Gary (1989) *Michel Foucault's Archaeology of Scientific Reason.* Cambridge University Press.

———— (ed.) (1994) *The Cambridge Companion to Foucault.* Cambridge University Press.

———— (2003) 'Michel Foucault'. *Stanford Encyclopedia of Philosophy*. Available at http://plato.stanford.edu/entries/foucault, date accessed 31 July 2005.

———— (2005) *Foucault. A Very Short Introduction.* Oxford University Press.

Habermas, Jürgen (1987) *The Philosophical Discourse of Modernity*, Frederick Lawrence (trans.). Cambridge, MA: MIT Press.

Hacking, Ian (1979) 'Michel Foucault's immature science', *Nous*, 13, 1 (March), 39–51.

———— (1981) 'The archaeology of Foucault'. *The New York Times*, 14 May.

———— (1984) 'Five parables', in Richard Rorty, J.B. Schneewind and Quentin Skinner (eds) *Philosophy in History. Essays on the Historiography of Philosophy.* Cambridge University Press.

———— (1986) 'The archaeology of Foucault', in David Couzens Hoy (ed.) *Foucault. A Critical Reader.* Oxford and New York: Basil Blackwell Inc.

———— (1988) 'Night thoughts on philology', in Barry Smart (ed.) (1994) *Michel Foucault: Critical Assessments*, vol. II. London: Routledge.

———— (2002) *Historical Ontology.* Cambridge, MA: Harvard University Press.

———— (2005) 'Les Mots et les Choses, forty years on'. Available from http://www. heymancenter.org/Storage/Hackinglecture.doc, date accessed 16 February 2006.

Hands, D. Wade (2001) *Reflection without Rules. Economic Methodology and Contemporary Science Theory.* Cambridge University Press.

Hausman, D. (2001) 'A new era for economic methodology', *Journal of Economic Methodology*, 8, 1, 65–8.

Hawkes, Terence (2003) *Structuralism and Semiotics*, 2nd edn. London and New York: Routledge.

Heckscher, E.F. (1955) [1931] *Mercantilism*, 2 vols. London: George Allen & Unwin.

Heilbroner, Robert L. (ed.) (1986) *The Essential Adam Smith*. With the assistance of Laurence J. Malone. New York and London: W.W. Norton & Company.

Heimann, Eduard (1945) *History of Economic Doctrines. An Introduction to Economic Theory*. London, New York and Toronto: Oxford University Press.

Henderson, W., Dudley-Evans, Tony and Backhouse, Roger (eds) (1993) *Economics and Language*. London and New York: Routledge.

Hodgson, Geoffrey (2001) *How Economics Forgot History: The Problem of Historical Specificity in Social Science*. London and New York: Routledge.

Hollander, Samuel (1973) *The Economics of Adam Smith*. London: Heinemann.

——— (1987) *Classical Economics*. Oxford: Basil Blackwell.

Howell, Wilbur S. (1975) 'Adam Smith's lectures on rhetoric: an historical assessment', in Andrew Skinner and Thomas Wilson (eds) *Essays on Adam Smith*. Oxford: Clarendon Press.

Hoy, David C. (ed.) (1986) *Foucault. A Critical Reader*. Oxford and New York: Basil Blackwell.

——— (1988) 'Foucault: modern or postmodern?', in Jonathan Arac (ed.) *After Foucault. Humanistic Knowledge, Postmodern Challenges*. New Brunswick, NJ: Rutgers University Press.

Huppert, George (1974) 'Divinatio et Eruditio: thoughts on Foucault', in Barry Smart (ed.) (1994) *Michel Foucault: Critical Assessments*, vol. II. London: Routledge, pp. 55–68.

Jasinski, James (2001) *Sourcebook on Rhetoric: Key Concepts in Contemporary Rhetorical Studies*. London: Sage Publications.

Jevons, William S. (1871) *The Theory of Political Economy*. London and New York: MacMillan and Co.

Kant, Immanuel (1933) [1781] *Critique of Pure Reason*, Norman Kemp Smith (trans.). London: Macmillan.

——— (1963) [1784] 'What is Enlightenment?', in Lewis White Beck (ed.) *On History. Immanuel Kant*, Lewis White Beck, Robert E. Anchor and Emil L. Fackenheim (trans.). Indianapolis and New York: The Bobbs-Merrill Company, Inc.

Kaushil, S. (1973) 'The case of Adam Smith's value analysis', *Oxford Economic Papers*, 25, 60–71.

Kermode, Frank (1973) 'Crisis critic: review of *The Archaeology of Knowledge* and *The Discourse on Language* by Michel Foucault, translated by A. M. Sheridan Smith', in Barry Smart (ed.) (1994) *Michel Foucault: Critical Assessments*, vols. I–III. London: Routledge.

King, Richard (1999) *Orientalism and Religion: Post-colonial theory, India and 'the Mystic East'*. London and New York: Routledge.

Klaes, Matthias (2003) 'Historiography', in Warren J. Samuel, Jeff E. Biddle and John B. Davis (eds) *A Companion to the History of Economic Thought*. Malden, Oxford, Melbourne and Berlin: Blackwell Publishing.

Klamer, Arjo (1984) *The New Classical Macroeconomics: Conversations with the New Classical Economists and their Opponents*. Brighton: Wheatsheaf.

——— (1987) 'The advent of modernism in economics', *Mimeo*.

—— (1990) 'The textbook presentation of economic discourse', in Warren J. Samuels (ed.) *Economics as Discourse. An Analysis of the Language of Economists*. Boston, Dordrecht, London: Kluwer Academic Publishers.

—— (1995) 'The conception of modernism in economics: Samuelson, Keynes and Harrod', in Sheila Dow and John Hillard (eds) *Keynes, Knowledge and Uncertainty*. Aldershot: Edward Elgar, pp. 318–33.

—— (2001) 'Late modernism and the loss of character in economics', in Jack Amariglio *et al.* (eds) *Postmodernism, Economics and Knowledge. Economics as a Social Theory*. London: Routledge.

Klamer, Arjo, McCloskey, D.N. and Solow, Robert M. (eds) (1988) *The Consequences of Economic Rhetoric*. Cambridge University Press.

Kritzman, Lawrence D. (ed.) (1988) *Foucault. Politics, Philosophy, Culture. Interviews and Other Writings 1977–1984*. New York and London: Routledge.

Kuhn, Thomas (1970) [1962] *The Structure of Scientific Revolutions*, 2nd edn. University of Chicago Press.

—— (1977) *The Essential Tension. Selected Studies in Scientific Tradition and Change*. Chicago and London: University of Chicago Press.

—— (1979) 'History of science', in Peter D. Asquith and Henry E. Kyburg, Jr. (eds) *Current Research in Philosophy of Science. Proceedings of the P.S.A. Critical Research Problems Conference*. East Lansing, Michigan: Philosophy of Science Association.

—— (1999) 'Remarks on incommensurability and translation', in Rema Rossini Fravetti, Giorgio Sandri and Roberto Scazzieri (eds) *Incommensurability and Translation. Kuhnian Perspectives on Scientific Communication and Theory Change*. Cheltenham and Northampton, MA: Edward Elgar.

Kusch, Martin (1991) *Foucault's Strata and Fields. An Investigation into Archaeological and Genealogical Science Studies*. Dordrecht, Boston and London: Kluwer Academic Publishers.

Lalande, André (1999) *Technical and Critical Vocabulary of Philosophy*. Sao Paulo: Martins Fontes.

Latour, B. and Woolgar, S. (1986) *Laboratory Life. The Construction of Scientific Facts*. Princeton University Press.

Laudan, Larry (1977) *Progress and its Problems. Towards a Theory of Scientific Growth*. London: Routledge & Kegan Paul.

Lawson, Tony (1997) *Economics & Reality*. London: Routledge.

Leary, David E. (1976) 'Essay review: Michel Foucault, an historian of the sciences humaines', *Journal of the History of Behavioural Sciences*, 12, 3, 286–93.

Le Bon, Sylvie (1967) 'Un positiviste desespere: Michel Foucault', *Les Temps Moderns*, 22, 1299–319.

Lebrun, G. (1985) 'Transgress the finitude', in R. Ribeiro (org.) *Remember Foucault*. Sao Paulo: Brasiliense.

Lecourt, Dominique (1975) *Marxism and Epistemology. Bachelard, Cangulhem and Foucault*. London: NLB.

Lemert, Charles C. and Gillan, Garth (1982) *Michel Foucault. Social Theory and Transgression*. New York: Columbia University Press.

Locke, John (1972) [1690] 'Of words', in Oswald Handling (ed.) *Fundamental problems in Philosophy*, 2nd edn. Oxford: Basil Blackwell.

Macdonell, Diane (1986) *Theories of Discourse. An Introduction*. Oxford and Cambridge, MA: Basil Blackwell.

Magnusson, Lars G. (1994) *Mercantilism: The Shaping of Economic Language*. London: Routledge.

—— (2003) 'Mercantilism', in Warren J. Samuels, Jeff E. Biddle and John B. Davis (eds) *A Companion to the History of Economic Thought*. Malden, Oxford and Victoria: Blackwell Publishing.

Major-Poetzl, Pamela (1983) *Michel Foucault's Archaeology of Western Culture. Toward a New Science of History*. Brighton: The Harvest Press Limited.

Marsden, Richard (1999) *The Nature of Capital: Marx after Foucault*. London: Routledge.

Masterman, Margaret (1970) 'The nature of a paradigm', in I. Lakatos and A. Musgrave (eds) *Criticism and the Growth of Knowledge*. Cambridge University Press.

Mautner, Thomas (2000) (ed.) *The Penguin Dictionary of Philosophy*. London: Penguin.

Mayer, Thomas (1993) *Truth versus Precision in Economics*. Aldershot: Edward Elgar.

McCloskey, D.N. (1983) 'The rhetoric of economics', *Journal of Economic Literature* 31, June, 482–517.

—— (1985) *The Rhetoric of Economics*. Madison: University of Wiscosin Press.

—— (1992) 'Commentary by Donald McCloskey', in Neil de Marchi (ed.) *Post-Popperian Methodology of Economics. Recovering Practice*. Boston, Dordrecht, London: Kluwer Academic Publishers.

McElroy, Davis D. (1969) *Scotland's Age of Improvement: A survey of Eighteen-Century Literary Clubs and Societies*. Washington University Press.

McHoul, Alec and Grace, Wendy (1995) *A Foucault Primer. Discourse, Power and the Subject*. London: UCL Press.

McKerrow, R.E. (1989) 'Critical rhetoric: theory and praxis', *Communication Monographs*, 56, 91–111.

Merquior, J.G. (1991) *Foucault*, 2nd edn. London: Fontana Press.

Mills, Sara (1997) *Discourse*. London and New York: Routledge.

Mirowski, Philip (1984) 'Physics and the "marginalist revolution"', *Cambridge Journal of Economics*, 8, 361–79.

—— (1986) 'Mathematical formalism and economic explanation', in Philip Mirowski (ed.) *The Reconstruction of Economic Theory*. Boston, Kluwer-Nijhoff Publishing.

—— (1988) *Against Mechanism. Protecting Economics from Science*. Lanham, MD: Rowan & Littlefield.

—— (1989) *More Heat than Light. Economics as Social Physics, Physics as Nature's Economics*. Cambridge University Press.

—— (1990) 'Woo's *What's Wrong with Formalization in Economics? An Epistemological Critique*: review essays', *Research in the History of Economic Thought and Methodology*, 7, 269–88.

—— (1991) 'The when, the how and the why of mathematical expression in the history of economic analysis', *Journal of Economic Perspectives*, 5, 1, 145–57.

Montes, Leonidas (2004) *Adam Smith in Context. A Critical Reassessment of some Central Components of His Thought*. London: Palgrave Macmillan.

Mossner, Ernest C. and Ross, Ian S. (eds) (1977) *The Correspondence of Adam Smith*. Oxford: Clarendon Press.

Naughton, John (1982) 'Thomas Kuhn's Revolutions'. Available from http://molly. open.ac.uk/Personal-pages/Pubs/Essays/kuhn.htm, date accessed 8 September 2009.

Negri, Toni (2004) 'A contribution of Foucault'. Available from http://www. generation-online.org/p/fpnegri14.htm, date accessed 16 September 2005.

Norris, Christopher (1994) '"What is Enlightenment?": Kant according to Foucault', in Gary Gutting (ed.) *The Cambridge Companion to Foucault.* Cambridge University Press.

Norton, David F. (1993) 'An introduction to Hume's thought', in David Fate Norton (ed.) *The Cambridge Companion to Hume.* Cambridge University Press.

O'Farrell, Clare (1989) *Foucault. Historian or Philosopher?* London: Macmillan.

——— (1996) *Unacceptable Imaginings: Artaud's Medieval Revolution.* Available from http://www.foucault.qut.edu.au/artaud.html, date accessed 17 December 2003.

——— (2005) *Michel Foucault.* London: Sage Publications.

Ormerod, Paul (1994) *The Death of Economics.* London: Faber & Faber Ltd.

Pears, David (2000) 'Wittgenstein', in Thomas Mautner (ed.) *The Penguin Dictionary of Philosophy.* London: Penguin.

Perelman, Michael (1996) *The End of Economics.* London and New York: Routledge.

Piaget, Jean (1971) *Structuralism,* Chaninah Maschler (ed. and trans.). London: Routledge & Kegan Paul.

Poster, Mark (1984) *Foucault, Marxism & History. Mode of Production versus Mode of Information.* Cambridge and Oxford: Polity Press and Basil Blackwell.

——— (1992) 'Foucault, the present and history', in *Michel Foucault Philosopher.* Timothy J. Armstrong (trans.). New York: Harvester Wheatsheaf.

Rabinow, Paul (ed.) (1984) *The Foucault Reader.* London: Penguin.

——— (ed.) (2000) *Ethics. Subjectivity and Truth. Essential Works of Foucault 1954–1984,* vol. 1, Robert Hurley *et al.* (trans.). London: Penguin.

Redman, Deborah A. (1991) *Economics and the Philosophy of Science.* New York: Oxford University Press.

Robinson, Douglas (1997) 'Speech acts', in Michael Groden and Martin Kreiswirth (eds) *The Johns Hopkins Guide to Literary Theory & Criticism.* Baltimore, MD: Johns Hopkins University Press. Available from http://www.press.jhu.edu/ books/hopkins_guide_to_literary_theory, date accessed 23 March 2005.

Rorty, Richard (ed.) (1967) *The Linguistic Turn. Recent Essays in Philosophical Method.* Chicago and London: University of Chicago Press.

——— (1986) 'Foucault and epistemology', in David Couzens Hoy (ed.) *Foucault. A Critical Reader.* Oxford and New York: Basil Blackwell.

——— (1995) 'Deconstruction', in Raman Selden (ed.) *The Cambridge History of Literary Criticism. From Formalism to Poststructuralism,* vol. 8. Cambridge University Press.

Rossetti, Jane (1992) 'Deconstruction, rhetoric, and economics', in Neil de Marchi (ed.) *Post-Popperian Methodology of Economics. Recovering Practice.* Boston, Dordrecht, London: Kluwer Academic Publishers.

Rotwein, Eugene (1955) (ed.) *David Hume. Writings on Economics.* Toronto: Thomas Nelson and Sons Ltd.

Russell, Bertrand (1946) *History of Western Philosophy and its Connection with Political and Social Circumstances from the Earliest Times to the Present Day*. London: George Allen & Unwin Ltd.

Schabas, Margaret (2005) *The Natural Origins of Economics*. London and Chicago: University of Chicago Press.

Schleifer, Ronald (1997) 'Structuralism', in Michael Groden and Martin Kreiswirth (eds) *The Johns Hopkins Guide to Literary Theory & Criticism*. Baltimore, MD: Johns Hopkins University Press. Available from http://www.press.jhu.edu/books/hopkins_guide_to_literary_theory, date accessed 23 March 2005.

Schumpeter, Joseph A. (1954) *History of Economic Analysis*, Elizabeth Boody Schumpeter (ed.). London: George Allen & Unwin Ltd.

Screpanti, Ernesto and Zamagni, Stefano (1993) *An Outline of the History of Economic Thought*. Oxford: Clarendon Press.

Sheridan, Alan (1980) *Michel Foucault: The Will to Truth*. London: Tavistock Publications.

Shumway, David R. (1989) *Michel Foucault*. Charlottesville and London: University Press of Virginia.

Skinner, Andrew (2001) 'Adam Smith, the philosopher and the porter', in Pier Luigi Porta, Roberto Scazzieri and Andrew Skinner (eds) *Knowledge, Social Institutions and the Division of Labour*. Cheltenham: Edward Elgar.

Skinner, Andrew and Wilson, Thomas (eds) (1975) *Essays on Adam Smith*. Oxford: Clarendon Press.

Smart, Barry (1985) *Michel Foucault*. Chichester, London and New York: Ellis Horwood Limited and Tavistock Publications.

——— (ed.) (1994) *Michel Foucault: Critical Assessments*, vols. I–III. London: Routledge.

Smith, Adam (1976) [1776] *An Inquiry into the Nature and Causes of the Wealth of Nations*, R.H. Campbell and A.S. Skinner (eds), 2 vols. Oxford: Clarendon Press.

——— (1983) 'Considerations concerning the first formation of languages', in J.C. Bryce (ed.) *Adam Smith. Lectures on Rhetoric and Belles Lettres*, A.S. Skinner (General Editor). Oxford: Clarendon Press.

——— (1986a) [1759] 'The theory of moral sentiments', in Robert L. Heilbroner (ed.) *The Essential Adam Smith*. With the assistance of Laurence J. Malone. New York and London: W.W. Norton & Company.

——— (1986b) [1776] 'An inquiry into the nature and causes of the wealth of nations', in Robert L. Heilbroner (ed.) *The Essential Adam Smith*. With the assistance of Laurence J. Malone. New York and London: W.W. Norton & Company.

——— (1986c) [1799] 'The principles which lead and direct philosophical enquiries; ilustrated by the history of astronomy', in Robert L. Heilbroner (ed.) *The Essential Adam Smith*. With the assistance of Laurence J. Malone. New York and London: W.W. Norton & Company.

Steiner, George (1971a) 'The mandarin of the hour – Michel Foucault', *The New York Times*, 28 February.

——— (1971b) 'Steiner responds to Foucault', *Diacritics*, 1, 2, 60.

Sturrock, John (ed.) (1979) *Structuralism and Since. From Lévi-Strauss to Derrida*. Oxford University Press.

Suppe, Frederick (1977) *The Structure of Scientific Theories,* 2nd edn. Urbana: University of Illinois Press.

Thurow, Lester C. (1984) *Dangerous Currents: The State of Economics.* New York: Vintage Books.

Toulmin, Stephen (1972) *Human Understanding,* vol. 1. Oxford: Clarendon Press.

Tribe, Keith (1978) *Land, Labour and Economic Discourse.* London: Routledge & Kegan Paul.

——— (1988) *Governing Economy: The Reformation of German Economic Discourse, 1750–1840.* Cambridge University Press.

——— (1999) 'Adam Smith: critical theorist?'. *Journal of Economic Literature,* 37, 2, 609–32.

Ward, Benjamin (1972) *What's Wrong with Economics?* London and Basingstoke: Macmillan Press Ltd.

Weintraub, E. Roy (ed.) (2002) *The Future of the History of Economics. Annual Supplement to Volume 34 History of Political Economy.* Durham and London: Duke University Press.

White, Hayden (1973) 'Foucault decoded: notes from underground', *History and Theory,*12, 1, 23–54.

——— (1979) 'Michel Foucault', in John Sturrock (ed.) *Structuralism and Since. From Lévi-Strauss to Derrida.* Oxford University Press.

Woo, Henry K.H. (1986) *What's Wrong with Formalization in Economics? An Epistemological Critique.* Neward: Victoria Press.

Young, Robert (ed.) (1981) *Untying the Text: A Post-Structuralist Reader.* London: Routledge & Kegan Paul.

Index